COSTS AND BENEFITS OF PROTECTION

ORGANISATION FOR ECONOMIC CO-OPERATION AND DEVELOPMENT

Pursuant to article 1 of the Convention signed in Paris on 14th December, 1960, and which came into force on 30th September, 1961, the Organisation for Economic Co-operation and Development (OECD) shall promote policies designed:

- to achieve the highest sustainable economic growth and employment and a rising standard of living in Member countries, while maintaining financial stability, and thus to contribute to the development of the world economy;
- to contribute to sound economic expansion in Member as well as non-member countries in the process of economic development; and
- to contribute to the expansion of world trade on a multilateral, non-discriminatory basis in accordance with international obligations.

The Signatories of the Convention on the OECD are Austria, Belgium, Canada, Denmark, France, the Federal Republic of Germany, Greece, Iceland, Ireland, Italy, Luxembourg, the Netherlands, Norway, Portugal, Spain, Sweden, Switzerland, Turkey, the United Kingdom and the United States. The following countries acceded subsequently to this Convention (the dates are those on which the instruments of accession were deposited): Japan (28th April, 1964), Finland (28th January, 1969), Australia (7th June, 1971) and New Zealand (29th May, 1973).

The Socialist Federal Republic of Yugoslavia takes part in certain work of the OECD (agreement of 28th October, 1961).

Publié en français sous le titre:

COÛTS ET AVANTAGES
DES MESURES DE PROTECTION

This study, requested by the OECD Council at Ministerial level in 1982, was conducted under the auspices of the Economic Policy Committee. It was discussed by a large number of OECD Committees, including those responsible for general economic policy, for trade policy and for industry policy. The project was carried out by OECD's Planning and Evaluation Unit consisting of Wolfgang Michalski, Henry Ergas and Barrie Stevens.

The Introduction, Summary and Conclusions were endorsed by the Economic Policy Committee and derestricted by the OECD Council, representing Member governments. At the April 1985 meeting of the Council at Ministerial level, Ministers welcomed the report. In their Communiqué they said "It has provided further substantial evidence that protection has yielded few, if any, benefits but imposed very substantial costs, chiefly on the protecting country. Not only are restrictive trade measures an inefficient means of sustaining employment, they also delay much-needed adjustment".

The analytical part of the report is issued under the responsibility of the Secretary-General.

Also available

LONG TERM OUTLOOK FOR THE WORLD AUTOMOBILE INDUSTRY (March 1984)
(70 83 04 1) ISBN 92-64-12523-X 118 pages   £7.60   US$15.00   F76.00

TRANSPARENCY FOR POSITIVE ADJUSTMENT. Identifying and Evaluating Government Intervention (September 1983)
(03 83 02 1) ISBN 92-64-12467-5 258 pages   £9.50   US$19.00   F95.00

TEXTILE AND CLOTHING INDUSTRY. Structural Problems and Policies in OECD Countries (May 1983)
(71 83 70 1) ISBN 92-64-12432-2 176 pages   £7.00   US$14.00   F70.00

POSITIVE ADJUSTMENT POLICIES. Managing Structural Change (February 1983)
(03 83 01 1) ISBN 92-64-12402-0 116 pages   £6.20   US$12.50   F62.00

PROBLEMS OF AGRICULTURAL TRADE (October 1982)
(51 82 05 1) ISBN 92-64-12368-7 178 pages   £9.00   US$18.00   F90.00

STEEL IN THE 80s. Paris Symposium, February 1980 (June 1980)
(58 80 02 1) ISBN 92-64-12081-5 278 pages   £10.00   US$22.50   F90.00

INTERFUTURES. FACING THE FUTURE. Mastering the Probable and Managing the Unpredictable (August 1979)
(03 79 03 1) ISBN 92-64-11967-1 456 pages   £8.90   US$20.00   F80.00

THE IMPACT OF THE NEWLY INDUSTRIALISING COUNTRIES ON PRODUCTION AND TRADE IN MANUFACTURE. Report by the Secretary-General (June 1979)
(11 79 04 1) ISBN 92-64-11943-4 96 pages   £5.90   US$12.00   F48.00

Prices charged at the OECD Publications Office.

*THE OECD CATALOGUE OF PUBLICATIONS and supplements will be sent free of charge
on request addressed either to OECD Publications Office,
2, rue André-Pascal, 75775 PARIS CEDEX 16, or to the OECD Sales Agent in your country.*

TABLE OF CONTENTS

Part III

PROTECTIONISM AND INTERDEPENDENCE

INTRODUCTION, SUMMARY AND CONCLUSIONS

I. MANDATE, AIM AND SCOPE OF THE STUDY

1.   Underlining its awareness of growing world economic interdependence and expressing its concern about mounting pressures on the open multilateral trading system, the OECD Council at Ministerial Level in 1982 "agreed on the importance of objective analysis of the costs and benefits of trade and trade-related measures, and of government support to research projects in this field". It invited the Secretary-General to "compile with the help of Member countries an inventory of on-going research in this field, in particular by existing national research institutes, and to make as required further proposals to promote and make more systematic use of such research".

2.   In implementing this mandate, the Secretariat report presents a critical assessment of the studies available, their methodologies and their results. Its principal objectives are:

— To broaden the basis of analysis, and to place the dynamics of adjustment to trade in a context of economic and political realities, particularly those bearing on employment prospects.
— To increase the visibility of the costs and benefits of trade protection by referring not only to its direct effects on trade but also to its broader impacts on medium-term efficiency and welfare.
— To highlight the relevance of research into protection to the main areas of current policy concern, namely employment, industrial adjustment, interdependence and sustainable growth.

3.   The main focus of the report is on import restrictions in OECD countries affecting manufactures. This obviously limits the range of cases examined, and the intended breadth of the study's results. The study does not deal with agriculture, mining, energy, high-technology products or services. Nor does it address the problems of government support for new promising activities and export promotion, including associated finance. This is not to say that trade issues in these other areas are less important. Some, such as agriculture, have been the subject of extensive academic research, the results of which point in the same direction as the broad conclusions of this report. Agriculture has also been examined in the OECD report on Problems of Agricultural Trade. Other areas, given their complexity and the weakness of available research, clearly require further separate study.

9

4.   It should be noted at the outset that though original work has been carried out for this report, it relies heavily on the publicly available research. This has the unfortunate effect of focusing the discussion on those countries for which the most research is available, namely the United States, Canada and Australia. Particularly in continental Europe, governments have shown little interest, if any, in promoting analysis of the costs and benefits of trade and trade-distorting domestic measures, even in areas of great and topical importance such as steel, textiles and clothing, automobiles and consumer electronics.

5.   In evaluating the results of research on the costs and benefits of import restrictions on manufactures, the analysis concentrates on six issue areas:
   —   How has trade policy in manufactures evolved over the last decade?
   —   What has been the effect of trade policy measures on trade flows and prices?
   —   Did import restrictions have a positive impact on employment in the industries being assisted and in the economy as a whole?
   —   What impact have trade policy measures had on the competitiveness and efficiency of industrial structures?
   —   What has been the impact of trade and trade-related measures on the countries against which the measures were originally taken, and to what extent has this fed back into the protecting economies?
   —   Have changes in the economic environment and in the policy process increased the receptiveness of political systems to demands for protection?

6.   The issues have been looked at from an economy-wide as well as from a sector-specific perspective. The examples included in this summary are illustrative cases. For a fuller presentation of their context, implications and underlying assumptions, recourse should be made to the main report.

II.   SUMMARY OF FINDINGS

7.   The key findings of the study can be synthesised as follows:
   —   The spread of protection has yielded few benefits, but imposed substantial costs. Protectionist measures have complex and pervasive effects throughout the economy, so that the outcome of such policies frequently differs from the original intentions and objectives.
   —   The effectiveness of rigorous demand management in ensuring sustained non-inflationary growth can be reduced if at the same time governments engage in defensive structural and trade policies which drive prices up.
   —   Protection has not proved to be an efficient means of sustaining employment. Jobs saved in the industries protected are often offset by viable jobs foregone elsewhere in the economy. On its own, protection is a poor alternative to positive adjustment policies.

10

— Discriminatory restrictions have a relatively limited impact on overall import volumes (because of trade diversion), provide large transfers to restricted foreign producers, and distort trade by penalising those with the greatest comparative advantage.
— Uncertainty about the future of trade regimes depresses investment and business confidence. Continued openness of the trading system would allow the recovery to diffuse throughout the international economy and encourage investment inside and outside the OECD area.
— The rapid upsurge in LDC exports after 1982 has been a crucial factor in keeping indebtedness within manageable limits. This experience underlines the importance of sustained growth in the OECD area, and the LDCs' ability to secure access to world markets and expand export earnings for coping with high indebtedness.

The factual results of the report, grouped by issue area, are set out in detail below.

The evolution of trade policy

8.   World trade in manufactures encounters lower tariff obstacles today than at any time in the past. Subsequent to full implementation of the reductions agreed to in the Tokyo Round, average MFN tariffs on industrial imports for 17 major OECD countries will stand at around 4.5 per cent. The results of the Tokyo Round also embody moves towards liberalisation of some major non-tariff barriers. Access by developing countries to OECD markets has been significantly broadened by the Generalised System of Preferences, now entering its second decade, reflected in the steadily rising share of the developing countries in OECD imports of manufactures.

9.   Despite a prolonged period of slow growth and high unemployment, the OECD countries' commitment to the multilateral trading system has ensured that the vast majority of manufactured trade goes free of hinderance and interference. However, a relatively small, but recently increasing number of sectors — accounting for more than a quarter of manufactured trade — is still subject to high nominal and effective tariffs, to severe non-tariff barriers and to distorting subsidisation. Though the sectors traditionally most affected by such measures include textiles, clothing, footwear, steel and shipbuilding, protection has more recently been extended to previously less- or un-affected sectors such as automobiles, consumer electronics and machine tools.

10.   The non-transparency of many of the trade barriers recently put in place makes it difficult to assess their extent or coverage, and any such assessment must be treated cautiously. On one plausible estimate, the share of restricted products in total manufactured imports increased over the period 1980 to 1983 from 6 per cent to 13 per cent for the United States and from 11 per cent to 15 per cent for the EEC. In 1983, the product groups subject to restriction accounted for around 30 per cent of total manufactured consumption in the countries covered, up from 20 per cent from 1980. These results are drawn from a study which adopts a relatively narrow definition of NTBs; the increases in non-tariff protection are even more dramatic in some of the other research reviewed.

11

11.   Within the protected sectors the scope of protection has both deepened and widened. Taking steel, automobiles, motorcycles, consumer electronic products, textiles and footwear together, it has been estimated that the absolute number of NTB's quadrupled between 1968 and 1983. While less than one per cent of OECD automobile trade (excluding trade within the EEC) was affected by discriminatory restrictions in 1973, this share had risen to nearly 50 per cent a decade later. Other estimates suggest that the proportion of trade under non-liberal treatment rose in recent years from 31 to 73 per cent in steel and from 53 to 61 per cent in textiles and clothing.

12.   Changes in the mix of policy instruments used to control imports have increased the extent of discrimination. There has been a marked shift away from Article XIX safeguards, applied on a non-discriminatory basis, towards bilateral instruments such as voluntary exports restraints and orderly market arrangements. From 1980 to 1983 the share of Japan's and the Asian NICs' exports affected by discriminatory restrictions rose from 15 per cent to over 30 per cent. At the same time, the range of supplying countries subject to such restrictions has also expanded.

13.   The spread of discrimination undermines the free flow of goods between countries which — at least in theory — are not subject to restrictions. Thus, measures adopted to prevent trans-shipment impose heavy documentation requirements on products from unrestricted sources. According to experts in trade procedures, the execution of the average transaction in international trade now requires 35 documents and 360 copies, partly as a result of trade restrictions. A study for Finland found that documentation costs amounted to 1.4 to 5.7 per cent of the total value of 1982 imports — a heavy burden, when set against the profit margins typically involved in foreign trade.

14.   Domestic subsidies, too, may be exercising an increasing impact on trade flows. Narrowly defined, the share of the OECD countries' GNP accounted for by financial transfers to enterprises has increased by over four-fifths since 1965, while the share of such transfers in the operating surplus of firms has more than doubled. Of course, not all subsidies are distorting; but it is important to note that the industries benefiting most from the increase in public assistance are by and large the same in the various OECD Member countries. Apart from high-technology activities they include steel, shipbuilding, textiles and clothing, and more recently, automobiles.

The impact on trade flows and prices

15.   It is frequently argued that the protectionist backlash has had a limited impact, since trade in manufactures, even in the product groups most subject to restrictions, continued to grow rapidly in the 1970s. Equally, the countries to whose exports most of the discriminatory measures apply, managed to increase their share of OECD imports. However, the trade performance of the more restricted product categories deteriorated markedly in the 1980s. It would seem that — after being largely ineffective in the earlier period (with the possible exception of the MFA) — protectionist measures were gradually reinforced and eventually began to bite.

16.   In the 1970s, the impact of discriminatory restrictions on trade flows was limited by pervasive trade diversion, as imports from the more restricted sources were replaced by imports from other suppliers. Trade diversion has been greatest in industries where there is a multiplicity of potential sources of supply and where trade is highly responsive to price and quantity signals — for instance, clothing and footwear. In the EEC, diversion as a result of MFA restrictions has occurred from the most affected Asian exporters to sources with preferential access to the EEC market, notably those on the Mediterranean rim (and the very small ACP suppliers). Over the period 1976 to 1980 the volume of EEC imports of MFA products from the Asian NICs increased at an average of 2.2 per cent annually, while the figure for the Mediterranean and ACP suppliers was 9.5 per cent.

17.   Nonetheless, trade diversion has also been important in less mobile activities such as steel and consumer electronics, mainly because of the growing diffusion of technological and industrial capabilities, improvements in worldwide marketing and distribution channels and the great sensitivity of multinational enterprises to opportunities for shifting the localisation of production. The 1977 Orderly Market Agreement for colour television receivers between the United States and Japan is a good illustration. Though at the time of the agreement Japan accounted for 90 per cent of US imports of complete receivers, its share two years later was down to 50 per cent, while that of the Asian NICs has increased from 15 to 50 per cent.

18.   In addition to changing the geographical origin of imports, quantitative restrictions have affected the nature of the products traded. In particular, faced with a volume limit on their exports, the more restricted suppliers have been encouraged to move up-market within the controlled group, thus maximising the value of a fixed total volume of exports. According to one estimate the share of luxury cars in Japanese automobile exports to the United States increased by 13 percentage points as a result of voluntary export restraint. There is also considerable evidence of such shifts in product composition occurring in the other industries reviewed.

19.   All these protection-induced changes in the country and product composition of trade have tended to undermine the specific objectives of import control. Governments have therefore come under continuous pressure from domestic producers to extend the number of countries subject to the restrictions, and to more precisely specify the product categories in which the restricted producers can operate. Thus, during MFA I, the United States had bilateral agreements with 19 countries but none of these agreements specified explicit limits on imports of so-called "sensitive items". During MFA II, specific limits were introduced into US bilateral agreements with seven countries; and during MFA III, this number rose to 14. Equally, for the EEC the number of countries covered by bilateral agreements increased from 33 in MFA I to 43 in MFA III, while the number of categories specified went from 23 to 48.

20.   The progressive extension of discriminatory restrictions suppresses an increasing volume of trade. Econometric evidence suggests that the tightening of the MFA at its second renewal has reduced imports of textiles and clothing into the OECD by nearly 10 per cent in volume terms. With the economic recovery and changes in exchange rates boosting demand, the restrictive impact of import controls has been compounded.

21.   Throughout the period discriminatory quantitative restrictions have created upward pressures on prices in protected markets: first, because the most restricted sources tend to be those with the lowest costs; and second, because these restricted sources raise their export prices to capture the rents from the restrictions. Particularly in industries where demand is — at least in the short term — fairly inelastic, these increases in import prices provide an important "price umbrella" for domestic producers. As restrictions tightened and the scope for offsetting effects diminished, the upward pressure on prices may have strengthened over the period.

22.   A study on the UK clothing industry suggests that the average increase in UK clothing retail prices due to the second MFA was already in the order of 20 per cent and for lower quality items such as jeans 30 to 50 per cent. Prices for children's wear — a highly labour intensive product — doubled. These changes can have a regressive impact on income distribution, because clothing accounts for a larger share of poorer households' consumption expenditure. One estimate finds that protecting the Canadian clothing industry costs lower-income households four times as much as it costs higher-income households.

23.   Protection, notably by voluntary export restraint, also provides large transfers to foreign producers. It is estimated that protection has increased the profit margin on Japanese steel sales in the US market by at least 10 per cent. This is around $200 million a year — about equivalent to half of Japan's annual expenditure (the world's highest) on steel R&D. As regards textile and clothing, UK restrictions under the MFA are estimated to transfer twice as much income to foreign exporters as to UK producers. A plausible overall assessment is that the annual transfer from OECD consumers to Asian NIC exporters of textile and clothing products is at least US $2 billion. This is equivalent to around 4 per cent of the total value of NIC exports to the OECD region.

The impact on employment

24.   Employment in industries (and regions) facing structural difficulties has declined faster than in manufacturing as a whole. Over the past ten years manufacturing employment in the EEC fell by 11 per cent, but in textiles and clothing the drop was about 40 per cent (i.e. 1.7 million jobs) and in steel over 40 per cent (equivalent to 330 000 jobs). As for the United States, total manufacturing employment fell 7 per cent between 1978 and 1982. In the same period employment in textiles and clothing declined by 16 per cent (almost 400 000 jobs) and in steel by 31 per cent (a job loss of 150 000). Employment declines of this magnitude, particularly in a period of overall recession, impose high adjustment costs on the labour force.

25.   Governments have therefore come under increasing pressure to attenuate the speed of the adjustment process and the rate of job losses. However, import restrictions appear to have only a limited positive impact on employment in the protected sectors. First, even in the sectors most exposed to international competition, trade flows are usually a fairly minor determinant of employment levels; second, because of trade diversion, discriminatory restrictions have a relatively limited impact on overall import

14

volumes; third, the scope for substituting domestic output for imports may be limited.

26.   Protection is most likely to be effective in maintaining employment in the few industries which have structurally low productivity, little scope for modernisation and hence compete mainly with developing countries: for example the clothing industry. It was estimated in 1980 that Canadian restrictions on apparel imports protected 7.5 per cent of the industry's jobs. Another study found that 1977 US tariffs on apparel preserved nearly 90 000 jobs, equivalent to 10 per cent of the industry's employment. Finally, a 50 per cent increase in allowable MFA imports of apparel under Swedish VERs would, it was concluded, reduce clothing employment by 6 per cent, twice as large a job loss as a similar increase in textiles imports would entail.

27.   In most other industries the proportion of domestic employment potentially protected by import restrictions is typically in the order of two or three percentage points, though in the very short term the effect may be larger. This is still a small sum relative to the changes induced by shifting macro-economic circumstances. On one estimate, the US-Japan automobile VER increased US employment by no more than 22 000 over the period to 1982, while the recession was cutting required labour input by more than ten times this figure.

28.   In the longer term, protection can accelerate capital-labour substitution, further reducing industry employment. Capital-labour ratios in the textile industry, for instance, have gone from being well below the manufacturing average in the 1950s to some 20 per cent above average now. Together with relatively slow demand growth, capital deepening accounts for two-thirds or more of the industry's long-run employment decline in the advanced OECD countries, with changes in import penetration being a rather minor factor. A recent UK study estimates that given the slow growth of demand, productivity growth in the UK textile industry will reduce employment by nearly 40 per cent over the period 1983-97. Abolishing the MFA would, over the same period, involve a fall in employment of only 7 per cent, equivalent to 13 000 jobs. "Saving" each of these jobs costs UK consumers annually about twice as much as the yearly wage of a textile worker.

29.   Productivity increases, partly as a result of accelerated offshore assembly, were also at work when employment in the US colour television industry declined despite protection, passing from 29 000 in 1977 to 26 000 in 1979 and 21 000 in 1981. It is, however, estimated that job losses between 1979 and 1981 would have been 1 000 to 1 500 greater, had import restrictions not been in effect. Saving each of these jobs cost US consumers over $60 000 a year (on the conservative assumption that the price of a $200 set increased by $5).

30.   The employees who benefit from protection have in a number of cases not been those at whom protection was originally aimed. This is because of major shifts in the regional and occupational composition of employment within the protected country. Thus, in the US textile industry, total employment was virtually constant from 1968 to 1977, but within this total the industry created some 60 000 white collar jobs, which

went to employees with considerably higher educational qualifications than the manual employees they were replacing. Over roughly the same period, and again with approximately constant total employment, the industry created some 50 000 jobs in the South, while suppressing 75 000 jobs in the North. Protection has done little for those workers who face the most difficult adjustment problems. Rather, whatever jobs have been created have gone to fairly mobile, better trained employees.

31.   Finally, job-maintenance in the protected industry may be offset by adverse macro-economic impacts. Protection sufficiently extensive to have a major impact on imports and employment in a wide range of industries is likely to lead to currency appreciations reducing total exports, thus curtailing employment in other sectors of the economy. Protection induced changes in price and wage behaviour can compromise the effectiveness of macro-economic policy and necessitate a tighter demand management stance.

32.   Restrictive trade policies are more likely to redistribute income and employment than to create new bases for growth. In most instances, import restrictions remove employment from one set of industries — those which are more export-oriented and more technology intensive — to industries which mainly compete with imports. The small number of lower-pay, lower-quality jobs being saved by protection are replacing other jobs which, over the longer term, would contribute more to overall productivity and higher real incomes.

The impact on structural adjustment

33.   By raising prices and increasing the domestic producers' share in the home market, import restrictions can increase the resources available for industrial adjustment. The improved cash flow of domestic firms makes it possible for them to carry out modernisation investments, underwrite the costs involved in adjusting capacity to demand, and/or diversify into more promising areas of activity. Moreover, protection can change the incentives for cooperation between foreign and domestic firms. At the same time, however, by reducing the pressures for adjustment to occur, and given the substantial costs adjustment entails, protection can perpetuate technical and economic inefficiency.

34.   In fragmented, labour-intensive industries such as clothing and footwear, competition occurs primarily on a cost basis. There is limited scope for product differentiation and capital-labour substitution. As a result, protection does little to establish durable market segmentation or to reduce the cost differential between OECD producers and major developing country exporters. In the clothing industry, for example, advanced technology is being introduced into ancillary operations such as cutting and grading, but stitching operations, which account for 80 per cent of value added, are — and in the medium term will remain — highly labour intensive. Cost differentials in this stage of production between developed and leading developing country exporters are in the order of 1 to 5 or 6; even by drawing on peripheral labour markets (such as home workers or the

"underground" economy) OECD manufacturers cannot reduce wage costs by this amount.

35.   The argument that protection facilitates a run-down in these activities is clearly contrary to the evidence. In effect, given low entry barriers, the rents created by protection in these activities simply attract new resources, not only labour and capital, but also entrepreneurship. In the United States, one-third of the clothing and textiles establishments existing at the end of 1982 had been created since 1976. In France over a fifth of new manufacturing firms are in the textiles and clothing industries. Protectionist measures have permitted adjustment only to the extent that they have allowed the international division of labour to operate through such indirect means as off-shore assembly and licit or illicit trade diversion.

36.   In oligopolistic industries, competition depends chiefly on product differentiation, economies of scale, technology, marketing and service. By changing industry behaviour, quantitative restrictions can provide a substantial flow of rents both to domestic and foreign producers. According to one analysis, the automobile VER increased the profitability of Japanese sales in the US market by 12 percentage points. Notably when their market share is restricted, foreign firms can seek to further increase the rents they derive from the protected market by selling technology and other intangible assets to domestic producers. Indeed, cooperative agreements between restricted foreign suppliers, particularly Japanese, and domestic firms have proliferated in the oligopolistic industries receiving protection.

37.   There are cases in which protection, coupled with adjustment programmes, has encouraged firms to utilise the resources made available for restructuring. Prominent examples are the car industry in the United States and certain parts of the steel industry in the European Community. Frequently, however, there are factors at work which impede adjustment from occurring. If price and quantity signals from the market place are distorted, import controls can make it difficult for firms to assess long-term relative costs and set investment plans accordingly. If there is widespread excess capacity, and modernisation investments would involve construction of large-scale plant, as is the case, for example, in the steel industry, the risk of reinvesting in the activity may outweigh the potential benefits. Firms may also face political or institutional constraints on their restructuring choices; for instance, if assistance has been granted to firms on condition that employment levels be maintained.

38.   Over time, the response of foreign suppliers to protection can also substantially narrow the domestic firms' adjustment options. To the extent that foreign rivals generally respond to quantitative restrictions on imports by product upgrading and moving upmarket, domestic firms face increased foreign competition in those sections of the market which are least price-elastic. This is precisely where their long-run competitive edge could otherwise lie. Foreign firms can also offset the benefits of protection to domestic rivals by investing in the protected market. In the longer term, neither the domestic nor the foreign firms may derive much net advantage, but real economic costs are incurred in the process, bearing largely on the protecting country.

17

Protection and developing countries

39.   Uncertainty about the future of trade regimes depresses investment and business confidence not only in many OECD economies, but also in developing countries. So far, OECD protection has had more impact on the composition than on the level of LDCs exports. However, the vulnerability of LDCs, and particularly those at an earlier stage of industrial development, to protectionist measures (or their threat) has remained very high. Moreover, as protectionist measures spread, narrowly economic feedback effects may be magnified throughout the multilateral trading system as income levels, financial solvency and capacity to import are affected.

40.   In the nine years up to 1982, LDC manufactured exports to the OECD area grew by less than 8 per cent per annum, a substantially slower rate than in the period prior to the 1973 oil shock. There are strong indications that in the absence of, or at least with less protection, these exports would have been higher. In the 1982-84 recovery they accelerated to well above 20 per cent per annum, despite protection, and import penetration of manufactured goods on some major OECD markets has continued to increase strongly. Moreover, the five major NICs — the main target of protectionist measures — have largely benefited from this upsurge. It seems plausible, therefore, that on the whole variations in the growth of aggregate demand in the OECD countries have had more impact on the rates of LDC export growth than has OECD protection.

41.   The spread of trade restrictions has changed the pattern of LDC exports. Developing countries, and particularly the more advanced NICs, have rapidly stepped up the diversification of their exports, moving into new regional markets and more skill intensive products. At the same time there has been a deliberate shift of certain production activities away from those countries particularly restrained by protection in industrial countries into less restricted low labour cost countries. Protection has compounded the impact of changing patterns of cost competitiveness in prompting and accelerating these developments.

42.   Other developing countries have captured market shares left by the more restricted exporting countries, benefiting in some cases from the shift of production facilities out of NICs. Attempts to circumvent quotas under MFA and to benefit from GSP tariff quotas have been important factors in this regard. Nonetheless as restrictions tighten, many of the second and third generation of manufacturing exporters, rather than the more flexible NICs, may run into mounting difficulties. These difficulties may include resistance from established exporters anxious to preserve market shares, and a network of trade restrictions which take effect quickly as export volumes expand fast from a low base.

43.   The manifest willingness of protecting countries to extend existing restrictions to new sources of supply plays an important role in this respect, discouraging investment in potential LDC exporters. A striking instance is provided by the US colour television receiver Orderly Marketing Agreement. Initially aimed at Japan, the emergence of Korea and Taiwan as alternative sources of supply led to the agreement's extension to these two countries. Though a number of other sources — for instance Mexico, Singapore and

Thailand – were well placed to enter the US market at that time, the deterrent effect of the initial extension was clearly sufficient to dissuade them.

44.　Debt service ratios for developing countries fluctuated around 15-16 per cent during the 1970s, but rose sharply to around 24 per cent in 1982/83. The recession, the dollar appreciation and the rise in interest rates which followed the second oil shock, played a larger part in this increase than did OECD protection. But had the developing countries been able to achieve in the 1980s even half the annual average growth rate in export earnings they recorded in the 1970s, their 1982 debt service ratio would have been more than 4 percentage points lower. Indeed, the rapid upsurge in LDC exports after 1982 has been a crucial factor in keeping indebtedness within manageable limits. This experience underlines the importance of both sustained growth in the OECD area and the LDCs' ability to secure access to world markets and expand export earnings for coping with high indebtedness.

45.　Sharply increased debt service ratios and the limited inflow of real resources mean that in many developing countries there will be a higher premium on the efficient use of capital. But uncertainty about future trade regimes makes it increasingly difficult for developing country exporters to predict market outlets. Resources tend to be diverted to activities which are highly protected domestically and/or where product mixes and production schedules are highly flexible rather than going to those with the greatest development potential.

46.　Any break in the complex chain of expanding LDC manufactured exports and imports, servicing external debt, and sustaining investment will work to the detriment of developing and developed countries alike. It has been estimated that a gradual increase in protection in the OECD region equivalent to a 15 percentage point rise in tariffs would cause a significant reduction by 1995 of GDP both in developing and developed countries. The middle income oil-importing LDCs would sustain a loss in GDP of 3.4 per cent; but the industrial countries would equally suffer a 3.3 per cent cut in their GDP as a result of the self-inflicted effects of their own protective measures.

47.　Beyond the purely economic feedback effects of protectionism, broader considerations are also relevant here. In the first place, the industrial countries have to avoid that the heavily indebted LDCs – partly on account of the spread of protection – see no politically and socially acceptable way of restoring their economic health in the foreseeable future. Second, although protectionism in many LDCs has been part of the landscape for many decades, its advocates consider their position vindicated by the attitude of pressure groups in industrial countries. Protectionism thus feeds on itself in a circular and cumulative process, undermining the open multilateral trading system. North-South relations are not the only ones at stake; trade among industrial countries and intra-LDC trade could be just as much affected.

The politics and economics of protectionism

48.　Ultimately, trade policy is determined by politics, domestic and international. Whether protectionism spreads, imposing major harm on the world economy, depends on three factors: the costs and benefits of trade for domestic political actors; these actors' access to and control over the process of government; and the extent to which international commitments and obligations with regard to trade policy are viewed as binding by national governments.

49. The process of growing economic interdependence, though making an important contribution to overall macro-economic performance, has created major adjustment pressures over the last decade. Shifts in the structure and dynamics of the OECD's trading relations, notably the emergence of new actors in the world economy, have increased the need for adjustment. But at least until the early 1980s, the flexibility of most OECD economies — and hence their capacity to adapt to change — diminished. The burdens this gives rise to have been aggravated by a context of slow growth and high unemployment.

50. In the mature oligopolies — automobiles, steel, consumer electrical equipment — intensified international competition has compressed profit margins, in a trend which the recent recovery has reversed, but unevenly. At the same time, there has been a strong association between greater import penetration and employment losses in industry, while the cost of losing one's job in these industries has increased. (According to one estimate, workers dismissed from the US steel industry suffer an earnings loss equal, on average, to 10-15 per cent of their lifetime earnings.) Moreover, import competition may have affected those who remained employed through its impact on wage setting.

51. While raising the "potential demand" for protection, the extent to which shifting trade patterns actually lead to protectionist measures will depend on the receptiveness of the political system to interest group pressures. Two salient changes can be identified: first, governments must deal with increasingly articulate, narrowly-defined pressure groups unconcerned by the macro-economic impact of their behaviour. This is partly because the growing scope of public involvement in the economy has itself encouraged more sectional interests to become politically organised, as the frequency and density of their contacts with governments rises.

52. Second, the range of policy instruments governments can use for responding to these pressures has diminished. Increasing economic interdependence constrains individual government's choices. Because of the inefficacy of macro-economic policy in maintaining full employment and budgetary constraints on social welfare programmes, consensus maintenance has become more difficult. The attractiveness of import protection — which is off-budget, highly visible to the protected group, but much less visible to others in terms of its costs — has consequently increased.

53. These changes in the domestic policy system have been paralleled by the diminishing efficacy of multilateral instruments in regulating, if not preventing, protectionist measures. This is partly the result of changed economic circumstances — the observance of international rules and regulations being to some extent a "fair-weather" phenomenon. However, it is also due to more far-reaching, and less readily reversible, changes in the structure of international relations. These include the growing range and diversity of participants in international negotiations; the widening agenda and increasing

technical complexity of the issues to be dealt with; and the emergence of a multipolar economic power system.

54. The medium-term prospects for the world trading system will depend on this interaction of economic and political, domestic and international, factors. While sustained recovery and greater flexibility in product and factor markets may reduce the costs of adjusting to change, it would be illusory to expect protectionist pressures to disappear. Moreover, the prospects for increasing the resilience of domestic political systems to interest group pressures should not be over-rated. Nonetheless, a decade of structural change in the OECD economies has produced new actors with a growing interest in an open trading regime — notably in the high technology and service industries. Much rests on the capacity of the multilateral system — and especially of its OECD participants — to respond to the needs of these new actors and resolve newly emerging problems and major long-standing issues, rather than concentrate on defending the industries and activities of the past.

III. CONCLUSIONS: PROTECTION AS AN INSTRUMENT OF POLICY

55. Protectionist measures are usually intended to meet two broad objectives: to provide visible and immediate relief to industries experiencing severe difficulties, and notably to their workforce; while allowing ongoing adjustment to changed circumstances. These objectives correspond to an employment and social equity concern on the one hand, and to a general goal of promoting greater economic efficiency and industrial restructuring on the other. Relative to the complexity of these objectives, protection is a fairly simple and blunt instrument of policy.

56. By reducing imports, protection seeks to raise the market share of domestic producers and the price they receive for their goods. Greater output and profitability in the domestic industry is presumed to increase employment and promote modernisation. The highly indirect nature of this link between the instrument — import controls — and the variables of policy interest — jobs and investment — provides a first source of ineffectiveness. Trade diversion reduces the impact of discriminatory restrictions on import volumes; domestic producers may not be able to provide an attractive substitute for imports; if the pressure of competition or of excess capacity on the home market is sufficiently strong, an increase in domestic output may involve little increase in employment, producers' profits or capacity to finance investment.

57. Even when protection does effectively transfer resources to the protected industry, the outcomes may still fall far short of policy goals. To begin with, the objectives of industry modernisation and job preservation are frequently incompatible, at least in the short run. More rapid modernisation usually involves shutting obsolete plants and reducing the industry's labour force. Conversely, preserving jobs may mean keeping these plants — often the industry's most labour-intensive ones — in operation, at an obvious cost

21

to efficiency. Protection may help achieve one objective or the other; in none of the cases surveyed did it achieve both.

58.   Moreover, the jobs saved or investments promoted may themselves not reflect the policy's original goals, notably with respect to income distribution. It has proved very difficult to ensure that whatever jobs are "saved" go to the less mobile and skilled workers located in problem regions. Equally, rather than promote investment and modernisation in the domestic industry, a large share of the rents from protection have accrued to their foreign competitors, notably in cases involving "voluntary" export restraints.

59.   Ultimately, the bluntness of protection as a policy instrument means that its precise effects — the extent of the "benefits" and their distribution — are extremely difficult to predict when the policy is being designed; while the outcome frequently fails to meet the objectives in some important respect. This creates pressures for yet more assistance to the industry in question. Trade diversion leads to demands for extending the import controls to new sources and products; the persistence of high adjustment costs for workers in the industry makes the social cost of cheap imports seem excessive; while the fact that the industry is not increasing its competitiveness relative to rivals casts a return to normal trading conditions as premature.

60.   The ineffectiveness of protection has a pervasive impact on its costs. The tangible costs to consumers — both individual households and, in the case of intermediate goods, user industries — have been extensively documented in this report. But to these must be added the indirect costs of protection which are less tangible and more difficult to quantify. Even in economies operating far from full employment, it may be possible to ignore the macro-economic impact of a single protectionist measure, but not the cumulative effect of the spread and persistence of such measures.

61.   Poorer economic performance as a result of protection is aggravated by a deteriorating environment for policy making. Macro-economic policy is more difficult to implement when a large part of the domestic economy expects to be shielded from the competitive discipline of product and labour markets. The "demonstration effect" of protection encourages more and more interest groups to become organised and active, diverting adjustment policy from promoting overall efficiency to arbitrating among competing sectoral claims. Protection itself becomes less effective in promoting adjustment when — as a result of the repeated renewal of protectionist measures — the firms being protected have no reason to expect that they will ever be exposed to the full challenge of international competition.

62.   Similar processes operate at an international level. Protectionist measures implemented by one country may seem to legitimate similar measures adopted by other countries. Retaliation is more likely to occur in an environment where protection is pervasive than when protectionist measures are a clearly confined exception to the rules. As countries act to neutralise the impact on their own producers of policies adopted elsewhere, it becomes more difficult for each country to predict and control the outcome of policy choices.

63.   Taken on their own, import controls have therefore not been a cost-effective instrument of adjustment policy. The disproportion between costs and benefits has been particularly great in cases involving highly discriminatory and complex restrictions imposed on a large number of potential suppliers — as, for example, in the MFA. Widespread discrimination and complexity results in cumbersome and costly adminis- tration, an extreme lack of transparency and uncertainty for all trading parties. Conversely, the costs of protection have been lower when the measures implemented were nondiscriminatory and transparent, with minimum distortion of the price system. The cases surveyed confirm that quantitative restrictions generally impose higher costs than tariffs, because the effective protection they accord increases as the domestic industry loses competitiveness, is particularly great in phases of cyclical recovery, and is inevitably less transparent.

64.   Equally important in determining the costs of protection is the scope it leaves for the domestic industry's ongoing adjustment to changes in the international division of labour. In the clothing industry, for example, tariff provisions favourable to outward processing trade are a major factor explaining why the industry has adjusted better in some OECD countries than in others.

65.   Some forms of protection are consequently less costly than others, but the "first-best" solution of returning to normal trading conditions should not simply be set aside. This does not mean providing no adjustment assistance whatsoever — in fact, certain assistance policies can clearly improve the functioning of market economies. But there are cases where the assistance being provided through protectionist measures is imposing costs far in excess of the conceivable benefits. Ultimately, choosing among these options depends on careful and ongoing assessment of the costs and benefits of policies — not only from a narrow budgetary point of view but in terms of the economy as a whole. A clear understanding of the costs protection imposes is essential to mobilising the groups it harms, particularly since these costs are frequently widely dispersed and indirect.

66.   Two priorities stand out in this respect. Firstly, the survey carried out by the Secretariat highlights the fact that the empirical and quantitative work on the costs and benefits of protection in manufacturing overwhelmingly originates in and refers to the United States, Canada and Australia. This is largely because these countries have institutional structures which promote public discussion of trade policy choices, make available the information needed for empirical research, and encourage academic research in this area. In contrast, in most of Continental Europe, there seems to be little public backing or encouragement for such work. Consequently there are very few publicly available studies on the costs and benefits of even very major public policy decisions — for example, with respect to the steel industry, or to trade in textiles and clothing.

67.   Secondly, in addition to achieving greater geographical balance in the research on protection, there are issue areas which will substantially influence the long-term development of the trading systems but which appear to be insufficiently covered by current research. Five such areas have emerged from this study:

- the macro-economic effects of sectoral protection;
- the impact of defensive domestic policies, and notably subsidies, on trade flows and economic performance;
- the effectiveness of policies for promoting high technology activities;
- the nature and extent of the potential gains from trade liberalisation in the service industries;
- the costs and benefits of government assisted export promotion, including through associated finance.

68.   Over the longer term, the strength of the multilateral trading system crucially reflects the depth of the political commitment sustaining it. This is not so much a question of the positions of this government or that; but of the appreciation throughout public opinion of the importance of liberal trade to achieving sustained growth and creating new jobs. It is in this broader domain, rather than simply in informing the day to day decisions of governments, that research on the costs and benefits of protection acquires its full significance.

Chapter I

RECENT TRENDS IN TRADE POLICY
FOR MANUFACTURED PRODUCTS

Part I

THE IMPACT OF PROTECTION:
AN ECONOMY-WIDE PERSPECTIVE

Preceded by a chapter summarising recent trends in trade and trade-related policies in the OECD area, this Part combines macro- and micro-economic approaches in analysing the impact of protection on trade flows, prices, employment, competitiveness and adjustment. Although the main emphasis of the presentation is on economy-wide implications, a major effort has been made to illustrate the various points with empirical material, drawn predominantly from the sectoral studies reviewed in Part II. Much attention is paid to industry characteristics and corporate strategies. Although often overlooked, they appear to be decisive in influencing the adjustment process, in forming attitudes towards protection and in determining its economic consequences.

Chapter 1

RECENT TRENDS IN TRADE POLICY
FOR MANUFACTURED PRODUCTS

1.   Since the late 1960s, tariff and non-tariff protection from imports in the OECD countries has concentrated on a small number of industries: textiles and clothing, footwear, some light consumer products and steel. In general, the multilateral trading system has held up well to the strains arising from prolonged slow growth and high unemployment. But the scope of protection has both widened and deepened in recent years:

  — Protection has been extended to previously less- or un-affected industries such as automobiles, consumer electronics and machine tools.
  — Within the protected industries, the share of trade subject to control has increased.
  — A growing range of countries is subject to discriminatory controls on their exports.
  — The share of these countries' exports subject to control has risen.

Tariff protection

2.   Tariff levels have declined steadily since the passage of the United States Reciprocal Trade Agreements Act in 1934. Bilateral trade agreements, mostly extended on an MFN basis, and multilateral agreements within the GATT, have permitted substantial reciprocal reductions in tariff rates. Until the late 1950s, while the United States cut its relatively high tariff rates considerably, the primary focus in Europe was on easing quantitative restrictions and payments controls[1]. Rather, the most significant multilateral tariff reductions occurred in the 1960s and 1970s in the Kennedy and Tokyo Rounds of the GATT, accompanied by regional liberalisation within and between the EC and EFTA.

3.   Measured by the ratio of customs duties to the value of imports[2], the incidence of tariffs was more than halved between 1965 and 1975 (Table 1.1). This process continued in the 1970s, though at a slower pace. By the end of the decade, customs duties accounted for some 2.5 per cent of the value of imports, half the ratio ten years earlier[3].

Table 1.1

RECEIPTS FROM CUSTOMS AND IMPORT DUTIES
ACCRUING TO OECD COUNTRIES AS A
PERCENTAGE OF THE VALUE OF THEIR IMPORTS: 1965–1980

	1965	1970	1975	1980	Percentage Change 1965–1980
Australia	9.62	12.30	12.21	10.13	+5.3
Austria	8.57	6.42	4.04	1.70	−80.2
Belgium/ Luxembourg	3.79	2.70	1.49	1.38	−63.6
Canada	7.95	5.66	5.46	4.62	−41.9
Denmark	2.84	2.19	1.46	1.02	−64.1
Finland	9.97	4.21	2.81	1.37	−86.3
France	6.05	2.33	1.43	1.07	−82.3
Germany	4.64	3.04	2.36	1.81	−61.0
Greece	11.73	9.81	5.55	5.51	−53.0
Ireland	15.75	14.02	10.43	0.90	−94.3
Italy	5.94	4.66	0.57	0.78	−86.9
Japan	7.55	7.03	2.96	2.46	−67.4
Netherlands	5.72	2.98	1.68	1.40	−75.5
Norway	4.03	1.05	1.32	0.86	−78.7
Portugal	11.72	10.28	6.63	3.41	−70.9
Spain	16.56	14.51	12.66	9.46	−42.9
Sweden	6.26	6.62	2.37	1.72	−72.5
Switzerland	6.93	4.15	2.95	1.57	−77.3
Turkey	53.55	52.71	29.80	15.20	−71.6
United Kingdom	5.97	2.76	2.25	2.17	−63.7
United States	6.75	6.08	3.79	3.08	−54.4
OECD average	6.77	5.05	3.32	2.43	−64.1

Source: Revenue Statistics of OECD Member Countries 1965–1981
OECD Historical Statistics of Foreign Trade 1965–1980
Secretariat calculations

4.   A broadly similar picture emerges from comparisons of average tariffs on industrial imports alone. Calculated on a trade-weighted basis for the EC 6, the United States, the United Kingdom and Japan, these declined from 11 per cent prior to the Kennedy Round to slightly over 6 per cent thereafter. After the implementation of the Tokyo Round, average MFN tariffs on industrial imports for 17 major OECD countries[4] will stand at around 4.5 per cent, a reduction of one third. The Generalised System of Preferences, implemented in the early 1970s, has allowed even more substantial cuts in tariff barriers

confronting imports from developing countries, over 40 per cent of these entering OECD markets duty free in 1984[5].

5.   Nominal tariff rates are now at an all-time low, being less than half those prevailing during the nineteenth century heyday of "free trade"[6]. However, post-war reductions in nominal tariff rates have been much greater for some commodity groups than for others. Effective rates of protection (i.e. the incidence of tariffs on value added) for particular products have not necessarily diminished by as much as the declines in average nominal rates suggest[7].

6.   In the early stages of import substituting industrialisation, countries tend to impose relatively low levels of duty on imports of essential raw materials and capital goods, for which there is no domestic industry, and relatively high tariffs on light manufacturing goods which can be produced domestically. This pattern of tariff differentiation is typically perpetuated as countries become more industrialised[8].

7.   This has two consequences. First, effective rates of protection tend to be higher than nominal rates, given the relatively low duties on materials as compared with semi-manufactured and finished goods, and the absence of tariffs on non-material, non-traded inputs[9]. Second, there has been a convergence of tariff escalation in industrialised countries with effective rates of protection considerably higher than nominal rates at later stages of processing[10]. The post-war process of trade liberalisation has substantially preserved this pattern.

8.   In the multilateral trade negotiations, cuts in nominal tariffs were much greater for chemicals, transport equipment and machinery than for iron and steel and especially footwear, textiles and clothing (Graph 1.2). Under the Tokyo Round, 18 per cent of all industrial tariff lines will receive duty-free treatment in the industrial countries; but only 3 per cent of textiles and clothing tariff lines will be so treated. Tariff rates above 20 per cent will be imposed on only 5 per cent of all industrial products; but on 25 per cent of textiles and clothing products. Since tariffs on textiles and clothing are higher on the more heavily traded items, the trade weighted average of tariff rates for these products is substantially higher than the simple average. The opposite is true for industrial products as a whole.

9.   As a result of these disparities, effective tariff rates may have declined less than their nominal counterparts; the general degree of escalation in industrial tariff structures, which had declined substantially in the Kennedy Round, has remained virtually constant thereafter; while in some industrial sectors — again, most notably textiles and clothing — the degree of tariff escalation has actually increased[11].

10.   A similar differentiation is apparent in the tariff reductions under GSP. Several of the light manufacturing products which received the smallest MFN tariff reductions have been excluded in whole or in part from the GSP. Thus, on average 90 per cent of industrial sector tariff lines in OECD countries are either covered by GSP or duty-free at MFN rates; but the ratio for textiles and clothing products is only 70 per cent. Textile products represent about 17 per cent of all industrial tariff lines, but they account for over one-half of industrial product exclusions for all the GSP schemes taken together[12].

Graph 1.2

AVERAGE TARIFFS FOR OECD COUNTRIES IN SELECTED SECTORS

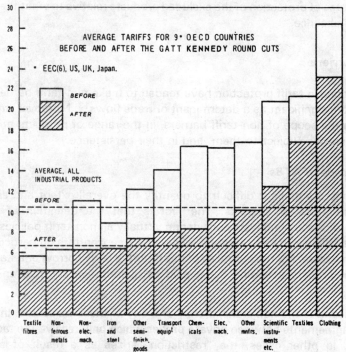

AVERAGE TARIFFS FOR 9• OECD COUNTRIES
BEFORE AND AFTER THE GATT KENNEDY ROUND CUTS

• EEC(6), US, UK, Japan.

BEFORE

AFTER

AVERAGE, ALL INDUSTRIAL PRODUCTS

BEFORE

AFTER

Textile fibres · Non-ferrous metals · Non-elec. mach. · Iron and steel · Other semi-finish. goods · Transport equip! · Chem-icals · Elec. mach. · Other mnfrs. · Scientific instruments etc. · Textiles · Clothing

Note : Tariff averages are weighted according to total OECD imports.
Source : UNCTAD document TD/6/Rev 1, 1968 «Evaluation des effets des négociations Kennedy sur les obstacles tarifaires», page 70.

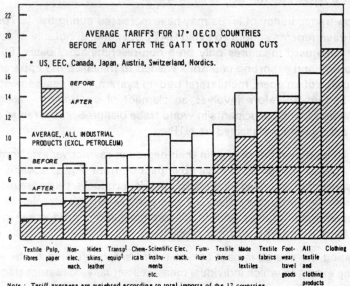

AVERAGE TARIFFS FOR 17• OECD COUNTRIES
BEFORE AND AFTER THE GATT TOKYO ROUND CUTS

• US, EEC, Canada, Japan, Austria, Switzerland, Nordics.

BEFORE

AFTER

AVERAGE, ALL INDUSTRIAL PRODUCTS (EXCL. PETROLEUM)

BEFORE

AFTER

Textile fibres · Pulp, paper · Non-elec. mach. · Hides skins, leather · Transp! equip! · Chem-icals · Scientific instruments etc. · Elec. mach. · Furn-iture · Textile yarns · Made up textiles · Textile fabrics · Foot-wear, travel goods · All textile and clothing products · Clothing

Note : Tariff averages are weighted according to total imports of the 17 countries.
Source : GATT and OECD estimates.

29

11.   The fact that the products excluded from GSP attract relatively high MFN duty rates, while the products covered by the Scheme generally enter duty free, may increase the effective rates of protection of the excluded products relative to what they would be in the Scheme's absence.

Non-tariff barriers

12.   Reductions in tariff protection have tended to make non-tariff barriers both more visible and more significant as a determinant of trade flows[13]. Moreover, there has been an increase in the scope of non-tariff barriers, in the range of products affected, in the number of countries subject to them, and in their persistence.

The overall scope of NTBs

13.   Three factors make it difficult to quantify the overall extent and significance of non-tariff restrictions on imports. The first is that the definition of NTBs varies considerably, with some analysts considering virtually all non-tariff policies which affect trade flows as falling into this category, while others concentrate on particular measures or classes of measure. For the purposes of this report, a fairly narrow orientation has been adopted, with primary attention being paid to quantitative controls on imports and exports.

14.   The second is the non-transparency of many of these measures. In some cases, they involve agreements between private parties which only receive the tacit consent of governments. In other cases, the "restriction" arises as a result of administrative procedures for processing, customs valuation, technical standards and health regulations, without a declared intention to limit trade.

15.   The non-transparency of NTBs may have increased during the 1970s. In part this was because governments sought to avoid GATT obligations, notably under Article XIX, which permit safeguard measures only on a non-discriminatory basis. But it was also because importing and exporting countries wished to minimise the apparent departures from the principles of an open, multilateral trading system. Any assessment of the scope of non-tariff barriers therefore involves an element of controversy, as governments, independent experts, and participants in world trade disagree on the range and incidence of measures appropriately classified as NTBs.

16.   Third, NTBs may differ greatly in their degree of restrictiveness: some quotas, for instance, may be set so high as to have no impact on trade flows; equally, though some countries require import licences for a broad range of products, these are granted liberally and do not hinder imports; conversely, certain administrative obstacles to imports – for example, type-approval procedures for telecommunications products – may impose so great a cost burden as to be virtually prohibitive.

17.   Estimating the overall impact of non-tariff barriers on imports therefore involves quantifying the extent to which individual measures actually do restrict trade, calculating the ad valorem tariff or bounty which would have an equivalent effect, and then

aggregating these estimates. Clearly, some simulation must at least implicitly be made of what trade flows would have been without the NTBs, but such calculations are inevitably complex and disputable. Moreover, unlike ad valorem tariffs, the restrictive impact of many NTBs, and notably of quantitative restrictions, varies greatly over time — e.g. as a result of cyclical shifts in relative costs and levels of demand. "Adding up" of unadjusted estimates may therefore give a misleading indication of the extent of restrictiveness at the margin.

18.   Given these difficulties, few studies have attempted to compute global ad valorem or subsidy equivalents for non-tariff barriers. Moreover, those which have, arrive at quite differing estimates[14]. Most of the studies carried out to date have focused on identifying the share of world trade subject to NTBs, without quantifying the degree of restriction involved. These studies do not allow comparison of the distortions due to NTBs with those arising from tariff protection, nor any overall assessment of the constraints imposed; but they do provide an indication of the changing scope of imports subject to differing types of non-tariff restriction, and of the distribution of affected imports by commodity group.

Table 1.3

MEASURES OF IMPORT RESTRICTIONS FOR MANUFACTURED
GOODS IN DEVELOPED COUNTRIES

			United States	European Common Market	Japan
I.	Restricted Imports as a	1980	6.20	10.80	7.20
	Share of Total	1981	5.53	1.38	–
	Manufactured Imports	1982	0.69	0.18	–
		1983	0.30	2.50	–
	Total affected:	end 1983	12.72	14.86	7.20
II.	Restricted Imports as a	1980	0.56	1.30	0.33
	Share of Total	1981	0.49	0.16	–
	Consumption of	1982	0.06	0.02	–
	Manufactured Goods	1983	0.03	0.25	–
	Total affected:	end 1983	1.14	1.73	0.33
III.	Consumption of	1980	20.3	23.7	15.7
	Restricted Manufactured	1981	12.4	2.3	–
	Goods as a Share of	1982	2.1	0.3	–
	Total Consumption of	1983	0.2	2.1	–
	Manufactured Goods				
	Total affected:	end 1983	35.0	28.4	15.7

Source: Balassa and Balassa (1984)

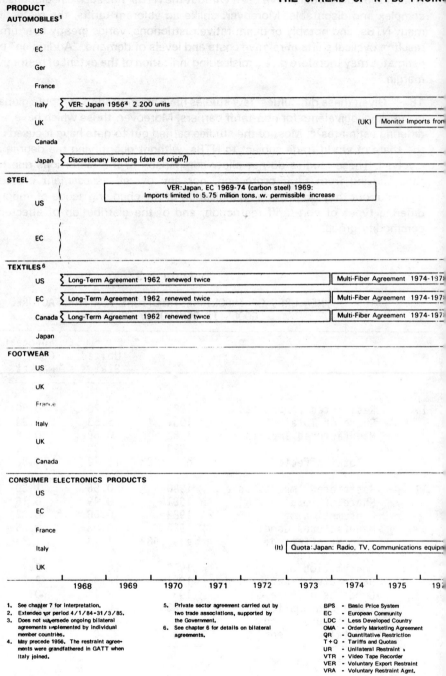

PRODUCT

AUTOMOBILES[1]

US

EC

Ger

France

Italy   VER: Japan 1956[4] 2 200 units

UK   (UK) | Monitor Imports from

Canada

Japan   Discretionary licencing (date of origin?)

STEEL

US   VER: Japan, EC 1969-74 (carbon steel) 1969:
Imports limited to 5.75 million tons, w. permissible increase

EC

TEXTILES[6]

US   Long-Term Agreement 1962 renewed twice   Multi-Fiber Agreement 1974-197

EC   Long-Term Agreement 1962 renewed twice   Multi-Fiber Agreement 1974-197

Canada   Long-Term Agreement 1962 renewed twice   Multi-Fiber Agreement 1974-197

Japan

FOOTWEAR

US

UK

France

Italy

UK

Canada

CONSUMER ELECTRONICS PRODUCTS

US

EC

France

Italy   (It) | Quota: Japan: Radio, TV, Communications equipm

UK

| 1968 | 1969 | 1970 | 1971 | 1972 | 1973 | 1974 | 1975 | 19 |

1. See chapter 7 for interpretation.
2. Extended for period 4/1/84-31/3/85.
3. Does not supersede ongoing bilateral agreements implemented by individual member countries.
4. May precede 1956. The restraint agreements were grandfathered in GATT when Italy joined.

5. Private sector agreement carried out by two trade associations, supported by the Government.
6. See chapter 6 for details on bilateral agreements.

BPS   - Basic Price System
EC   - European Community
LDC   - Less Developed Country
OMA   - Orderly Marketing Agreement
QR   - Quantitative Restriction
T+Q   - Tariffs and Quotas
UR   - Unilateral Restraint
VTR   - Video Tape Recorder
VER   - Voluntary Export Restraint
VRA   - Voluntary Restraint Agmt.

Termination Date

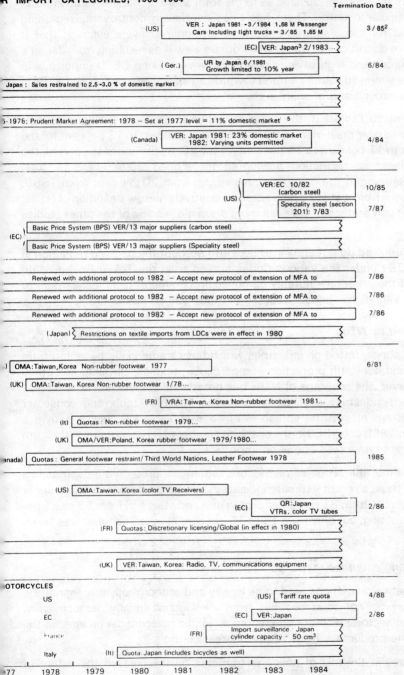

(US) | VER : Japan 1981 -3/1984 1.68 M Passenger Cars including light trucks = 3/85 1.85 M | 3/85[2]

(EC) VER: Japan[3] 2/1983 ...

(Ger.) | UR by Japan 6/1981 Growth limited to 10% year | 6/84

Japan : Sales restrained to 2.5 -3.0 % of domestic market

5-1978; Prudent Market Agreement: 1978 — Set at 1977 level = 11% domestic market[5]

(Canada) | VER: Japan 1981: 23% domestic market 1982: Varying units permitted | 4/84

(US) | VER:EC 10/82 (carbon steel) | 10/85

Speciality steel (section 201): 7/83 | 7/87

(EC) | Basic Price System (BPS) VER/13 major suppliers (carbon steel)

Basic Price System (BPS) VER/13 major suppliers (Speciality steel)

Renewed with additional protocol to 1982 — Accept new protocol of extension of MFA to | 7/86

Renewed with additional protocol to 1982 — Accept new protocol of extension of MFA to | 7/86

Renewed with additional protocol to 1982 — Accept new protocol of extension of MFA to | 7/86

(Japan) Restrictions on textile imports from LDCs were in effect in 1980

OMA:Taiwan, Korea Non-rubber footwear 1977 | 6/81

(UK) OMA:Taiwan, Korea Non-rubber footwear 1/78...

(FR) | VRA:Taiwan, Korea Non-rubber footwear 1981...

(It) Quotas : Non-rubber footwear 1979...

(UK) OMA/VER:Poland, Korea rubber footwear 1979/1980...

anada) Quotas : General footwear restraint/Third World Nations, Leather Footwear 1978 | 1985

(US) OMA:Taiwan, Korea (color TV Receivers)

(EC) | QR:Japan VTRs, color TV tubes | 2/86

(FR) Quotas : Discretionary licensing/Global (in effect in 1980)

(UK) VER:Taiwan, Korea: Radio, TV, communications equipment

OTORCYCLES

US | (US) Tariff rate quota | 4/88

EC | (EC) VER:Japan | 2/86

France | (FR) | Import surveillance : Japan cylinder capacity · 50 cm³

Italy | (It) Quota: Japan (includes bicycles as well)

77 | 1978 | 1979 | 1980 | 1981 | 1982 | 1983 | 1984

19.   Given differences in methodologies and in definition of non-tariff restrictions, the studies come to quite differing conclusions as to the total share of manufactured imports affected in any particular country. There has been continuing controversy regarding Japan's low demand for manufactured imports, with some analysts claiming that it reflects administrative distortions to trade, while others view it as resulting from Japan's lack of natural resources and high savings rate[15]. However, taking OECD imports as a whole, all the studies surveyed identify a trend towards an increasing coverage of NTBs in terms of commodity groups and of suppliers.

20.   Thus, according to Table 1.3, the share of restricted products in total manufactured imports increased over the period 1980-1983 from 6 per cent to 13 per cent for the United States and from 11 per cent to 15 per cent for the EC. By the end of the period, the product groups subject to restriction accounted for around 30 per cent of total manufactured consumption in the countries covered, up from 20 per cent from 1980. These results are drawn from a study which adopts a relatively narrow definition of NTBs; the increases in non-tariff protection are even more dramatic in some of the other studies referred to[16].

21.   The studies surveyed do not appear to take into account the ongoing reduction in certain important NTBs under the various Codes agreed to in the Tokyo Round. With respect to several of these codes — notably on public procurement, technical barriers to trade, and customs valuation — impact assessment may still be premature[17].

The products affected by NTBs

22.   NTBs remain concentrated on industries which have traditionally benefited from high levels of tariff and non-tariff protection — in particular, textiles, clothing, and steel. More recently, however, the coverage of NTBs has broadened somewhat, extending to relatively unprotected industries such as automobiles, machine tools and consumer electronics. This pattern of sectoral spread is obvious in Table 1.4, which shows a quadrupling between 1968 and 1983 in the absolute number of NTBs, notably in the form of discriminatory quantitative restrictions on imports.

23.   At the same time, the scope of restrictions within the protected industries has tended to increase. Thus, a recent estimate indicates that the proportion of trade under non-liberal treatment rose from 31 to 73 per cent in iron and steel and from 53 to 61 per cent in textiles and clothing, but only from 13 to 15 per cent in other manufactures taken as a whole.

The range of exporting countries restricted

24.   Many quantitative restrictions tend to be legally and economically discriminatory: legally, because they do not treat supplies from all sources equally; economically, because their uneven sectoral distribution creates an implicit discrimination against the major suppliers of the products subject to the tightest controls.

25.   Recent changes in the mix of policy instruments have increased the extent of discrimination. There has been a marked shift away from Article XIX safeguards, applied

on a non-discriminatory basis, towards bilateral instruments such as voluntary export restraints and orderly marketing agreements. Thus out of 22 major trade actions implemented by the United States, Canada and the EC in the period 1981 to 1983, at least 14 resorted to VERs[18].

26.   Growing recourse to anti-dumping action and countervailing duties has also accentuated this trend. These measures can be a perfectly legitimate response to unfair trading practices. But it must also be recognised that to the governments imposing these measures — and to the firms soliciting them — anti-dumping and countervailing duty actions can appear to be attractive as they are rapidly implementable, highly selective in the products and sources affected and not requiring prolonged negotiations with supplying countries. Moreover, they can effectively eliminate the intense price competition characteristic of exports from the NICs and Centrally Planned Economies.

27.   Traditionally, discriminatory restrictions have focused on a small number of supplying countries, mainly Japan and the Asian NICs, and recently the number of restrictions to which these countries are subject has risen. Table 1.5 shows that in 1980, 15 per cent of the exports of Japan and the Asian NICs were affected by NTBs; by 1983, new actions brought this share to over 30 per cent. (To correct for the impact of restrictions on the composition of trade, this is calculated using 1980 trade weights.)

28.   The number of suppliers affected by NTBs has also increased. The evolution of the Multifibre Agreement provides a striking example. During MFA I, the United States had bilateral agreements with 19 countries; but none of these agreements specified explicit limits on imports of so-called "sensitive items". During MFA II, specific limits were introduced into US bilateral agreements with seven countries; and during MFA III, this number rose to fourteen. Equally, for the EC the number of countries covered by bilateral agreements increased from 33 in MFA I to 43 in MFA III, while the number of categories specified went from 23 to 48, much of the rise actually occurring in MFA II. Similar trends are apparent for other countries participating in the MFA.

29.   The spread of discrimination also undermines the free flow of goods between countries which — at least in theory — are not subject to restrictions. Measures adopted to prevent trans-shipment impose heavy documentation requirements on products from unrestricted sources. These increase the delays and costs involved in exporting and thus discourage trade. This applies not only to free trade areas, but also to the EC, where the spread of discriminatory measures applied individually by Member countries to imports from third countries has been reflected in a growing number of certificate of origin requirements on goods in intra-EC trade[19].

30.   The cost of documentation requirements should not be underestimated. According to experts in trade procedures, the execution of the average transaction in international trade requires 35 documents and 360 copies[20]. Within the EC, where it was recently decided to adopt a single customs document replacing the seventy-odd papers now needed, the transactions cost due purely to administrative procedures at customs exceed 1 per cent of the value of shipments — a large sum when set against the profit margins typically involved in foreign trade[21]. This is consistent with a study for Finland which

Table 1.5

VALUE ($m) OF MANUFACTURED EXPORTS
TO OECD COUNTRIES SUBJECT TO TRADE RESTRICTIONS

Country of origin	Total manufactured exports 1980	Subject to restrictions (a)	
		in 1980	in 1983
Japan	61 688	6 963	21 813
Korea	10 070	2 260	3 175
Taiwan	12 034	1 984	2 216
Hong Kong	11 769	3 423	4 150
Singapore	3 579	209	276
Total	99 140	14 839	31 630(b)
		(=15 %)	(=32 %)

a) Product items subject to restrictions are:

Japan — 1980: steel; television receivers to US; ships.
1983: steel; one-third of television receiver exports to EEC; ships; automobiles; motorcycles to US.

Korea — 1980: one-half clothing and textile exports; one-third footwear exports; television receivers to US.
1983: two-thirds clothing and textiles; one-half footwear to EC; one-half steel.

Taiwan — as per Korea.

Hong Kong — 1980: two-thirds clothing and textiles; 1983: four-fifths clothing and textiles.

Singapore — 1980: one-third clothing and textiles; 1983: two-thirds clothing and textiles.

b) To correct for the impact of restrictions on the composition of trade, this is calculated using 1980 trade weights.

found that documentation costs amounted to 1.4 to 5.7 per cent of the total value of 1982 imports[22].

The persistence of NTBs

31. Finally, temporary protection has been very much the exception rather than the rule. Of the four industries surveyed in Part II, the only major trade restrictions which have

been allowed to lapse are the US OMA in consumer electronics and (most recently) VER in automobiles. In the other industries they have been systematically renewed and even strengthened, extending virtually indefinitely the "breathing space" provided to domestic firms.

Trade-distorting domestic measures

32.   In an increasingly interdependent world economy, the boundaries between "trade" and "domestic" policies have become progressively blurred. This has led a number of observers to question the concentration of trade policy analysts on measures applied at national borders. A common theme underlying this growing literature is that governments are intervening more in the process of structural and industrial change. These interventions may alter the distribution of world output and trade, particularly (but not only) through the provision of subsidies to industries or regions facing severe difficulties and to promising industries or activities.

33.   There has been an upward drift in subsidies to industry in the OECD region since the 1950s (Table 1.6). There may also have been some change in the volume of indirect subsidies provided, for instance, through public procurement, exemptions from competition law, etc; but no comprehensive studies exist in this regard.

34.   Clearly not all subsidies can be considered to be distorting; nor do all subsidies alter trade flows. For a domestic subsidy to durably affect the pattern of trade it must be discriminatory (or selective) so as to alter the relative cost position of a country's industries, thus shifting the pattern of comparative advantage. At the same time it must not be entirely offset by changes in exchange rates or in the other parameters of internal and external balance.

35.   Subsidies provided to all or a broad range of activities are unlikely to meet these criteria. A generally available subsidy to the use of a particular factor will only significantly advantage the industries intensive in that factor if the subsidy provided is fairly sizeable. But precisely if the subsidy is sizeable, it is likely to be at least partly offset by changes in factor prices or in real exchange rates[23].

36.   Equally, once-off grants, including capital transfers, in principle do not alter the discounted present value of incremental costs. Consequently, they will not affect a firm's optimal level of output and hence its long-term market share. They may nonetheless induce the installation of new capacity at the margin and can hence distort trade flows over the longer term.

37.   From a pragmatic point of view, this suggests that the subsidies which may affect trade are those which
   a)   are concentrated in a few sectors of the economy and
   b)   have a substantial and recurring impact on these sectors' cost positions relative to other sectors.

38.   In many OECD countries, there has been an increase in both the volume and share of public assistance provided to the fairly small number of industries experiencing severe

37

Table 1.6

GROWTH OF SUBSIDIES (1) IN ALL OECD MEMBER COUNTRIES
1960-1983

Index: 1965 = 100

	As share of GDP		As share of operating surplus	
	Index	%	Index	%
1960	75	0.72	73	2.63
1965	100	0.96	100	3.60
1970	119	1.15	131	4.71
1975	157	1.52	199	7.18
1976	157	1.52	197	7.10
1977	161	1.56	202	7.27
1978	169	1.63	207	7.44
1979	169	1.63	208	7.48
1980	172	1.66	219	7.89
1981	175	1.69	224	8.05
1982	183	1.77	236	8.51
1983	194	1.87	241	8.67

1. Grants on current account by the public authorities to (i) private industry and public corporations and (ii) government enterprises to compensate for losses which are clearly the consequence of the price policies of the public authorities. Current grants to producers of private non-profit services to households are excluded.

Source: OECD National Accounts 1960-1983.

---

adjustment difficulties. These industries are by and large the same in the various Member countries; they include steel, shipbuilding, textiles and clothing and more recently automobiles. Many of these industries have been subject to below-average reductions in effective rates of tariff protection and benefited from the spread of NTBs. However, there have also been growing subsidies to technology-intensive industries frequently working for export markets.

39. The concentration of public assistance on industries in difficulty can readily be illustrated.

— In *Germany,* while federal government subsidies to industry (excluding transport) increased by only 23 per cent at constant prices over the period 1967-1983, the share of steel and shipbuilding in these subsidies went from less than 1 per cent to 9.6 per cent.

— In *Sweden,* a 114 per cent rise in the value of industrial subsidies at constant prices from 1976/77 to 1981/82 was accompanied by an increase in the share going to steel, shipbuilding, mining, textiles and clothing, and pulp and paper from 72.5 to about 79 per cent, though this has more recently been reversed through a sharp reduction in the level of direct financial assistance to industry.

- In the *United Kingdom*, steel, shipbuilding and coal mining accounted in 1982/83 for 25.5 per cent of total government support to industry, up from 7.5 per cent six years earlier.

- In *France*, shipbuilding and steel accounted for 35 per cent of total sectoral aids over the period 1970-78; this share appears to have increased subsequently.

- In *Italy*, while overall government assistance to industry increased 180 per cent at constant prices during the 1970s, the share of the steel, transport equipment and chemicals industries went from 44 per cent in 1970 to 54 per cent in 1979.

- Finally, in the *United States*, the relatively small volume of public assistance to domestic manufacturing almost doubled during the second half of the 1970s; in 1982, shipbuilding and automobiles accounted — according to one estimate — for some 70 per cent of the implicit protection these transfers accorded[24].

40.   The fact that internationally, subsidies are heavily concentrated in the same industries may very much reduce their overall effect on trade flows. A large share of the subsidies provided may simply counteract support policies implemented elsewhere, with high budgetary costs but little net impact.

41.   However, it must be recognised that a major difficulty encountered in this study has been the scarcity of serious applied research on the impact of domestic policies on trade flows, let alone any quantitative assessment. This can be explained partly by the conceptual, methodological and statistical problems raised, and partly by the fact that much of the research work in the area of international trade is carried out in countries mainly relying on border measures of import protection.

42.   Bearing these caveats in mind, a broad pattern nonetheless emerges from the information presented above. Interventions in the trading system have become increasingly polarised and sector specific. Most manufactured products entering world trade face relatively few barriers; however, a small but growing range of products is subject to persistent tariff and non-tariff distortions. These products tend to be the same in the various OECD countries: the list includes textiles and clothing, footwear, steel and automobiles. Legacies of successive phases of industrial development, these products share some characteristics which set them apart from the manufacturing average: notably slower growth rates of demand and lower R&D intensity. There are, however, also important structural differences amongst them. A central theme of this report is how these differences have shaped the impacts of growing protection.

NOTES AND REFERENCES

1. The average rate of duty on dutiable imports in the United States fell from an average of 50 per cent in 1931-1935 to 16 per cent in 1946-1950 and then to 11.5 per cent in 1955-1960. See Kenen: 1964, p.69.

2. This measure may understate the extent of tariff reductions, since cuts in prohibitive tariffs tend to lead to an *increase* in duties collected. Morgan stresses the importance of reductions in prohibitive tariffs as a factor expanding trade in the post-war period. See Morgan and Martin: 1975 and Batchelor, Major and Morgan: 1980. However, it may also overstate the reduction in tariffs, since trade may increase more rapidly in products with below average rates of duty.

3. It should be noted that a substantial part of this decline was due to the increase in petroleum products' share in the value of imports, since these products typically attract very low rates of duty.

4. The United States, EEC, Canada, Japan, the Nordic countries, Austria and Switzerland.

5. OECD; 1983 (The Generalised System of Preferences: Review of the First Decade), p.12.

6. The average rate of duty on UK imports in the 1880s and 1890s was between 5 and 7 per cent (Imlah: 1958, pp.121 and 160); these were, of course, accompanied by substantial non-tariff distortions to trade, particularly as regards UK colonies (see, for instance, as regards India, de Cecco : 1970). Average nominal rates of tariff protection in this period were higher in other countries, in Germany for instance being in the order of 9-10 per cent (Glismann and Weiss: 1980, p.6). For the United States see Hawke: 1975, Andersen: 1972, Lerdan: 1957.

7. The effective tariff rate can be conveniently defined as the percentage addition made possible by the existence of the tariff to the domestic industry's value added, with prices being calculated at free trade levels. It should be noted that calculations of effective rates of protection are highly sensitive to assumptions made about substitution elasticities in production, so that differing studies yield greatly differing results. See Corden: 1957, Corden: 1974, Deardorff and Stern: 1984.

8. See Maizels: 1963.

9. The overall ratio of effective to nominal rates based on 1962 data was 1.85 for Sweden, 1.82 Japan, 1.79 United Kingdom, 1.72 United States, 1.65 Canada, 1.56 Common Market. See Melvin and Wilkinson: 1968, pp.31-32.

10. B. Balassa: 1965.

11. See, however, Andersen: 1972, pp.57-76, who found a greater reduction in effective than nominal rates for the United States over the period 1939-1958. For other surveys, see Cline: 1978, Dancet: 1980, Henner: 1972; Lafay: 1979; UNCTAD: 1968, Grubel and Johnson: 1971; Deardorff and Stern: 1984; Deardorff and Stern: 1982; and GATT: 1984, pp.69-70.

12. OECD; 1983 (The Generalised System of Preferences); GATT; 1984, p.71.

13. Clearly a quota or other NTB will not affect trade flows if the tariff on the product being restricted is such as to limit trade below the quota level. As tariffs are reduced, quotas therefore appear to be increasingly restrictive.

14. Nonetheless, a number of these studies suggest that overall the protection provided by NTBs now nearly equal that due to tariffs. Compare for instance, the tariff equivalents reported by Baldwin: 1970, Brown and Whalley: 1980 and Morici and Megna: 1983. See also Jager and Lanjouw: 1977. Looking at all commodity groups for the United States, Baldwin estimated that after the Kennedy Round reductions, NTB distortions accounted for 33 per cent of the average total effective rate against 25 per cent in 1958. He found that between 1964 and 1972, the effective rate of protection afforded by non-tariff measures rose from 3 to 5 per cent. More recently, Morici and Megna: 1983 estimate that US NTBs have a net impact, economy-wide, approximately equal to that of tariffs. See more generally Deardorff and Stern: 1983.

15. On differences in estimate see Cline (1981) who estimated that close to 45 per cent of US manufactured imports were subject to major NTBs; while Balassa and Balassa (1984) set this proportion at closer to 12 per cent. A similar difference with respect to the United Kingdom can be found by comparing Page: 1980 with Jones: 1983. On Japan, see Saxonhouse: 1984.

16. Page: 1980, for example, estimates that between 1974 and 1979 the amount of trade by market economies affected by formal non-tariff measures rose from 40 to 46 per cent. In manufactures, the share leaped from 13 to 20 per cent. The changes for European countries' imports were from 34 per cent to 41 per cent for all goods and from 2 to 14 per cent for manufactures.

17. It is interesting to note though that Deardorff and Stern: 1983 estimate that the world welfare gains from the Public Procurement Code exceed those due to the multilateral tariff reductions agreed to in the Tokyo Round. Nonetheless, it is also notable that unlike MTN tariff cuts these codes are not applicable on an MFN basis, reducing the extent of their potential impact.

18. Calculated from GATT: 1982; see also Balassa and Balassa: 1984.

19. House of Lords: 1982; Holmes and Shepherd: 1983.

20. Economic Commission for Europe, Working Paper IX on Facilitation of International Trade Procedures, INF.68.

21. Holmes and Shepherd: 1983.

22. Koskinen: 1983.

23. Deakin and Pratten: 1982, pp.145-147 find that the UK temporary employment subsidy did have a discernible impact on British exports of labour intensive products, notably clothing and footwear. However, they also find that within a twelve months period the indirect effects of the subsidy offset nearly two-thirds of the initial job-creating effect. It should be noted that a subsidy may of course act as a tax on the non-traded sector to the benefit of the traded sector as a whole; even in the absence of a shift in comparative advantage such a subsidy would alter trade flows. However, in the absence of restrictive assumptions on relative factor intensities in the two sectors, this subsidy would have to come very close to being a pure export subsidy of the type proscribed under the GATT. It is therefore not dealt with in this discussion.

24. Grilli and La Noce: 1982 emphasize the partial substitutability of tariffs and subsidies in the Italian case. Carlsson: 1983; de Carmoy: 1978; Franko: 1980; Morici and Megna: 1983; Mutti: 1982; Ranci: 1983; "Subsidies in the Federal Republic of Germany" (European Economy: 1983); Deutscher Bundestag: 1983.

Chapter 2

THE IMPACT ON TRADE FLOWS AND PRICES

1. World trade in the product groups most subject to restrictions increased rapidly in the 1970s. Notably in the case of clothing and footwear, growth rates of OECD imports were well above those for manufactured products as a whole (Graph 2.1). Equally, the countries most subject to discriminatory restrictions on their exports managed to steadily increase their share of OECD imports (Graph 2.2). However, the more restricted product categories did not sustain this strong performance into the 1980s. It would seem that — after being largely ineffective in the earlier period (with the possible exception of the MFA) — protectionist measures were gradually reinforced and eventually began to bite.

The effect of protective measures in the 1970s

2. Restrictions on imports are generally intended to reduce the foreign supply of a product to a particular market, lowering the level of imports for that product, raising its price and thus reducing also home demand. The domestic industry is presumed to benefit from both the increase in price and in domestic sources' market share.

3. In practice, the forms of quantitative restrictions currently in most widespread use — namely discriminatory "voluntary" export restraint and orderly marketing agreements — induce complex shifts in foreign supply which at least partially offset these intended impacts.

4. First, the *sources* of the imports may change. In particular, discrimination against certain sources of supply may simply divert demand from "more" to "less" restricted foreign countries, rather than to domestic suppliers.

5. Secondly, the *composition* of imports may change, as a result of the uneven sector — and product — incidence of the restrictions:
- Sector-specific measures, especially when adopted in a context of overall trade liberalisation, can lead to major changes in effective rates of protection along chains of processing; these then give rise to offsetting shifts in the degree of processing of traded products, for instance, restricted imports of

Graph 2.1

OECD IMPORTS OF ALL MANUFACTURED GOODS AND OF THOSE SUBJECT TO RESTRICTIONS 1965-83

1965 = 100

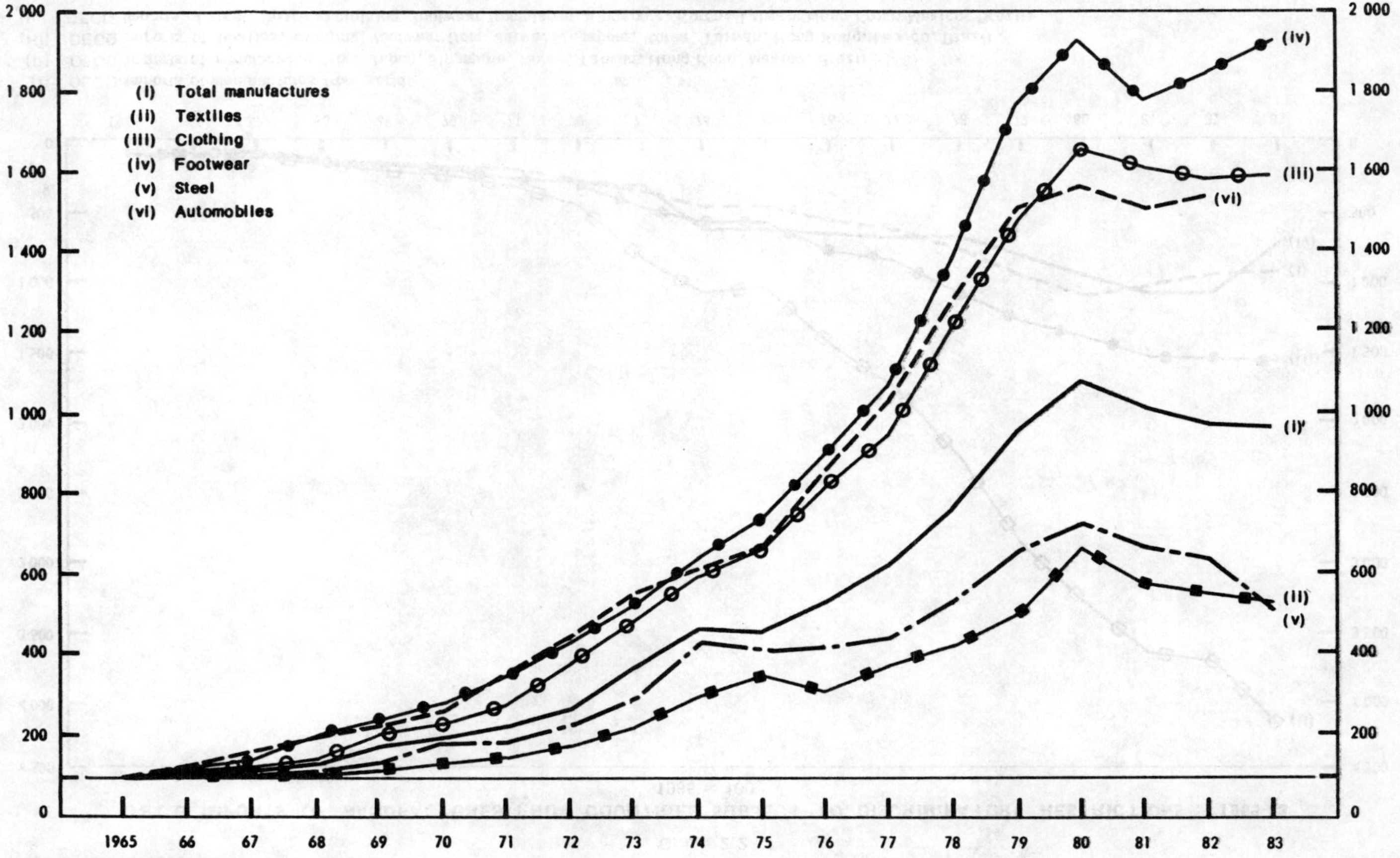

(I) Total manufactures
(II) Textiles
(III) Clothing
(IV) Footwear
(V) Steel
(VI) Automobiles

Note : Includes Intra-EEC trade.

Source : OECD, Foreign Trade Statistics.

43

Graph 2.2

OECD IMPORTS OF MANUFACTURES FROM COUNTRIES SUBJECT TO DISCRIMINATORY RESTRICTIONS : 1965-83

1965 = 100

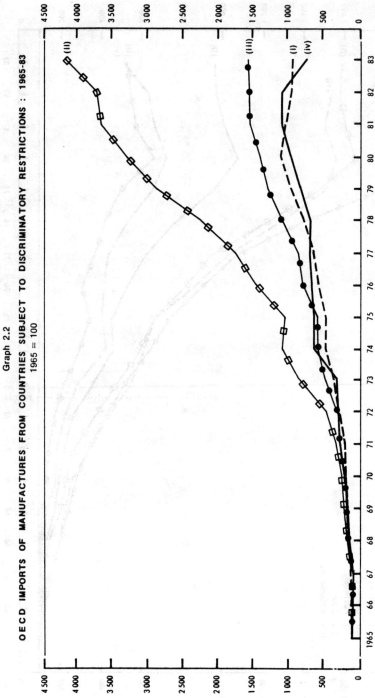

(i)   OECD imports of manufactures from world.
(ii) OECD imports of manufactures from Japan, Singapore, Korea, Taiwan, Hong Kong, Mexico, Brazil.
(iii) OECD imports of textiles, clothing, footwear from Japan, Singapore, Korea, Taiwan, Hong Kong, Mexico, Brazil.
(iv) OECD imports of steel, textiles, clothing, footwear from Japan, Singapore, Korea, Taiwan, Hong Kong, Mexico, Brazil.

Source : OECD, *Foreign Trade Statistics.*

finished products being replaced by unrestricted imports of components.

- Within the protected sector, the degree of restrictiveness typically varies greatly among products, so that the primary impact may fall on the composition of imports rather than on their total volume.
- These compositional changes are compounded by the incentives quantitative restrictions create for foreign suppliers to move among the restricted product categories: from those with lower to those with higher value added, and from those with higher to lower elasticities of demand[1].

6.   Three factors increased the importance of trade diversion during the 1970s. These were: the nature of the restrictions imposed; the industrial characteristics of the sectors being protected; the growing interdependence of the world economy.

The nature of the restrictions imposed

7.   The extent of offsetting changes is partly dependent on the inherent "restrictiveness" of the protective measures, and notably the leeway they provide for source and compositional shifts in imports. The process by which these measures were adopted in the 1970s ensured that they embodied considerable latitude in this respect.

8.   The modalities of VERs and OMAs used to be negotiated between the importing and the exporting country. These negotiations did not generally give rise to formal compensation for the exporting country, but the need to ensure a mutually acceptable outcome tended to lead to a compensatory element being built into the final agreement:

- Typically, negotiators from the protecting country — while seeking to placate domestic pressure groups — wished to avoid undue or too obvious harm to the trading system. They were therefore willing to make concessions on product categories not considered as sensitive, incorporate flexibility provisions in the protective measures, and exempt smaller supplying countries from these measures.
- Negotiators from the exporting countries learned that a strategy of rejecting restrictions altogether was unlikely to succeed. But one which maximises the degree of flexibility and of product substitutability in the final agreement could minimise the measures' cost — and might even yield benefits to suppliers in the form of product upgrading and diversification, controls on "excessive competition" and improvements in the terms of trade[2].

Features of the protected sectors

9.   The industrial characteristics of the sectors being protected were also such as to allow offsetting shifts in foreign supply, given the scope for such shifts embodied in the protective measures.

10.   Changes in sources of imports in response to discrimination depend on:

— the size of the cost differential between foreign and domestic suppliers;
— the ease with which new sources of supply can enter and exit the market in response to the opportunities for trade diversion which cost differentials create.

Both of these factors vary over time. Investment in physical and human capital may be needed if economic agents are to exploit opportunities for trade diversion; the longer run response is therefore likely to be stronger than that in the short term. In the longer run, however, the domestic industry itself is likely to change, altering the extent to which profitable trade diversion can occur. (These longer term impacts are discussed in Chapter 4.)

11.   In the short run, the critical factor affecting the response to trade diversion opportunities is the structure of the protected activity's cost function. Activities dependent on complex technology, capital intensity, or static and dynamic scale economies display substantial barriers to entry and exit. The established producers' vulnerability to "hit and run" behaviour by new entrants is low. The impact of import restrictions on trade flows and prices depends on the responses they elicit from existing suppliers, rather than on the threat and fact of entry. These responses consist largely of compositional shifts, for instance in product quality or degree of processing. Nonetheless, in the longer term, the persistence of above average price-cost margins in the restricted market may encourage the development of new sources of supply either in unrestricted source countries or in the restricted market itself.

12.   In contrast, in highly labour-intensive activities — such as clothing, footwear, or other light manufactured products — variable costs dominate the cost structure and the sunk costs required to penetrate markets are relatively low. In the language of contemporary industrial organisation theory, these markets are "contestable"[3]. Moreover, a large and persistent cost differential separates the protecting OECD countries from a wide range of potential suppliers. Discriminatory controls on established foreign suppliers are therefore quickly offset by the emergence of new suppliers, despite the possibility that the initial restrictions will eventually be extended.

13.   During the 1970s, the bulk of the restrictions in place affected precisely these "footloose" sectors of activity. As is apparent from the sector surveys for textiles and clothing and consumer electronics, this created great scope for trade diversion, in terms of both the product and country composition of trade. The footwear industry highlights the speed with which this scope was taken up. In 1977, the United States negotiated an Orderly Marketing Agreement on non-rubber footwear with Korea; at the time, 70 per cent of Korea's footwear exports were non-rubber and 30 per cent rubber. By 1978, these percentages had reversed while the value of Korea's overall footwear exports actually increased.

Growing economic interdependence

14.   Finally, broader structural changes in the world economy increased the responsiveness of product and factor markets to the opportunities for diversion which discriminatory and sector-specific controls created. These structural changes include:

- The greater homogeneity of demand patterns world-wide, and notably among the developed economies, made it easier for suppliers facing a restriction in one importing country to divert products to less restricted markets.
- The spread of industrialisation and of industrial capabilities to an increasingly broad range of developing countries reduced the concentration of world supply and facilitated replacement of products from restricted exporters by products from other sources.
- The integration of world capital markets, and improved access by developing countries to these markets, accelerated the pace at which capital flowed to profitable opportunities for trade diversion.
- The growing share in world trade of flows occurring within multinational enterprises operated in the same direction, since these enterprises are presumably well placed to identify arbitrage opportunities and rapidly internalise their benefits[4].
- The increased concentration of distribution channels in the developed economies introduced new actors in the international economy, who systematically scan world markets for new low-cost sources and can quickly modify their procurement patterns; at the same time, it reduced the costs new exporters face in penetrating advanced markets[5].

15. It is not surprising, therefore, that econometric studies of international trade find little evidence that protection significantly affected the expansion of total exports of manufactured goods until the late 1970s. Since then, however, three important changes have reduced the extent of these diversion effects and heightened the trade constraining effects of restrictions.

Diminishing scope for shifts in the 1980s

16. To begin with, the very extent of diversion has created strong pressure on a number of OECD governments to extend the country and product coverage of the restrictions, so as to provide more protection to the domestic industry. Notably in the textiles and clothing industries, this has led to a generalised system of discriminatory import controls applying to most non-OECD sources and virtually all sensitive product categories. The econometric evidence discussed below (see Chapter 6) suggests that on its own, the tightening of the MFA at its second renewal reduced OECD imports of textiles and clothing by nearly 10 per cent in volume terms.

17. Second, the manifest willingness of protecting countries to extend their restrictions to new sources has become an increasingly credible entry deterrent. A striking instance in this respect is provided by the US colour television receiver Orderly Marketing Agreement of 1976-81. Initially aimed at Japan, the emergence of Korea and Taiwan as alternative sources of supply led to the agreement's extension to these two countries. Though a number of other sources — for instance Mexico, Singapore and Thailand — were well placed to enter the US market at that time, the deterrent effect of the initial extension was clearly sufficient to dissuade them[6].

18.   Finally, the focus of import restrictions has shifted. At the beginning of the 1970s, the steel industry was virtually the only capital intensive industry with important sector-specific non-tariff barriers. By the early 1980s, such restrictions had spread to a range of products whose characteristics made them less vulnerable to trade diversion. These include automobiles, video-recorder equipment, and numerically controlled machine tools. Discriminatory restrictions in these industries were more likely to effectively control the level of total imports.

Price effects

19.   The narrowing of diversion opportunities has aggravated the upward pressure on prices which the initial restrictions – despite the pervasiveness of offsetting impacts – provoked.

... due to cost differentials

20.   Thus, extensive shifts in import source have raised prices when (as is usually the case) the "less" restricted sources are producers operating at a higher cost than the "more" restricted sources. Moreover, even in fairly "footloose" activities, some economic costs are involved in altering sourcing patterns. These cost differentials are reflected in differentials in the profitability of exports from the various sources, with a Ricardian rent accruing to the lowest cost producer:

- Trade restrictions have driven a wedge between prices in the protected market and world market prices. Particularly in markets with easy entry and exit, this wedge reflects cost differentials between more and less restricted sources of supply, rather than price discrimination.
- The tighter the restriction is – in terms of excluding low cost sources at the expense of home demand – the greater the wedge between domestic and world price. The differential is particularly large in periods when domestic demand is strong, since this is when the quantitative limits have the greatest constraining effect. The price effect of the measures in place has therefore tended to increase in the recovery underway.

21.   In the clothing industry, for example, manufacturing costs in the Asian NICs for similar items involving a high direct labour input – e.g. women's coats or knit blouses – are around half those in the United States and a third lower than those in the EC; the fact that these can be profitably produced in the United States and the EC is a straightforward indication of the price rises due to protection. Between a third and a half of these price increases accrues to the Asian exporting NICs as a quota rent. A plausible estimate is that the annual transfer from OECD consumers to Asian NIC exporters is at least US$2 billion. This is equivalent to around 4 per cent of the total value of NIC exports to the OECD region.

22.   Equally, in the steel industry, US transaction prices for cold rolled sheet steel in January 1984 were around 20 per cent higher than prices in the European market and nearly 40 per cent higher than prices on third markets. The marginal profitability of

exports to the US market was therefore very high (and continued to increase with the appreciation of the dollar): it was sufficiently high already in the 1970s to ensure that foreign producers captured as much as one half of the total income transferred to the steel industry by US protection.

... due to commodity composition

23.   Shifts in the composition of trade as a result of import restrictions have also involved economic costs resulting in price increases, typically associated with changes in relative prices within the protected product group:

- Changes in degree of processing due to shifts in effective rates of protection alter cost relativities between components and final products, both in the restricted market and (when the protecting country accounts for a large share of total demand) on the world market.
- Moves "up-market" by restricted producers leave the supply of the lower-quality varieties to the domestic producers, who have higher costs of production. Together with the effects of reduced supply, this increases the price of lower-quality varieties of the product, often at the expense of poorer consumers.

24.   Again, the clothing case is relevant here. The average increase in UK clothing retail prices due to the second MFA was in the order of 10-20 per cent and for lower quality items such as jeans 30-50 per cent. Prices for children's wear — a highly labour intensive product — doubled. These changes have a regressive impact on income distribution, also because clothing accounts for a larger share of poorer households' consumption expenditure. One estimate finds that protecting the Canadian clothing industry costs lower-income households four times as much as it costs higher-income households.

... and due to price-cost margins

25.   Finally, while the effects of source and composition changes on prices reflect additional costs, import restrictions have also lead to price rises by increasing price-cost margins, notably in oligopolostic industries:

- The reduced competitive pressure of foreign supply encourages the dominant domestic firms to increase their output price, since the firm price elasticity of demand is now lower.
- Domestic firms may find it easier to collude (overtly or covertly) amongst themselves than with foreign suppliers, given similar cost structures and access to information. By excluding or at least restricting the foreign suppliers, the import controls facilitate oligopolistic coordination.
- Faced with a binding import restriction, the foreign suppliers have a greater interest in colluding (both amongst themselves and with their foreign rivals within the importing country) so as to jointly maximise profits, than they would have in the absence of such a constraint. Notably in the case of voluntary export restraints, the fact that quotas are administered by exporters has facilitated such collusion, since a high level of cooperation and

consultation between firms is needed to allocate export quotas and set official minimum export prices.

26.   A simulation study of the US automobile industry's experience under voluntary export restraints highlights these impacts. Prior to the VER, intense competition between Japanese suppliers, and the search for long run market share, kept Japanese car prices in the US market well below the level corresponding to joint profit maximisation. By limiting market share competition, and hence raising price-cost margins, the VER increased the profit position of Japanese manufacturers in the US market by some 18 per cent. A tariff with an equivalent impact on trade would have reduced Japanese profits by around 40 per cent, since Japanese producers would absorb a large share of the tariff through lower margins. Consequently, the prices charged by US suppliers would have been largely unchanged and there would be little positive impact on domestic profitability. The VER, in contrast, increased domestic suppliers' net income by almost as much as for the Japanese, with General Motors and Ford obtaining the largest absolute and relative gain.

27.   Overall, the evidence highlights the inherent limits of the "new" forms of protection — voluntary export restraint, orderly marketing agreements and so on — as instruments for the control of international trade. Fundamentally, these instruments are attractive to governments since they avoid an escalation of bilateral trade conflicts into the multilateral arena — though this in and of itself is a cause for serious concern (see Chapter 10 below). However, precisely because of their discriminatory character, they create great opportunities for trade diversion, which in an increasingly integrated world economy are rapidly taken up.

28.   To make the restrictions binding, governments therefore extend import controls. But the country allocation of quotas arising from this process may — as in the MFA — bear little obvious relation to that which would emerge in a market regulated by non-discriminatory instruments. As a result, the ultimate price effects can be substantially greater than those needed to reduce imports to the desired level.

NOTES AND REFERENCES

1.   A useful survey of the relevant literature can be found in Baldwin: 1982. Useful illustrations are provided, for example, by Consumers' Association: 1979, and Industries Assistance Commission: December 1983.

2.   This learning process is documented in Yoffie: 1983. The viewpoint of protecting country negotiators is well captured by the concept of "embedded liberalism" set out in J.G. Ruggie: 1982, pp.379-415.

3.   Baumol et al., 1982; Bailey and Friedlaender: 1982.

4. A recent econometric study by K. Flamm on *The Volatility of Offshore Investment* (mimeo, University of Massachusetts, 1983) provides empirical evidence on the response speed of assembly oriented foreign investment to shifts in costs and in political risk.

5. In France, for example, 95 importers accounted for nearly 50 per cent of all 1979 merchandise imports, with concentration being very much higher in individual product lines. See Candot and Dubarry: 1982 and Messerlin: 1982. Similar trends are apparent in other countries, see for instance Utton: 1982 for the UK. See Keesing: 1983, pp.338-342 for a more general discussion. The role of increasing concentration of retail and distribution in the growth of world textiles and apparel trade is discussed in United Nations: 1981, pp.218-227.

6. See G. Gregory in *Far Eastern Economic Review,* July 1979.

Chapter 3

THE IMPACT ON EMPLOYMENT

1.   One of the principal rationales for import restraints is to expand or at least preserve domestic employment, especially for sections of the labour force that might otherwise face adversity. But to what extent are protectionist measures effective in maintaining output in the domestic industry? How close is the link between output and jobs when protectionist measures are introduced? And what happens to the composition of jobs? These questions are central to evaluating the effectiveness of protectionist policies in achieving their goals. They are the first set of issues addressed in this chapter. The analysis shows that the relationship between sectoral protection and sectoral employment is a very indirect one. The links between trade and output growth and between output and employment are more complex than appear at first sight.

2.   The effects of protectionist measures spread from the protected sector through the economy, affecting employment opportunities in other sectors. Theoretical work on these issues has concentrated on what happens in flexible economies or after sufficient time has elapsed for full adjustment to the new conditions. But protectionist pressures in Member countries today usually arise because there are rigidities in economies and because adjustment costs are magnified when unemployment is high.

3.   Protection may, at a cost to overall living standards, be able to preserve a pre-existing level and pattern of employment, but only in special circumstances. Normally, exchange rates and cost movements will cancel out or even reverse the initial sectoral effects of protection. Negotiated voluntary export restraints to protect oligopolistic domestic industries appear to have the least favourable prospects for adding to economy-wide employment. Generalised tariffs may have less unfavourable effects, but are still likely to be inferior to other policies.

4.   A final set of issues concerns the effects of wide-spread trade controls on overall economic performance and hence on medium-term employment growth. Any general re-orientation of policies alters the behaviour of economic actors, affecting the evolution of potential output. Protectionist policies are no exception in this regard.

Effects of trade restrictions in the protected sector

5.   OECD area employment in the "highly protected" industries declined more rapidly in the 1970s than in manufacturing as a whole (Graph 3.1). Certainly protection was not

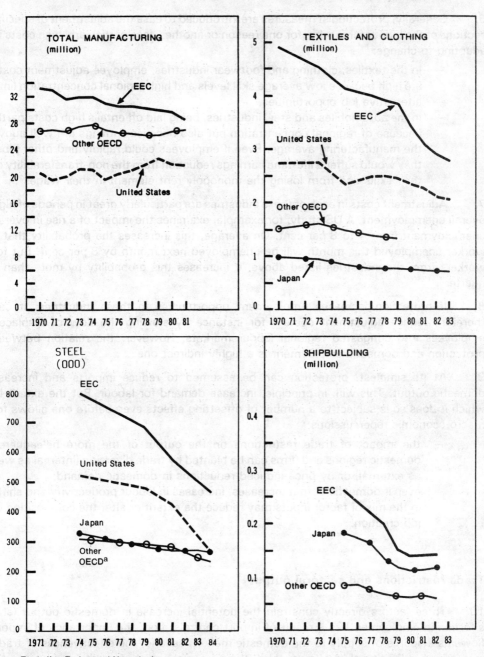

Graph 3.1

EVOLUTION OF OECD EMPLOYMENT IN MAJOR MANUFACTURING INDUSTRIES

TOTAL MANUFACTURING
(million)

EEC

Other OECD

United States

TEXTILES AND CLOTHING
(million)

EEC

United States

Other OECD

Japan

STEEL
(000)

EEC

United States

Japan

Other
OECDa

SHIPBUILDING
(million)

EEC

Japan

Other OECD

a. Excluding Turkey and Yugoslavia.

Source : OECD, ILO Yearbook of Labour Statistics.

53

sufficient to fully offset the adverse impacts of changes in competitiveness and in patterns of demand, though it may have slowed the rate of decline.

6.   Generally, protectionist measures are introduced to ease the adjustment of specific sections of the labour force who, for one reason or another, face particularly high costs in adapting to change:

—   In the textiles, clothing and footwear industries, employee adjustment costs are high because low average skill levels and high regional concentration limit alternative job opportunities.

—   In the automobiles and steel industries, being laid off entails high costs partly because of regional concentration but also because earnings are well above the manufacturing average. Even if employees could rapidly find other jobs, they would suffer a life-time earnings reduction from the non-transferability of their skills and from losing the monopoly rent element in their wages[1].

7.   Adjustment costs in each of these industries are particularly great in periods of high overall unemployment. A US study, for example, examines the impact of a rise in overall unemployment from 4 to 8 per cent. On average, this increases the probability that a worker unemployed this month will be unemployed next month by 8 per cent. But for workers from the industries listed above, it increases this probability by more than a quarter[2].

8.   If protection increases employment opportunities in these industries, it can therefore reduce adjustment costs — for instance by slowing the flow of displaced employees into congested regional labour markets. However, the relation between protection and domestic employment is a highly indirect one.

9.   At its simplest, protection can be assumed to reduce imports and increase domestic output. This will, in principle, increase demand for labour. But the extent to which it does so is subject to a number of offsetting effects even before one allows for macro-economic repercussions:

—   the impact of trade restrictions on the output of the more beleaguered domestic regions and firms can be blunted by trade diversion (internal as well as external) or by price-induced reductions in domestic demand;

—   even if domestic output increases, increases in labour productivity and shifts in the mix of factor inputs may reduce the extent or alter the composition of job creation.

Trade restrictions and sectoral output

10.   Three factors directly constrain the potential increase in domestic output (and a fortiori in employment) as a result of import controls: first, the importance of import flows as a source of supply to the domestic market; second, the effectiveness of trade restrictions in limiting these flows; third, the ease with which domestic output can be substituted for the products previously imported.

11.   The extent of import penetration varies significantly among the products identified as "heavily protected". Nonetheless, in the US and Japan, as well as in the EC, if intra-trade is excluded, the ratio of imports to domestic supplies is actually fairly low, particularly as regards imports from LDCs. Even a considerable increase in trade flows would have little effect on output and hence employment. Thus, it has been estimated that even a doubling from the 1977 level of both imports and exports between the EC and developing countries would only require 1.5 to 2.5 per cent of workers in manufacturing to change sectors — far less than the proportion who actually do so each year[3]. The converse of this limited impact is, of course, that the potential for durably boosting output (and hence employment) through import controls is relatively small, even in the most heavily protected industries.

12.   Moreover, it is questionable whether actual import controls come close to realising this potential. The problems of trade diversion have been discussed above (see Chapter 2); at least until the late 1970s, these partially offset the trade and output effects of discriminatory restrictions. To these must be added the redistributive effects of diversion within customs unions and free trade areas. Thus, the MFA may substantially curtail net flows of imports into the EC and EFTA; but the positive impact on domestic output is likely to be concentrated on Italy and Finland (see Chapter 6 below).

13.   Finally, it is clearly incorrect to assume that each percentage reduction in imports will lead to an equal increase in domestic output. If domestic costs are higher than foreign costs (as is usually the case in industries seeking protection from imports), the extent of the increase in domestic output will be constrained by the price elasticity of demand. Furthermore, if the foreign and domestic products are differentiated (in the sense of having different product characteristics), even a substantial increase in the relative price of the foreign good may not lead to a shift in consumer demand towards the domestic product.

14.   In the case of differentiated goods subject to quantitative restrictions, imperfect substitutibility can lead to situations in which prices are not market clearing, at least in the short term. Purchasers, rather than buying the domestic substitute, prefer to queue for limited supplies of imported products. When current market share affects future market share, foreign producers may prefer to ration through waiting lists rather than entirely through prices; this certainly appears to be the case in the automobile industry[4]. Similar effects have been noted in the steel industry[5] and even in the supply of apparel[6]. In turn, the availability of the imported product on a waiting list basis limits the transfer of demand towards domestic producers.

15.   Seen overall, trade measures even in the form of quantitative restrictions have therefore only a limited impact on the sector concerned. In larger economies very little leverage can be obtained by regulating the year-to-year changes in imports, which are in total a small fraction of domestic output. In smaller, more specialised economies, the import share may be higher but the degree of substitutability between imports and domestic production is likely to be much lower. There is a contrast here with macro-policy which can affect an industry's entire demand and supply conditions.

16. In fact, the impact of trade policy instruments on domestic output has frequently been swamped by changes in the macro-economic environment. In the case of the US automobile industry, for example, the US-Japan voluntary export restraint agreement increased 1982 demand for domestic passenger cars by no more than 100 000 units, less than 1 per cent of industry sales. In contrast, changes in the macro-economic environment reduced US demand for automobiles by some 4 million units in 1982 relative to 1978 (see Chapter 7).

17. The domestic output effects of such trade instruments as quantitative restrictions therefore tend to be most significant at overall cyclical peaks. Unless they are nearly prohibitive or are varied across the cycle they may not be binding when overall demand is weak. Such restrictions may therefore boost an industry's demand in cyclical upswings and be quite ineffective at other times.

Output and employment

18. Even if domestic output does increase as a result of import restrictions (at least relative to what it would otherwise have been), this may not give rise to a sustained expansion in employment, or even prevent a continuing loss of jobs. In the short term, protected industries are frequently operating with substantial margins of excess capacity, and can increase output without additional labour or capital input[7]. Moreover, if labour is in fact a quasi-fixed input – for example, because severance costs are high, notably in Europe[8] – domestic firms may be reluctant to expand employment in the face of possibly short-lived increases in demand. Protection could only offset this reluctance if firms expected it to provide a long-term guarantee of markets: in fact output in most of the key protected sectors has continued to decline (albeit at a slower rate) and – notably in fragmented sectors – trade protection provides little output guarantee for individual firms.

19. Over the longer term, the accumulated rents from protection may encourage an increase in the industry's capital stock and hence employment potential. However, in a context of slow industry growth, investment will generally go to replace existing plant, usually with equipment permitting higher levels of labour productivity. Protection and policy measures likely to accompany it (such as investment or rationalisation subsidies) may accentuate this capital deepening process, partly by moderating any potential increase in the demand for labour, and partly by actually encouraging the scrapping of older labour intensive plant.

20. First, by improving their cash flow, protection will permit firms to carry out investments which were in any case profitable, but could not be made because of financial constraints.

21. Second, protection can be expected to decrease the cost of capital relative to labour in the industry:

- By signalling to the capital market that the government is willing to socialise part of the industry's risk it will reduce the risk premium firms must pay to raise capital.
- At the same time, the flow of rents from protection will presumably be reflected in the market price of equity, raising the ratio of capitalised value to book value of assets and hence the industry's optimal capital intensity.
- Some part of the rents from protection may accrue to the industry's workforce as higher wages, increasing the relative price of labour.

22. Finally, in a number of countries border protection has been accompanied by industry policies aimed at promoting rationalisation. These policies typically involve provision of investment funds at subsidised rates, thus reinforcing the effects of the border measures on relative factor prices.

23. The textiles industry (see Chapter 6) provides a useful example of the combined impact of these factors. Over the period 1973-1982, production in the OECD textiles industries diminished at an annual average rate of 1.5 per cent; but employment declined three times faster, at an annual average rate of 4.5 per cent. Much of the fall in employment was therefore due to productivity increases, rather than to the direct effect of changes in import penetration on domestic output and hence employment. In the United States, for example, the direct effects of net trade on domestic employment were in fact positive in the 1970s, with all of the employment decline being due to greater productivity[9]. In the United Kingdom, direct productivity gains accounted for 60 per cent of the 1970-1979 job loss[10].

24. Clearly, the pressure of imports provided strong incentives for textiles firms to increase productivity levels. Moreover, the potential for such increases has largely been due to innovations in the textiles machinery industry, which do not depend on demand pressures coming from the textiles industry itself[11]. But it is questionable whether capital deepening at the observed pace and scale (capital-labour ratios going from well below the manufacturing average in the 1950s to some 20 per cent above average now) could have been financed in the absence of public intervention.

25. It is estimated that in France nearly 90 per cent of firms operating in the textile industry received some government financial assistance in the period 1981-83, permitting a 30 per cent increase in industry investment[12]. A UK study of investment assistance provided to firms in the woollen textiles industry found that assistance had increased recipients' rationalisation investments by some 20-30 per cent[13]. Equally, econometric studies of the US textiles industry have found that import restrictions have had a marked positive impact on industry profitability, which in turn increased investment and capital intensity[14].

26. Employment increases due to import restrictions are therefore likely to be greatest in industries with low levels of capital intensity and of labour productivity and with little scope for raising these through additional investment, a description that fits only a few industries, such as parts of the clothing industry. But these are precisely the industries which provide jobs at below average rates of pay, with few skill requirements or training

possibilities, and little job security. As is clear from the studies surveyed in Chapter 6 below, persistent protection in the clothing industry has increased employment – the question is the quality of the jobs this involved.

Protection and the composition of employment

27.   Whether protection eases employee adjustment costs will also depend on the distribution of whatever job opportunities it saves or creates: in particular, do the protected jobs go to those segments of the labour force which face the greatest difficulties in responding to industrial change?

28.   Clearly, in the very short term, the occupational and regional structure of an industry's labour force is pretty well fixed[15]. However, the industry's labour force itself is constantly shifting, as a result of "churning" in the labour market. There will thus be workers and enterprises constantly entering even static and declining industries and thus benefiting from their protection. This is true even for the steel industry with its relatively low turnover rates. During the period 1975-1980, employment in the EEC steel industry declined, as a combined result of quits and dismissals. But while the industry dismissed 100 000 manual workers and experienced a substantial net decline in employment, it hired 350 000 to offset the departure of 387 000 workers. As a number of studies have shown, many of the steel industry employees who benefited from extremely generous severance and early retirement provisions in the 1980s, had been attracted to the steel industry only a few years previously[16]. Clearly, the steel industry does have a core of employees who have few alternative job opportunities. The benefits from generous severance and other social provisions, however, go not only to these employees but also to a much more mobile fringe which protection may attract, including – for example – those working in newly established mini-mills.

29.   Superimposed on this churning are structural and regional changes in the pattern of industry's demand for labour. These changes are the natural result of competitive pressures and technological opportunities; but they too drive a wedge between the benefits of protection and the employee groups at which protection was originally targeted. Two such changes are of particular importance in the industries considered here.

30.   First, these industries have typically had a substantially lower ratio of non-manual to manual employees than manufacturing as a whole. In the United States, for example, the share of white collar employees in the "trade-impacted" industries' employment in 1970 was 10 percentage points below the manufacturing average and nearly 20 points below the average for export-oriented industries. This reflected a more general gap in employee skill levels and educational qualifications[17].

31.   Over time, structural change has tended to reduce this gap, as firms in trade-impacted industries raise the quality of their products and processes, increase capital per employee and place greater emphasis on marketing and distribution functions. In 1968, production workers accounted for nearly 90 per cent of US textile industry

Table 3.2

PRODUCTION WORKERS AS A SHARE OF TEXTILE INDUSTRY EMPLOYMENT

	Belgium	Denmark	Germany	Ireland	Italy	Luxembourg	United Kingdom	United States
1963	97.7(a)	80.4	83.1	81.5	93.7(b)	85.7(c)	86.6	89.7
1973	87.9	78.7	79.3	88	74.2	77.9	82.5	87.5
1974	87.5	77.4	78.5	88.4	73.2	69.5	82.4	86.7
1975	86.3	77.4	77.9	88.4	71.5	67.6	81.8	86.3
1976	86.6	78.3	78.1	-	71.9	69.9	81.6	86.8
1977	85.3	76.3	78	86.4	71.6	70.9	81.6	86.6
1978	86.3	76.3	77.5	86.2	71.3	70.8	81.3	86.6
1979	86.7	76.7	77.5	-	70.1	72.4	81.3	86.4
1980	86.3	76.8	-	-	69.7	-	80.5	85.9
1981	-	76.6	-	-	-	-	-	-

a) 1962.
b) 1961.
c) 1958; Textiles, Clothing and Footwear.

Source: The Growth of World Industry 1953-1965; Yearbook of Industrial Statistics, United Nations, 1981.

employment; by 1977 this proportion had declined by 10 percentage points[18]. A similar trend is evident in the European textile industry (Table 3.2), and in the other industries identified as receiving above average protection.

32.   Secondly, the regional pattern of industry employment has tended to change, though at differing rates in the various protecting countries. This trend has been most marked in the United States, where it forms part of a broader shift in the regional structure of the economy[19]. In 1959, the North Atlantic region accounted for 30 per cent of US textiles employment and nearly 60 per cent of apparel employment; by 1976, those shares were down to 20 and 34 per cent respectively[20]. In Europe, too, the geography of the textiles and clothing industries has changed: textiles tending to become more regionally concentrated, clothing somewhat less so[21].

33.   Thus many of the jobs "saved" by long-term protection do not go to those who face the greatest adjustment burden. Rather, they go to better trained workers living in regions which are in any case experiencing above-average rates of growth. In the US textile industry, total employment was virtually constant from 1968 to 1977, but within this total the industry created some 60 000 white collar jobs, which went to employees with considerably higher educational qualifications than the manual employees they were replacing[22]. Over roughly the same period, and again with approximately constant total employment, the industry created some 50 000 jobs in the South, while suppressing 75 000 jobs in the North[23]. Both in the case of the regional and occupational shifts, it is difficult to argue that the employees who benefited from these shifts — and hence indirectly from protection — would otherwise have incurred a disproportionate adjustment burden. The phenomenon of trade diversion thus occurs *within* economies just as much as between countries. In general within an industrial sector there will always be some strong and some weak firms and it is the former that are likely to gain by protection[24].

34.   Protection is therefore a very blunt instrument of policy. It can increase employment in a sector or slow its decline, relative to what would otherwise have occurred; but the impact is likely to be small and is often felt when and where it is least needed. Moreover, protection may undermine rather than assist any accompanying adjustment-promoting measures.

Protection and aggregate employment

35.   A single sector can thus benefit from protection, albeit in a limited and somewhat perverse way. The question remains, however, whether such an initial gain will actually be a *net* addition to employment, or whether the job gains in the protected sector will be offset by employment losses in other sectors.

36.   Clearly, if other countries retaliate, the benefits of protection may be completely eroded, though it is jobs in the export sector that are likely to be worst hit. Retaliation cannot be ruled out but it may be limited if the protecting economy is small or if the authorities have credibly promised that their action is temporary. But even in the absence of retaliation, there can still be major side-effects on other sectors through macro-economic linkages.

37.   In economies which are reasonably flexible, but which for some reason are operating with excess resources, sectoral protection may increase aggregate employment. Given excess resources and an elastic response of output to market signals, the protected industry can rapidly benefit from the demand stimulus coming from protection. Particularly if there are unexploited economies of scale to production, the increase in the protected sector's output may involve little or no rise in marginal costs — so that inflationary pressures are not transmitted into the economy as a whole. The resulting increase in real incomes will presumably lead to higher import volumes for other goods and services, but this will be associated with a higher level of activity and employment than prevailed prior to protection.

38.   Such a scenario is not impossible, but the assumption of flexibility hardly seems applicable to the industries and economies where the pressures for protection have been strongest. By and large, protection has been granted to industries with persistent difficulties in adjusting output to changes in the level and pattern of demand. Moreover, far from being self-equilibrating, the macro-economic context of sectoral protection has in recent years been one of persistent unemployment, high inflation, substantial excess capacity and the perception that floating exchange rates do not automatically ensure economy-wide competitiveness.

39.   In these circumstances, attempts to boost output and employment through sectoral protection quickly run into constraints imposed by product and labour market rigidities, creating costs for other sectors of the economy. Three inter-related factors are at work[25].

40.   The first is interdependence in factor markets, notably for labour. Even in an economy with substantial registered unemployment, the scope for adding new jobs without accelerating inflation may be very small indeed because of inflexibilities in labour and product markets. When observed unemployment, however high it may be, corresponds to the "natural rate" compatible with non accelerating inflation, net job creation can only be secured and sustained by improving the functioning of markets. For a given natural rate, the short-run effect of sectoral protection will then merely be to bid away employment from other industries, thus shuffling jobs around. But, over the longer run, the reductions in allocative efficiency and market flexibility brought about by import controls can be expected to actually increase the natural rate of unemployment, aggravating the problem which protection was intended to solve.

41.   The second is interdependence in product markets, in particular through pricing and wage setting decisions. Attempts to switch demand from foreign to domestic sources have invariably led to large increases in the domestic price of the protected goods (see Chapter 2 above). When intermediate goods are being protected, this raises costs to user industries; while protection of consumer goods reduces the purchasing power of wages. Unless these changes in relative prices are absorbed through reduced margins in user industries and lower real incomes, the result must be upward pressure on nominal wages and prices throughout the economy. The net outcome will depend on the extent and pattern of these increases, but it is hardly likely to involve a rise in aggregate employment, particularly if a more restrictive macro-economic stance is adopted to counter inflationary pressures.

42.   Finally, changes in prices and wages and in the level of economic activity will alter external competitiveness, feeding back on domestic employment. In particular, export industries are likely to be penalised by greater domestic inflation, and by any tendency for the exchange rate to appreciate as protection reduces demand for imports. Though the linkages affecting exchange rates are complex, the outcome may be a combination of higher inflation and a higher exchange rate than would otherwise have prevailed – compounding the burden on export industries[26].

43.   The likelihood that sectoral protection will increase aggregate employment in inflexible economies is therefore very small. Rather, any jobs saved or created in the protected sector will endanger employment elsewhere in the economy. It follows that for sectoral protection to be an acceptable tool of policy, social actors must be willing to bear a high burden in living standards so as to preserve the existing structure of employment.

44.   Sectoral import controls could have a less adverse aggregate impact in economies which are reasonably flexible. But there is little reason in such economies to select protection as an instrument of policy over other policy options. The only potential advantage of protection might lie in the exploitation of terms of trade gains and the possibility that tariff revenues may be used to subsidise wages at the expense of profits, which itself raises longer-term implications for employment. But these possibilities are foregone when protection is by arrangements such as VERs rather than tariffs. Moreover, there are major disadvantages to sectoral protection. Medium term efficiency losses will arise from the relative shift of resources to the internationally less competitive sectors of the economy. Insulation of economic agents from the need to adjust can only aggravate the loss of economic efficiency.

45.   More generalised, non-sector specific protection – such as that used in responding to balance of payments difficulties – is less obviously futile. But even fairly generalised tariffs can be highly inappropriate as a macro-economic tool in correcting large-scale imbalances. This can be seen by considering what scale of import controls would – under plausible assumptions about foreign trade elasticities – be required as an alternative to a 20 per cent devaluation: that is, a devaluation of the magnitude implemented by the French Government between 1981 and 1983[27]. Acting on the import side of trade only would have required tariffs (or quota equivalents) of 40 per cent. Working on industrial imports only (60 per cent of the total) would push the required tariff rate up to 65-70 per cent, while restricting only the half of imports generating the most import penetration would push the figure to 130-140 per cent. Such import tariffs (or quota equivalents) on half of industrial imports would inevitably have very serious implications for domestic prices and wages and hence for the competitiveness of unprotected tradeable goods.

Job creation in the medium term

46.   In most cases, the aggregate employment effects of a single protectionist measure are probably very small, regardless of whether they are positive or negative. But a spread of protection may alter the behaviour of groups in an economy in important ways. Thus, a

series of protectionist measures has effects different from the sum of the effects of each measure.

47.   To begin with, as each large firm or organised group of workers comes to expect that it will be protected against loss of jobs or market share, wage and price setting behaviour will become more aggressive. This is especially likely with sectorally "tailor-made" protection. Empirical studies confirm that particularly in oligopolistic or highly concentrated industries, reduced competitive pressures will lead to prices which respond less to cyclical variations in costs and demand. The burden of adjustment to shifting circumstances will therefore fall on movements in quantities — notably output and employment — rather than in nominal prices and wages[28].

48.   Greater collusion on domestic markets, and union resistance to changes which adversely affect employment (productivity improvement will seem less important if jobs can be secured through protection) can also slow adjustment to new growth opportunities. Since the sectors being protected (and hence, in relative terms, expanded) are in any case those with below-average productivity, long-term income growth must be reduced. The jobs being protected typically have lower skill requirements and make fewer demands on a country's capacity to develop and diffuse new technologies: the pressures for innovativeness throughout the economy and society can be expected to weaken. Both for Canada and Australia, econometric studies have found that persistent and widespread protection of manufacturing industry has imposed a "hidden tax" on the more export-oriented activities, constraining the growth of per capita income and hence earnings[29].

49.   Highly protected economies may therefore experience both lower growth of living standards and greater fluctuations of actual from potential income. This in and of itself generates further social conflict and inflationary pressures, as actors try to obtain by redistribution the higher incomes they would otherwise obtain from growth. Such an outcome seems particularly likely if protection has been presented as an option which can promote employment without reducing living standards, thus creating an additional gap between actual and expected real wages. In this "zero-sum" context, high and rising employment must become more difficult to achieve and whatever sectoral job gains protection may achieve will be dissipated.

NOTES AND REFERENCES

1. Surveys of employee adjustment costs are provided by Jacobson and Thomason: 1979 and Adams and Mueller: 1982. For a discussion of the rent element in wages see Geroski, Hankub and Knight: 1979.

2. Parsons: 1980.

3. Sapir and Schumacher: 1985. Even in clothing, imports from LDCs accounted for only 14 per cent of OECD apparent consumptions in 1981, nearly five times more than the ratio for textiles narrowly defined. The overall ratio for manufacturing import penetration from LDCs was around 2 per cent, not enough to really leave any impact on aggregate employment.

4. Parry: 1981 and USITC: 1985, p.X.

5. *L'Expansion,* 5th October 1984, p.104.

6. Consumers' Association: 1979.

7. However, it should be noted that the rate at which excess capacity is scrapped or excess labour released may be slowed by protection.

8. Gennard: 1979.

9. Krueger: 1980.

10. Soete, Clark and Turner: 1982.

11. Rothwell: 1976 and Pavitt: 1982 discuss the "dependent" nature of innovation in the textiles industry.

12. Stoffaes: 1984, pp.380-383.

13. Potter, Davies and Gibbs: 1983.

14. Pelzman: 1984 and Isard: 1973.

15. Freeman in Ehrenberg: 1977 finds that changes in occupational structure over time typically result from inter-industry rather than intra-industry shifts in the composition of employment.

16. See, for example, the "Rosenwald Report" on the French steel industry, Le Monde, 28th January 1984.

17. Aho and Orr: 1979; Appendix Table 3.

18. Pelzman and Andrews; this data source differs slightly from that used in Table 3.4.

19. Stanback, Bearse, Noyelle and Karasek: 1981.

20. Krueger: 1980.

21. EC *Regional Survey,* 1977; Bisault *et al.,* 1983.

22. Pelzman and Andrews, p.27 and pp.34-35.

23. Krueger: 1980, p.143; data refer to 1965-1976.

24. A recent French study of the financial situation of industrial firms noted that there was almost as much variation within sectors as between them. Weak sectors contained still many healthy firms, likely to be those most able to profit from protection. See INSEE: 1985, Annex 3.

25. Much analysis of the macro-economic effects of protection is weakened because the ability of the economy to sustain full employment is implicitly taken as an assumption and is not derived as a conclusion. But even when observed unemployment is above the natural rate, the final consequences of protectionist policies depend on complex macro-economic linkage effects between employment, prices, wages, and the exchange rate. These relationships, which may counteract the direct job creating effect, are not yet wholly understood, notably as regards sectoral protection. The relevant theory is in its infancy — see however various contributions to Major: 1979; RIIA: 1984; Krugman: 1982, and the classic analysis by Mundell: 1961. The empirical evidence apart from certain historical material (Capie: 1983; Weinstein: 1980) and studies of developing countries (Khan and Zhaler: 1982), relies mainly on simulations with macro-econometric models (Cable: 1983; Aislabie: 1984); the results of such models can be highly sensitive to the assumptions built in.

26. The link between an improvement in the current account and an exchange rate appreciation is by no means automatic, but it is plausible (see Hacche: 1983, p.25). Monetary factors may also lead to the appreciation of the currency of a protecting economy (or a failure of its currency to fall as far as it otherwise would), through their effects on capital flows. Thus, protection may lead to inflows (or the expectation of inflows) of foreign investment in the protected sector. At the same time, the price rises induced by protection may reduce the real money stock and hence push up interest rates. It would therefore be imprudent to calculate the consequences of protection on the assumption of exchange rate stability. The likelihood is that with some lag, export sector jobs will be destroyed as import-substituting jobs are promoted.

27. P. Holmes, unpublished manuscript, Sussex University, 1985.

28. De Rosa, Dean and Goldstein: 1981; and especially Encaoua: 1983; this contrasts with the underlying (and apparently unrealistic) assumption of the "Cambridge Group" (see Coutts, Godley and Nordhaus: 1978; Cripps, Francis and Godley: 1978) who claim that protection would not alter target wage and price setting and could hence improve UK GNP growth. See also Hindley: 1977 and Scott, Corden and Little: 1980 for a discussion of the Cambridge view.

29. See, for example, Harris: 1984, and the *Annual Reports* of the Industries Assistance Commission.

Chapter 4

PROTECTION, COMPETITIVENESS AND EFFICIENCY

1.   Historically, protection invoked the "infant industry" argument. This has changed in advanced industrial countries, where sectoral protection responds to the specific needs of firms in difficulty. Supporters of import controls claim that the "breathing space" it provides allows restructuring and adaptation to change. But to what extent do protected industries regain competitiveness and/or adjust otherwise, thus enabling protection to be temporary?

2.   Answering this question requires a more precise definition of "competitiveness" and of how it is lost and won. Three major points emerge:

  — The scope a firm has for improving its competitive position depends to a large extent on the activities in which it operates.
  — In some of the most heavily protected industries, competition occurs primarily on the basis of labour costs, so firms in high wage countries have little chance of competing successfully.
  — The picture is more complex in oligopolistic industries supplying differentiated products. By increasing profit margins and altering competitive behaviour, protection can increase the resources available for restructuring; but they are only likely to be used for this purpose under the special circumstances of a small initial cost advantage and a large and rapidly growing home market.

The parameters of competitiveness

3.   "Competitiveness" can be defined as the capacity of firms to earn an acceptable rate of return on investment in a particular activity, operating under normal conditions of market competition. Over time, this capacity can change in three respects.

4.   First, the value of firms' *ownership advantages* may deteriorate. These are the intangible assets which provide a firm with a competitive edge over its rivals[1]. Changes in the value of these assets redistribute the rents available to the activity as a whole:

  — Technical change can erode the value of a firm's physical capital, accumulated know-how and proprietary technology.
  — Changes in tastes and in customer awareness may reduce returns on past investments in product and brand differentiation.

66

- Shifts in up-stream and down-stream activities and in distribution channels can alter the optimal degree and pattern of vertical integration and/or diversification, imposing large transition costs.
- New entrants may be less vulnerable than previous entrants to retaliation – e.g. against price-cutting – for instance if they are operating from a protected home market. Investments in a reputation for active entry-deterrence may then have to be written off.

5.   Second, changes specific to individual countries may diminish the profitability of firms operating at particular *locations:*

- Movements in relative factor prices will alter cost levels at different sites.
- Even with factor prices constant, changes in the activity's cost function – for instance an increase in the weight of direct labour costs as a result of product and process standardization – may induce shifts between locations in cost attractiveness.
- Changes in the competitiveness of up-stream domestic suppliers can alter the performance of the activity itself.
- Government regulations – for instance, for pollution control – may impose cost penalties on plants in particular countries.
- Differences in market growth rates will affect the location of capacity expansions, notably in activities with highly "lumpy" increments to potential output[2].
- Exchange rate adjustments may accentuate the impact of initial cost/demand growth differentials.

6.   Finally, structural shifts may reduce the long-term *profit potential* of the activity as a whole[3]. These shifts include:

- Increases in the price of key inputs or complements which make the activity's product less attractive than substitutes;
- Slowing or negative demand growth due to saturation which accentuates market share competition and entails capacity write-downs;
- Reductions in entry barriers and the expansion of fringe producers under-mining pricing stability and profit margins.

The costs of adjustment

7.   The extent of the adjustment difficulties due to changes in competitiveness will depend on the number of parameters affected and on the magnitude and pace of the changes.

8.   For example, if firms' ownership advantages are preserved, but the pattern of locational advantages changes, the activity's geography may be reshaped relatively smoothly through multinationalisation. In the late 1950s and early 1960s, exchange rate misadjustments and changes in growth rates of demand altered the relative competitiveness of US and European locations. However, US firms retained a distinct advantage

over their European competitors in terms of organisational, production, product design and marketing know-how. U.S. firms were therefore in a position to internalise the benefits of shifts in competitiveness through direct investment in the European market. The wave of acquisitions of European firms by their US rivals provided a profitable exit route for weaker firms, while allowing US companies to gradually absorb changes in locational structure[4].

9.   In contrast, when overall profitability in an activity is declining, locational shifts must be accomplished through absolute reductions in capacity rather than relative changes in its international distribution. In such an environment, only firms operating from least-cost locations can maintain earnings by enlarging their share of a shrinking market.

10.   Firms with few intangible assets will be poorly placed to shift to lower-cost sites, both because of cash constraints on foreign direct investment and because they will lack any distinctive advantages in those markets relative to their competitors. Faced with a reduced salvage value of their assets, and hence high costs of exit from the activity, firms in the sites adversely affected may prefer to retain capacity in place so long as the product price exceeds the variable cost of operating plant. The fact that the loss of competitiveness may apply to a number of firms, operating within the same national territory, will increase the attractiveness of a protectionist response. It will also make it easier for each single firm adversely affected to rally support from industry and trade union sources.

11.   The US steel industry illustrates these impacts. Slowing demand growth, the increasing attractiveness of substitute products and changes in entry barriers have eliminated the industry's potential for above-average profits. At the same time, adverse movements in factor costs and exchange rates have made production at US sites increasingly uncompetitive. But the industry is not in a good position to engage in direct foreign investment, since it has no intangible assets which would give it an advantage in competing with domestic firms at lower cost sites, or compensate for the additional risks on investments abroad.

12.   Moreover, there is virtually no market for the industry's product-specific assets, notably its large integrated steel plants. On exit, firms could obtain for these assets no more (and possibly less) than the present value of revenue over variable cost *minus* a possibly hefty risk premium for the purchaser. From this sum, the exiting firms would have to subtract severance costs, since a reduction in manning would almost certainly be a condition for the transfer.

Options for adjustment

13.   Firms facing severe difficulties have two long-run adjustment options: they can either try to improve their competitive position in the activity; or they can exit from the activity, through liquidation or diversification.

14.   Many firms do succeed in sharply improving a poor relative performance in the ordinary course of competitive strategies. Thus they can increase the value of their *intangible assets* by product and brand differentiation, selective specialisation and innovation. The unfavourable impact of shifts in *locational advantages* can be offset by cost and asset-reduction. By improving their cooperation with foreign suppliers (and among themselves), firms in the importing country can seek to restore the *potential profitability* of the activity as a whole.

15.   If these strategies fail, firms may have to exit from the activity. But the exit choice typically involves high costs for firms with largely industry-specific assets[5]. Thus, large severance payments may be incurred in plant shut downs. Penalty clauses may also be built into long-term procurement and sales contracts. Even if the firm succeeds in selling its assets, it is unlikely to realise any economic rents in doing so; in fact, it may have to write off investments in intangible assets such as brand name, product/service reputation, or knowledge of customer requirements.

16.   Even for a diversified firm, exit from a particular activity may impose costs in other factor and output markets. The stock exchange may react badly to the extraordinary losses incurred in divesting assets; activities which shared inputs and assets with the activity being discontinued may face higher costs; customers adversely affected by the decision to discontinue supply may be reluctant to buy other products from the firm; the corporate image, and "goodwill" may suffer.

17.   The exiting firm may have limited opportunities to shift human and financial resources to more promising activities, because of cash constraints and a lack of transferable assets and technological expertise. Indeed, particularly in family firms, managers or owners may be highly committed or psychologically tied to the firm's original activity.

18.   These costs encourage companies to postpone exit so long as the product's price exceeds the variable cost of operating plant. They give added importance to the other exit route, namely bankruptcy proceedings, which, if carried out quickly and in orderly conditions, can permit "creative destruction".

The impact of protection

19.   The critical question is whether the protective measures alter the balance between these options for industrial adjustment. It must be noted that adjustment strategies are not equally applicable in fragmented activities, which approximate conditions of perfect competition and oligopolistic activities with highly differentiated products.

... in fragmented activities

20.   Firms in activities such as clothing or footwear have few ownership advantages. Product differentiation advantages, to the extent to which they persist, are primarily appropriated by large distributors. Marketing channels, particularly in the mass merchandising trade, display extensive economies of scope and hence are not amenable

to vertical control. Technology is highly standardised and is widely available from specialised equipment suppliers[6]. There are few economies of scale in production[7]. Capital requirements are low, minimum efficient scale is a small fraction of total output, and the sunk costs involved in entry are negligible. This makes the market highly vulnerable to "hit and run" entry. Attempts to raise margins through collusion are unlikely to succeed.

21.   Even in these activities, differentiation and specialisation strategies can be effective in some market segments. In the clothing industry, for example, certain product groups are highly (and increasingly) capital intensive – e.g. hosiery, or items based on advanced knitting and moulding technologies. In addition, the higher quality parts of the clothing market, and those which are most fashion-oriented, are less sensitive to price and cost differentials. However, these segments account for a small share of total output and could hardly absorb a substantial part of the resources currently employed in the activity.

22.   Moreover, the nature of product and process technologies limits the cumulative learning advantages accruing to firms operating in these segments. Imitability, even of proprietary trademarks and designs, remains high[8]. Finally, suppliers in high wage countries face increasing competition in these segments from the Asian NICs, who are moving up-market, at least partly due to protection itself[9]. As a result, the benefits of product differentiation/ specialisation strategies are highly transient. The very low intra-industry variance of rates of return, both in apparel and in footwear[10], suggests that few firms succeed in durably out-performing the activity as a whole, for instance through market segmentation.

23.   In this environment of cost competition, the locational effects of protection dominate. Import controls drive a wedge between domestic and foreign costs and prices. Though *net* resource use may diminish, the argument that import controls are simply facilitating a run-down in the protected activities is clearly contrary to the evidence. In effect, with low entry barriers, most of the rents this creates for established domestic suppliers are bid away through expansion of output by incumbents and entry by new firms[11]. The scale of this latter phenomenon highlights the diversion of entrepreneurial talent. In the United States, one-third of the clothing and textiles establishments existing at the end of 1982 had been created since 1976. In France over a fifth of new manufacturing firms are in the textiles and clothing industries.

24.   Even when output expands as a result of import restrictions chronic profitability problems persist. This is reflected in the persistence over time of the low ratio of the activity's profitability to that in manufacturing as a whole (see Graph 6.8).

25.   Nonetheless, there is some scope for firms in the industry to improve their profitability. In particular, they can seek to improve their cost position by changing the labour markets in which they operate and to internalise some of the benefits of the international division of labour through offshore subcontracting and assembly.

26.   Both of these strategies play an important role in the clothing industry. Firms have sought untapped reserves of low-cost labour in peripheral labour markets. In the United

States, this has primarily involved a shift in production to un-unionised sites in the less industrialised states. In many European countries, a similar effect has been obtained through heavy recourse to migrant labour, in some cases drawing on the "black economy". The Italian pattern has been more original: phases of the production process have been concentrated in particular villages and small towns, generally in rural areas well away from the centres of heavy industrialisation; firms in these areas are largely family-based, with incentive systems closely tied to net income; the result is great flexibility in real incomes and product prices in the face of fluctuations in competitive conditions[12].

27.　Nonetheless, cost differentials between the OECD countries and the major developing country exporters are too great to be closed by internal locational changes. Stitching operations, which account for 80 per cent of value added, are – and in the medium term will remain – highly labour intensive. Cost differentials in this stage of production between developed and leading developing country exporters are in the order of 1 to 5 or 6[13]; even in peripheral labour markets, OECD manufacturers cannot reduce wage costs by this amount. The cutting and finishing stages of clothing manufacture, on the other hand, are increasingly automated. There are some advantages to locating these stages in the advanced industrial economies – for instance, lower maintenance costs on machines[14].

28.　For labour-intensive stages of production, offshore assembly or, as it is commonly known, outward processing trade (OPT) therefore remains an attractive proposition. OECD manufacturers retain control of product design, the initial and final stages of production, and act as the interface to distribution channels; this allows them to appropriate at least part of the rents from protection. In exchange, the developing country exporter usually obtains access to OECD markets more easily than in arm's length transactions.

29.　The extent to which OECD manufacturers have made use of offshore assembly varies greatly. The United States and Germany are the countries in which these strategies are of the greatest importance. Offshore assembly has been of little importance in the United Kingdom.

30.　Two factors have been at work. First, US and especially German firms have retained ownership advantages which allow them to effectively control vertical links in production. In particular, the specialisation / differentiation strategies pursued by German firms (and the fact that only domestic producers can engage in outward processing) provide them with an edge, relative to arm's length importers, in dealing with distribution channels.

31.　Second, there are differences in government policies with respect to OPT. There is some evidence that quota and tariff provisions have been more favourable to OPT in the United States than in the EC market[15]. The United States has considerably higher tariff levels on textiles and clothing products than the EC: on a weighted average basis, some 19 per cent as against 11.5 per cent. The duty exemptions on re-imported inputs provided under US Tariff Schedule item 807 therefore have greater incentive effect than similar exemptions offered on a lower tariff.

32.   In addition to the incidence of MFA quotas, the growth of OPT in certain European countries, notably in France, may also have been hindered by restrictions on capital outflows – at least insofar as OPT required foreign investment – and by an overall policy stance aimed at preserving domestic employment.

33.   Overall, the importance of OPT should not be exaggerated. Imports of clothing under item 807 account for 8 to 10 per cent of total United States clothing imports. The proportion for some EC countries is roughly similar. Despite OPT, a large share of the higher cost phases of the production process remains concentrated in the OECD countries.

34.   Domestic changes in location and offshore assembly have therefore had a limited overall effect on the cost differential between the OECD countries and the major developing country exporters operating in these activities. This differential, reflected in substantially higher prices in OECD markets, can only persist because of protection; but protection does little to reduce it, even in the long run. Protection has only facilitated adjustment to the extent to which it has been ineffective, providing opportunities for the international specialisation to operate through such devious means as offshore assembly and licit or illicit trade diversion. As the protectionist measures are reinforced, these opportunities dwindle.

... in oligopolistic activities

35.   The scope for regaining competitive advantage may be greater in activities supplying differentiated products under conditions of oligopolistic competition. Three features characterise these activities.

36.   First, cost structures are complex and labour costs alone are rarely sufficient to give competitors a permanent advantage. Moreover, firms can exercise some market power in the determination of their factor prices. As a result, the adverse effects of location can be offset by:

- Abandoning the least profitable market segments, notably those with a cost structure unfavourable to existing sites.
- Reducing factor and input costs, through renegotiation of wage levels and supply contracts, changes in manning and work rules, and by concentrating production at the least-cost domestic sites.
- Investing in new plant and equipment so as to diminish production and overhead costs and shift the cost structure in the direction of local factor endowments.
- Transferring part of production to lower-cost locations in other countries through foreign direct investment, international subcontracting, or by purchasing parts and components overseas.

37.   Second, competition in product markets occurs only partially on the basis of price, with quality, availability, delivery and service also being major factors. Faced with a decline in cost competitiveness, a firm can seek to recreate its ownership advantages relative to rivals by:

72

- Refocusing its product portfolio on market segments with a low price elasticity of demand and a cost structure appropriate to its locational pattern.
- Upgrading the quality of proprietary products and processes, for instance through greater R&D expenditure, thus obtaining an important "bargaining chip" relative to distributors and competitors.
- Strengthening control over distribution and marketing channels, so as to reduce the vulnerability of its products to displacement.

38.   Finally, the number of major competitors is limited, and they are aware of their interdependence in pricing and output choices. Given the height of entry barriers, price-cost margins are mainly determined by the similarity of incumbent firms' cost levels and strategic objectives. Firms threatened by import competition can try to alter the functioning of market competition, for instance by:

- Changing industry structure, for example by acquiring equity positions in foreign competitors.
- Creating a clearer perception by foreign rivals of their commonality of interest with domestic suppliers, for instance by: penetrating foreign rivals' home markets; establishing joint ventures for the supply of parts and for product distribution; licensing agreements for proprietary technology; and by becoming important purchasers of their rivals' products.
- Developing new pricing arrangements, in which the foreign firms sacrifice market share growth to higher margins.

39.   Protection can affect the implementation of these strategies in two major respects:

- By improving the cash flow of domestic firms, and changing the incentives foreign and domestic firms have to cooperate, it can increase the resources available for adjustment.
- However, by reducing the pressures for adjustment to occur, and given the substantial costs adjustment entails, it can perpetuate technical and economic inefficiency.

"Adjustment-enhancing" impacts

... profitability

40.   Strategies to increase competitiveness frequently require high levels of invest-ment: to pay exit costs from market segments no longer viable; to modernise plant and equipment; to upgrade product and process development. The capacity to finance these investments is closely related to current cash flow, since, in the case of firms in a liquidity crisis and facing bankruptcy risk, capital markets will attach a high risk premium to future earnings. Increases in cash flow can therefore expand capital availability by more than their immediate flow-of-funds impact implies. In turn, increases in cash flow will depend on firms' capacity to raise price-cost margins.

73

41. There is considerable evidence that, in concentrated industries, import competition imposes major constraints on domestic firms' price-cost margins. This is because entry barriers typically have a weaker deterrent effect on established foreign suppliers than on potential domestic competitors[16]:

- An established foreign firm can enter the domestic market at a relatively low scale and does not need to fear the effect of its entry on price;
- Moreover, if it is marginally diverting sales from its established home and export markets to a new export market, the foreign entrant will have much less to lose by existing firms' defensive predatory policies, than would have a newly established domestic firm. If prices are slashed, it can simply withdraw from the new market until prices rise again.
- The foreign firm can also react more rapidly than domestic entrants to new opportunities for profit. If domestic firms increase their price-cost margins, the time required to build new capacity will retard domestic entry; but foreign firms will be able to quickly divert their sales from other markets.

42. As a result, even activities with high sunk costs can become contestable through foreign entry, reducing the entry-inducing price. To this must be added the fact that differences in cost structures and strategic objectives are likely to be greater between domestic and foreign suppliers than among domestic suppliers. The scope for stable oligopolistic coordination is consequently reduced by international competition.

43. Import restrictions ease this constraint. So long as domestic suppliers are capable of coordinating their price and output decisions, they can seek to durably raise price-cost margins, thus improving their cash flow. In these cases, the returns to lobbying for protection can be high.

44. The United States steel industry illustrates this statement. The industry has historically been a tight oligopoly in which the US Steel Corporation has had a commanding market share and exercised unquestioned price leadership. As the industry has lost competitiveness, the effectiveness of price leadership in maintaining margins has been eroded by the growing competitive fringe of imports. The industry has successfully obtained protection from this fringe, through the Trigger Price Mechanism (TPM) and a series of voluntary restraints agreements and quota restrictions.

45. Given the huge volume of US steel sales — over a quarter of OECD steel consumption — even the modest increase in price-cost margins due to protection has effected a massive transfer of resources to domestic producers. On one estimate, the transfers due to the TPM on the increment in steel output were equivalent in 1979 to $110 per ton of steel, compared with a direct cost of $350-450 per additional ton produced.

... coordination with foreign suppliers

46. In addition to facilitating collusion on the home market, protection may alter the incentives foreign competitors have to coordinate their pricing, output and investment decisions with domestic suppliers. This is particularly true in the case of quantitative

restrictions and voluntary restraint agreements, which modify industry conduct in a number of important respects.

47.   Quantitative restrictions alter the trade-off between current and future profitability. In industries supplying differentiated products, profitability can critically depend on market share[17]. Foreign entrants consequently have an interest in sacrificing present income to market share expansion, since this increases future earnings flows. If the restriction is perceived as durable, the attractiveness of such a strategy is very much reduced. Foreign firms will consequently attach greater importance to current net earnings — increasing their incentives to collude, tacitly or overtly, with erstwhile domestic competitors.

48.   This impact can be reinforced by the "commitment" effect of the restriction. The fact that the domestic industry has secured a visible political commitment from its government can clearly discourage foreign producers from "going too far" in their efforts to capture the market. Foreign competitors are basically being told that they will have to co-exist with their domestic rivals — so that even in the face of major differentials in costs, joint profit maximisation is attractive.

49.   Combined with restriction-induced collusion among foreign suppliers, these changes in industry behaviour could lead to an increase in import prices by more than is needed to price-ration the quota. More generally, they highlight the extent to which protection can create rents for domestic and foreign producers exceeding those due to the pure effect of the quantitative restrictions on supply.

50.   Along with these price impacts (discussed and illustrated above in Chapter 2 above) changes in industry behaviour may be reflected in other aspects of firm conduct. In particular, foreign firms may have greater incentives to share technology and other intangible assets with their former competitors subsequent to a trade restriction. This is partly because the restrictions reduce the opportunity cost of such sharing arrangements; in the extreme case when the foreign firms are completely excluded from the domestic market, the sale of these assets will be the only means through which the foreign firms can obtain any share of the rents available in the protected country.

51.   The restricted suppliers may also view cooperation with domestic suppliers as a way of defusing protectionist pressures. The longer-term rewards to cooperation in terms of market access may be even more important than the immediate financial returns from joint ventures, technology licensing arrangements and so on. As far as the domestic industry is concerned, the potential this offers for upgrading the quality of products and processes can be fundamental to improvements in competitive position. Indeed, agreements for the sharing of intangible assets between restricted foreign suppliers, notably Japanese, and domestic firms have proliferated in some of the oligopolistic industries receiving protection.

52.   In the automobile industry, US and European firms have entered into a number of cooperative arrangements with Japanese manufacturers, covering the exchange of equity, technology transfer, purchases of parts, components and even assembled vehicles, and cooperation in manufacturing process development[18]. Subsequent to a

voluntary restraint agreement covering video-tape recorder exports to the EC, Japanese firms seem to have opted for a policy of product licensing and joint ventures[19]. A number of joint ventures have been announced in steel and shipbuilding involving European or US firms on the one hand, and Japanese firms on the other[20].

53.   In summary, protection in oligopolistic activities provides domestic firms with a range of credible threats to be used against foreign entrants. At one end of this range are anti-dumping and countervailing duty measures taken or initiated against a particular supplier or group of suppliers. From the domestic industry's point of view, these *ad hoc* measures have the advantages of being readily available, highly targeted in their implementation, and of relatively low political visibility. At the other end of the range are quantitative restrictions and voluntary restraint agreements. Negotiated between governments (or with their tacit support) these provide more permanent protection and signal a high level political commitment.

54.   The oligopolistic equilibrium which results from protection provides some compensation for the entrant in the form of higher margins and a guaranteed market share; but it also provides the domestic firms with improved access to the financial, managerial and technological resources needed to restructure, without however forcing them to do so.

Constraints on adjustment

55.   In practice, two factors can offset the expected impact of import restrictions on industrial competitiveness:

— The firms benefiting from protection may face economic, political and managerial constraints on their restructuring choices.
— Over the medium term, the advantages that firms derive from protection can be seriously eroded by changes in domestic and international competitive conditions.

The risks and costs of change

56.   There are a number of factors which deter protected firms from carrying out the restructuring needed to improve competitiveness. To begin with, the risks of re-investing in the activity may appear to outweigh the benefits. This is particularly likely when demand for the activity's product is stagnating or declining, but modernisation investments would involve construction of large scale plant and hence addition to net capacity.

57.   Thus, to regain competitiveness, US steel firms would have had to undertake major investments in modern large scale plant and equipment. In a context of declining demand, the resulting expansion in potential output would have to be absorbed in a market already glutted by excess capacity. This could have seriously undermined the stability of pricing arrangements, which were in any case strained by foreign competition. While the industry has frequently been criticised for not carrying out a large scale modernisation effort, this choice may actually have been quite rational.

58.   Second, firms may face political or institutional constraints on their restructuring choices. Corporate efforts to regain competitiveness almost inevitably involve reductions in employment, as part of a broader cost-cutting process[21]. However, particularly in Europe, assistance has in a number of cases been granted to firms on condition that employment levels be maintained either generally or in particular plants and regions. Moreover, if the firms are concerned to receive protection in future, and believe that trade union support will be important in this respect, they may choose to maintain employment levels higher than they would otherwise be.

59.   Third, managerial factors may also inhibit restructuring. In owner-managed firms, the owner may be highly committed to a particular way of carrying out the business and simply not be capable of transferring entrepreneurial skills to other activities. Change in these firms is often associated with the liquidation of original ownership rights and a professionalisation of management[22].

60.   But large, complex organisations also display resistance to change. This is particularly true of well established, high market share firms operating in mature businesses. These firms are frequently characterised by intricate hierarchical systems and managerial career structures, which give managers an "ownership interest" in their jobs and impede quick strategic decisions[23]. As a result, radical change is an extremely costly process in organisational terms. The temptation is to use the "breathing space" offered by protection to avoid change.

61.   Even if there is a willingness to change, protection itself aggravates the constraints of bounded rationality under which complex organisations operate. These organisations derive their information from a broad range of sources; but the price and quantity signals emerging from marketplace competition still play an important role. By altering and distorting these signals, import controls can make it difficult for firms to assess long-term relative costs and adjust investment and capacity expansion plans accordingly.

62.   Given these multiple constraints, it is not surprising that protected firms frequently postpone or avoid radical restructuring. From the firm's point of view, output at current high cost levels may well be preferable to measures which can bring cost levels down. The postponement choice avoids the risks of modernisation investment, prevents serious internal dislocations, and minimises the clash with trade unions and political forces. The rents from protection are consequently used to finance technical inefficiency in production.

The diminishing advantages of protection

63.   In the longer term, powerful economic forces can reduce the extent to which the domestic firms benefit from protection-created rents, and further narrow their adjustment options. Even in highly oligopolistic activities, competition among incumbents may progressively erode the producer rents from protection. This is particularly likely when the protected industry is itself not cohesive; there is widespread excess capacity, and major differences exist between firms in cost levels and strategic objectives. The contrast between the United States and the EC is particularly striking in this respect.

77

64. Unlike its US counterpart, the European automobile industry no longer displays stable patterns of price and output leadership in the face of reductions in demand. This is mainly because of the size of the cost and productivity disparities between producers, and because of the differences in objectives between firms. Import restrictions have not, therefore, had the same durable effect in raising price-cost margins as in the US industry.

65. Furthermore, even in activities with substantial entry barriers, persistently high price-cost margins incite domestic entry. This makes collusion increasingly difficult, so that prices eventually decline to the level set at the margin of capacity expansion. Thus, in the steel industry, the direct reduction — electric arc furnace route has reduced investment costs per ton of capacity by around 50 per cent, relative to traditional integrated steel plants. Both in the United States and in the EC, persistent protection has encouraged the entry of "mini-mills", undermining price leadership by the dominant firms.

66. Competing entry may also come from the restricted foreign firms seeking to appropriate a greater share of the rents by investing in the protected market. Indeed, protection does not, in itself, reduce the ownership advantages of the foreign firms — it simply alters the optimal locational pattern for exploiting these advantages. If the foreign firms control proprietary technology or product differentiation skills, they will continue to do so once the restriction is in place. In fact, the flow of rents foreign firms derive from the restriction can be re-invested in expanding their portfolio of intangible assets. In the short term, the foreign firms may react to protection by leasing some part of these intangible assets to their domestic competitors. Over the longer term, however, they may find it more advantageous to resort to direct investment in the protected market.

67. The process is illustrated by consumer electronics. The threat of US restrictions on imports of colour television receivers from Japan prompted the Japanese industry to establish production plants in the United States. Once protective measures were enacted, the Japanese suppliers were in a position to obtain the flow of rents both from the resulting increase in export prices to the US market *and* from the increase in domestic output and prices in the United States. A substantial part of these rents was invested in upgrading production facilities and developing new product lines, notably in video technology.

68. A similar pattern of response is occurring in the automobile industry. This industry is less footloose than consumer electronics. Particularly, Japanese firms attach great importance to proximity to subcontractors of inputs, which, being smaller firms, have greater difficulties in going overseas. Nonetheless, Japanese manufacturers have recently announced a number of major foreign direct investment projects in protected markets.

69. It should be noted that entry by foreign direct investment, particularly when induced by import restrictions, may have quite a different effect on industry performance than has import competition. The foreign direct investment decision generally involves high sunk costs. Notably when plants being acquired cannot easily be used to serve markets in other countries, the return on this investment will depend on maintaining

pricing stability in the protected market. These plants are to some extent "hostages" the domestic industry has obtained from its foreign competitiors. The greater the extent of the foreign firms' commitment, the more likely it is that they will at least tacitly cooperate with their domestic rivals if and when the restrictions are removed.

70.　While competing entry alters the industry's pricing behaviour, the response of foreign rivals to protection also narrows product and marketing options. As a result of product upgrading and moving up-market by restricted competitors, the higher cost domestic firms face increased foreign competition in those sections of the market which are least price-elastic — which is precisely where their long-run competitive edge may otherwise lie. The expansion of domestic output is therefore likely to occur at the lower quality end of the protected product range.

The longer-term outcome

71.　The critical question is what determines the long-run balance between these two sets of contending forces put into motion by protection:

- The increased potential for adjustment arising from higher price-cost margins and a more cooperative attitude on the part of foreign producers;
- The economic and political factors which deter change, encourage technical inefficiency, and erode domestic firms' adjustment options.

72.　The balance between these forces will be mainly influenced by two factors. The first is the extent and nature of the domestic firms' competitive disadvantage. If this disadvantage is large and reflects not only weaknesses in the activity itself but in its environment (suppliers, distribution channels, the national system of science, education and technology, the functioning of domestic factor markets), the scope for fundamentally altering competitive positions through sectoral protection is inevitably limited and attempts to do so will be perceived by domestic firms as costly and risky.

73.　The second is the size and growth of the domestic market. The incentive-blunting effects of protection are weakened in markets large enough to sustain a number of competing firms. Particularly when the market is growing, firms will take advantage of its large absolute size to build new plant at minimum efficient scale; the fact that this can lead to short-term excess capacity will be offset by the anticipated gains of operating at lower cost. Collusion may be even less sustainable in a growing market where firms are jockeying for long-term positions, than in one which is declining[24].

74.　The US bicycle industry illustrates these points. The industry first obtained protection in the form of a substantial tariff increase in 1955. This was reconfirmed in 1961 and persisted through to the late 1960s. Tariffs were subsequently decreased in the Kennedy and Tokyo MTNs.

75.　The industry's response to protection was facilitated by the fact that domestic demand for bicycles increased rapidly as the "baby boom" generations reached bicycling age: apparent consumption went from some 2.5 million units in the mid-1950s to over 10 million units in the early 1970s. At the same time, new product designs, pioneered by the US industry, substantially eroded the product advantage of foreign brands: these designs included the "middleweight" bicycle in the 1950s, the "high-rise" model of the early 1960s, and the current "motor cross" style.

76.   These developments offered considerable scope for the more efficient firms in the US industry to restructure, improve their competitiveness and expand. In 1955, the nine manufacturers who petitioned for import relief produced 1.5 million bicycles. By 1979 only six of these companies or their successors were still in existence. But their level of production had increased to over 9 million units. As production rose, the surviving companies built new plants, located in lower wage cost areas, while increasing labour productivity by some 10 per cent annually.

77.   It is arguable whether protection played much role in this outcome. Probably the more efficient firms would in any case have taken advantage of product innovations and rapid demand growth to restructure. Nonetheless, in the given context, tariff protection, with a perspective of gradual reductions, may have hastened the process[25].

78.   Conversely, in situations where domestic firms operate under a major competitive disadvantage, and where the size and growth of the domestic market is insufficient for the full exploitation of static and dynamic scale economies, protection can result in extensive inefficiency in industrial structures.

79.   In some of the smaller OECD economies, import restrictions aimed at selectively promoting industrialisation have partially insulated a relatively high wage manufacturing sector from international competition, so that firms have been primarily oriented to the domestic market. Given the small scale of this market, the result has been a "branch plant" industrial structure, in which large, mainly foreign owned, firms operate sub-optimal scale plants, producing a product range too broad to achieve economies of scale, dependent primarily on imported and somewhat out-of-date technology, and cut off from export opportunities. Once in place, such a structure is difficult to change, since the adjustment costs relative to existing patterns of employment, training and investment are high.

80.   Canada and Australia provide clear evidence in this regard[26]. Though overall effective rates of assistance in these countries have declined over time — in Australia's case going from 36 per cent in 1968-69 to 26 per cent in 1977-78 — "made-to-measure" protection has continued to be provided to industries suffering from a large international cost disadvantage. Econometric studies find that in both countries, protection at ad valorem rates above 20 per cent has made suboptimal scale production feasible. This has amplified the natural protection arising from international transportation costs and accentuated the scale disadvantages of a small market. In addition to technical inefficiency, protected firms, notably in concentrated industries, have priced up to the tariffs, inducing allocative efficiency losses in the economy as a whole. The resulting industrial structure — dominated by foreign owned firms which carry out little domestic R & D — has been locked into a pattern of dependency.

81.   Even in the larger economies, a similar long-term outcome may be emerging. It can be argued that the spread of protection in oligopolistic industries has inevitably involved a

learning process. The foreign firms affected by the "new" forms of protection are now more aware of the threats and opportunities protection creates than they were a decade ago. They move more rapidly to establish production facilities in the protected market. Even if these facilities are higher cost than those in the home country, or do not fully exploit scale economies, they at least pre-empt the flow of rents to domestic rivals. The foreign firms also act more strategically in their cooperative relations with firms in the protected market — maintaining a mix of cooperation and competition which can narrow the domestic firms' adjustment options.

82.   The effectiveness of protection in promoting industrial restructuring may therefore be diminishing. In fragmented industries protection is clearly an inefficient policy instrument in this respect. In oligopolistic industries, the pattern is admittedly more complex and it is difficult to draw a line between trade policy and competition policy. The interdependence of firms' decision-making in these industries creates additional degrees of freedom. But as firms become increasingly aware of how protection can alter their interaction, the foreign firms can act so as to offset the benefits to domestic rivals. In the long term, probably neither the foreign nor the domestic firms derive much net advantage — but real economic costs are incurred in the process, bearing largely on the protecting country.

NOTES AND REFERENCES

1.   Dunning: 1981; Caves: 1982. This section draws on the "eclectic theory" of international trade elaborated by Dunning.

2.   Hekman: 1978; Porter: 1980; Spence: 1979.

3.   Porter: 1980; Harrigan: 1982.

4.   Dunning: 1981, pp.72-100; Vernon: 1977; Kitching: 1974.

5.   There is a rapidly growing literature on the "costs of exit": see Bulow and Shoven: 1979; Harrigan and Porter: 1983; Harrigan: 1982; Harrigan: 1980; Harrigan: 1982; Howe: 1980; Nelson: 1981.

6.   On clothing, see OECD: 1983 (Textiles and Clothing Industries), Pavitt: 1982; Kurt Salmon Associates: 1979; Passeron: 1983; Rush and Hoffmann: 1984; strikingly similar results to those for clothing are obtained in a study of innovation in the footwear industry — Duchesneau, Cohn and Dutton: 1980 — who stress the limited scope for competing on the basis of technology.

7.   On clothing, the most detailed study is Mariotti: 1982; see also Scherer: 1981, pp.81-151; George and Ward: 1975; Gold: 1981; Caves, Khailzadeh-Shirazi and Porter: 1975 for surveys on, and discussions of, scale economies and plant size.

8.   Owen: 1971 is the best case study.

9.   See the survey "Putting on the style" in *Far Eastern Economic Review,* 4th September 1981; *Business Week,* 7th June 1982, p.90; and *Far Eastern Economic Review,* 30th April 1982, p.46.

10. Bureau of Economics, Federal Trade Commission: 1969, pp.144-183 and Porter: 1979.

11. Hazeldine: 1980; see also the very weak results on the impact of protection on clothing profitability in Pelzman: 1984 (The Multifibre Agreement and its impact on the profit performance of the US textile industry).

12. A useful discussion of regional shifts in Germany can be found in Schatz and Wolter: 1982, p.247. On Italy see CENSIS: 1984; Forcellini: 1978, pp.127-160; Frey: 1975; Fornengo: 1978; Gavidi: 1983.

13. Toyne *et al.*, 1984, p.101 provide comprehensive data on labour costs and unit labour costs in textiles; the differentials here are considerably smaller than those in clothing — see also Cable: 1983 — but they are in the order of 1 to 4.

14. Fröbel: 1980, p.129.

15. GATT: 1984, p.104-105; on Germany, see Fröbel: 1977 and Schatz and Walter: 1982, pp.248-251.

16. Useful surveys are Jacquemin: 1982 and Lyons: 1979. See also Bloch: 1974, Encaoua: 1983, Geroski and Jacquemin: 1981, Pugel: 1980; Turner: 1980; White: 1974.

17. Buzzell, Gale and Sultan: 1975 and Gale and Branch: 1982.

18. OECD: 1983 (Long Term Outlook for the World Automobile Industry), pp.85-86; United Nations: 1983; Black: 1984.

19. *Fortune,* 16th May 1983, pp.146-150; "Friendlier Foes?", *Wall Street Journal,* 18th May 1983, p.7; *L'Usine Nouvelle,* 1st September 1983, p.36.

20. Over the period 1981-83, 227 industrial joint ventures involving Japanese firms were reported in the financial press. Of these, 30 per cent covered electrical machinery, 20 per cent transport equipment and 13 per cent steel.

21. The literature on cost-cutting strategies places a great deal of emphasis on the importance of labour-shedding to successful cost control. See especially the empirical studies reported in Grant: 1984; Hambrick and Schecter: 1983; Hamermesh and Silk: 1979; and Mayes: 1983.

22. Harrigan: 1980, Porter: 1980; see also Barna: 1962, pp.58-59 and Scitovsky: 1962, pp.38-39 and pp.129-130 on family firms and corporate adjustment.

23. There is extensive evidence of this in the cases analysed by Mintzberg: 1983 and the "contingency" theory of organisation. See also Berry: 1983, Quinn: 1980 and Midler: 1980 for analyses of the impact of organisational structure on corporate decision-making, notably with respect to major changes in strategic orientation.

24. One of the best analytical discussions in the context of foreign trade remains Scitovsky: 1962, pp.110-135. See also Dalton and Rhoades: 1974, Caves and Uekusa: 1976 (who explain intense competition on the Japanese market as a result of rapid market growth) and the theoretical model of collusion in industries with high fixed costs developed by Rotemberg and Saloner: 1984.

25. United States International Trade Commission: 1982, pp.43-57. The extent to which this success story can be attributed to protection should not be exaggerated. To begin with, the import relief accorded the industry was only partial: though imports declined in 1956/57, import penetration averaged around 20 per cent of the market, and fluctuated from 16 to nearly 40 per cent. Secondly, there is little evidence that protection had a durable effect on price-cost margins and hence on investment financing: bicycle prices declined subsequent to protection though somewhat less rapidly than the increase in productivity. Finally, the

industry's best performance came in the eary 1970s, when the protective tariffs were being phased out. This suggests that given the industry's innovation performance and favourable demand conditions, the more efficient firms would have adjusted in any case.

26. On Canada see Bloch: 1974; Caves, Porter and Spence: 1980; Cox and Harris: 1983; Eastman and Stykoit: 1967; and Melvin and Wilkinson: 1968. On Australia see Caves: 1984; Davidson and Stewardson: 1974; Industries Assistance Commission *Annual Report* (various years); Industries Assistance Commission *Approaches to General Reductions in Protection* (1980 and 1982); Krause: 1984; Scitovsky: 1962 presents an excellent analysis of the impact of trade protection on industrial efficiency. An important discussion clarifying the theory of scale economy loss under protection is in Ethier: 1982. For empirical applications see especialy Carlsson: 1972; Müller: 1983, Müller and Owen: 1984 and Owen: 1981.

Part II

PROTECTION IN SELECTED INDUSTRIES

The following chapters review protective measures taken in a few industries. Though far from exhaustive, the coverage illustrates different situations and problems, many of which have been evoked in Part I above. Each chapter contains a brief description of the characteristics of the industry and of its evolution in the post-war period. The protective measures discussed concern essentially import restrictions by industrial countries — concentrating on the most topical ones — but an effort has been made to bring together trade policy moves made by other countries as well as the relevant domestic policy measures. Finally, the prospects for the industry are surveyed, notably as regards industrial adjustment, and their implications for policy assessed.

Chapter 5

STEEL

1.   Steel is a set of widely traded standard products. Setting aside trade within the EC and Comecon, a tenth of world steel production was internationally traded in 1950. By 1983 the figure had reached 19 per cent. Especially in recent years, steel trade has given rise to international frictions. These tensions are associated with major changes in both supply and demand conditions.

Characteristics of the steel industry

Patterns of supply and demand

2.   In the OECD region steel is a mature industry. Typically, over 60 per cent of steel production goes to capital goods industries. But the OECD economies already have in place their steel intensive infrastructure, such as roads and railways, housing and factories. Consumer goods industries, notably motor cars and durables, have also lost their momentum in mature markets. Use of thinner steels and substitute materials means less steel is required to achieve a given purpose.

3.   As a result, after 1973, the trend in apparent steel consumption in the OECD region declined by an average of 1 per cent annually. This compared with a 5 per cent growth in trend consumption of the non-OECD market economies, whose share of world steel consumption increased from 9 per cent in 1973 to nearly 15 per cent in 1983.

4.   Major shifts in supply brought new steel producers to prominence. In 1960, the United States and the nine EC countries produced 78 per cent of the market economies' steel output; in 1982, their share had nearly halved, falling to 44 per cent. In contrast, Japan's share in steel production jumped from 9 per cent in 1960 to 24 per cent in 1974, and thereafter remained stable. More recently a new group of steel producers has emerged. These "newly steel active countries" comprise South Africa, South Korea, Taiwan, Argentina, Brazil, Mexico and Venezuela. Their share of the market economies' steel output rose from 4 per cent in 1970 to over 12 per cent in 1982, about equal to the output of Germany and the United Kingdom combined.

5.   Changes in the pattern of supply have broadly corresponded to differences in growth rates of demand within individual countries. Broadly speaking, domestic demand

86

has been the main engine of growth or cause of decline for each producer. But supply shifts have aggravated the problem of local demand changes in three important and inter-related ways.

6.   Firstly, increasing self-sufficiency in regions with rapid demand growth has cut export opportunities for producers facing low growth rates of domestic demand. The self-sufficiency ratio for non-OECD market economies as a group rose by 9 percentage points from 1970 to 1982. In particular, the "newly steel active countries" were net importers in 1970 to the extent of some 10 per cent of apparent consumption; by 1982, their net exports were equivalent to 17 per cent of their apparent consumption.

7.   Secondly, supply changes modify relative cost positions. Steel is a "capital dominated" industry. Although capital charges account for a relatively modest part of total costs, the scale and technology of a steelworks are the overwhelming determinants of its production potential and productivity[1]. By adopting best practice process technology, new entrants can secure substantial cost advantages, providing their home market can support plants of minimum efficient scale and they are operated at high levels of efficiency[2].

8.   During the 1960s, a rapidly growing home market encouraged Japanese investment in large scale integrated plants, located on coastal sites to benefit from reductions in transport costs for bulk raw materials and for shipping the finished product. By the mid 1970s, over two-thirds of Japanese steel was made in works with a capacity exceeding 8 million tonnes. No U.S. plant achieved this size. These new plants incorporated cost saving, quality enhancing technology, notably low energy ironmaking, basic oxygen steelmaking, continuous casting and mills with automated process control[3].

9.   A similar pattern is evident among some newly steel active countries. Despite world-wide overcapacity, these producers are investing in anticipation of continued growth in their home market. In East Asia steelmakers enjoy a substantial cost advantage from lower plant construction and employment costs. At the large Japanese-style works at Pohang in South Korea, virtually all the equipment is less than ten years old. Average construction cost was $422 per tonne of standing capacity, well below the $1,000 a tonne which has been the world norm for the past decade[4]. A well trained labour force is employed at a cost per hour a quarter of that found in Japan and only 13 per cent of that in the United States; effective labour costs are even less if allowance is made for sub-contract workers. It can be argued that POSCO is the world's most cost competitive steel producer, trading profitably at domestic and export prices 10 per cent below those found in the nearby Japanese home market, and at two-thirds of US list prices. However, South Korea — and perhaps Taiwan — are to some extent exceptional among the new producers. In particular, potential cost advantages in Latin America are often diminished by lower levels of production efficiency and poor capacity utilisation compared with East Asia.

10.   Oil producing countries hope to benefit from investing in direct-reduction/electric arc furnace technology as an alternative to the conventional blast furnace/oxygen

steelmaking route. These direct reduction processes rely on natural gas, an abundant and often under-utilised resource in oil-producing economies. Direct reduction and electric melting techniques offer high labour productivity in relatively small plants with an initial capital outlay per tonne half of that required by a normal integrated works[5]. Middle East countries are currently marginal producers. But they account for 20 per cent of the market economies' planned capacity expansion over the period to 1990. More than four-fifths of this new capacity intends to use direct reduction/electric arc processes.

11.   Thirdly, more fragmented supply has made the world steel industry more competitive (Graph 5.1) and established oligopolies have become less stable. Major cost differences now evident between producers have led to price cutting and erosion of traditional patterns of price leadership and customer loyalty[6].

12.   Market instability has been especially acute in the face of falling world demand and growing excess capacity. Overall, the industry price elasticity of demand is low. Yet individual low cost producers face a high own price elasticity of demand, and are therefore tempted to cut prices In 1978, the long-run equilibrium price for steel — the price at which only least-cost suppliers would earn a return on investment sufficient to maintain capacity levels — was estimated to be around $450 per tonne (and has probably remained about the same since)[7]. Transaction prices per tonne of steel plate — a product in considerable surplus world-wide — are currently well below this level, being at around $320 in the European market and $350-$400 in the United States.

13.   In the face of any demand upswings, ready availability of steel from plants currently operating at low capacity utilisation rates prevents rises in prices above incremental cost, at least for the standard specifications. Moreover, entry barriers in the steel industry have fallen, notably through reductions in capital requirements due to the direct-reduction/electric arc route[8]. Imminent technical developments, such as thin slab continuous casting, are likely to cut initial capital outlays still further. With low entry barriers, any potential the industry once had for above-average profits has pretty well disappeared[9].

The capacity to adjust

14.   The steel industry therefore faces a complex of severe structural and cyclical changes. Although the most efficient Japanese and Canadian companies have broadly maintained profitability, the result for many leading OECD steel companies has been chronic losses. But key features of firms in the OECD industry make adjustment to international competitive pressures unusually difficult.

15.   To begin with, the world steel industry shows a remarkably high degree of domestic ownership and operation. All the larger OECD steel companies are domestically owned and run. Low multinationalisation has prevented firms from "internalising" the benefits of geographical shifts in demand growth and comparative costs. Only in the "mini-mill" sector has there been significant multinational operation, by Ferrco of Canada and the now bankrupt Korf of Germany. The Austrian national steelmaker, Voest, has extended its operations in Germany and the United States. Certain Japanese and German

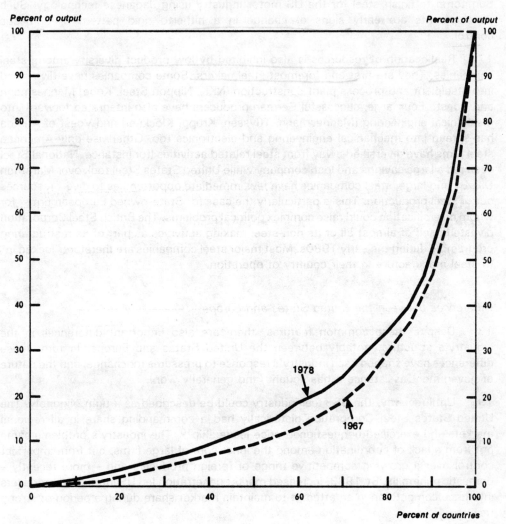

Graph 5.1
LORENZ CURVES FOR MARKET ECONOMIES STEEL PRODUCTION
1967 AND 1978

Percent of output

Percent of output

1978

1967

Percent of countries

Source : Crandall 1981 page 100.

companies have limited interests in plants overseas, notably Brazil. These are, however, rare exceptions.

16.   One side effect of sustained US steel trade protection has been to encourage recent entry into the US market by foreign firms seeking to partially circumvent trade controls. Three Japanese firms have taken equity shares in US companies; NKK in

89

National Steel, Nisshin in Wheeling-Pittsburgh; and Kawasaki in a consortium to re-open part of Kaiser's old works in California. In addition, LTV have a joint venture with Sumitomo to finish steel for the US motor industry using Japanese technology. Such developments are early signs of change in a hitherto rigid pattern of domestic control.

17.   Reallocation of resources is also inhibited by low product diversity among steel companies. They are first and foremost steelmakers. Some companies have diversified into steelplant and process plant construction (NKK, Nippon Steel, Kobe, Mannesmann and Voest). Four large, successful German producers have also integrated forward into mechanical engineering (Mannesmann, Thyssen, Krupp, Klöckner) and Voest of Austria has spread into mechanical engineering and electronics too. Otherwise only American steel firms have diversified away from steel related activities (for instance, National Steel acquired a large savings and loan company while United States Steel took over Marathon Oil). By and large, steel companies have few immediate opportunities to divert resources out of steel production. This is particularly the case for State-owned European firms, for whom diversification could raise complex political problems. The British Steel Corporation divested itself of almost all of its non-steel making activities as part of its restructuring programme during the early 1980s. Most major steel companies are therefore "locked in" to steel manufacture in their country of operation.

Differences between the United States and Europe

18.   Despite these common features, there are also important differences in the industry's structure, notably between the United States and Europe. In turn, these differences have shaped each industry's response to pressures for change, and the nature of government assistance it has sought (and generally won).

19.   Until recently, the US steel industry could be described as a tight oligopoly. The United States Steel Corporation historically had a commanding share in all regional markets and exercised unquestioned price leadership[10]. The industry's problems came not from a lack of coordination among the inner core of large firms, but from imperfect control over a growing competitive fringe of foreign producers and — more recently — domestic mini-mills. By 1983, increased market penetration led US integrated producers into price competition in an attempt to maintain market share during a period of strong recovery.

20.   Three features characterise the US integrated steel producers' response to growing competition:

- Recognition that the competitive fringe now has a substantial cost advantage in a broad range of product areas: the mini-mills in rod and bar products, overseas producers in flat products, structurals, pipe and tube and special steels. A long-run shift of capacity away from the inner core of leading domestic producers is therefore inevitable.
- Given these trends, the rational strategy is to avoid capacity expansion and limit modernisation investment. In effect, the industry is running down its

capital stock, while setting price in such a way as to maximise return on existing assets[11].

- The slower the expansion of the fringe, the more profitable this strategy will be. The main concern of the US industry has therefore been to slow down penetration by competitors, mainly through protection from imports, while accepting a continuing loss of market share, notably to domestic entrants.

21.   By contrast, the European industry is more fragmented and spread across individual countries. The largest US steel firm accounted in 1979 for nearly a quarter of US raw steel capacity; in Europe, the largest firm accounted for less than 15 per cent. The Herfindahl-Hirschman index of industrial concentration is a good 10 percentage points lower for the European steel industry than for its American counterpart[12].

22.   Moreover, cost differentials are as large among European producers, as between these producers and those in other regions. In 1983 reported differences in cost per tonne between near neighbours Britain and France ($435 in UK; $500 in France) are as great as those between Britain and South Korea (whose costs per tonne are below $400)[13].

23.   Most importantly, adjustment in the European steel industry has been subject to greater social and political constraints than in the United States:

- In Europe, the steel industry has been, and to an extent remains, a symbol of national prestige and a focus for industrial and regional development. There are high levels of State ownership, at least among integrated firms, though Germany is an important exception[14].
- In a number of countries, Britain and Germany for example, the steel industry has been obliged to use expensive local sources of coal, rather than importing cheaper or better quality feedstock, so as to protect national mining employment.
- Closure of steel plant is perceived as having a disproportionate social impact as they are often a major source of regional economic activity. Many European governments have sought to slow the rundown of employment in the industry, especially in nationalised steel firms, through support for continued high output operation at times of declining demand[15].

24.   In consequence, the European steel industry has faced two major problems: reconciling social and political constraints with the need for financial solvency; and retaining price stability despite marked differences between firms in operating costs and strategic objectives. In these circumstances, price maintenance has become the main preoccupation of European Community steel policy.

Policies for the steel industry in the United States and EEC

25.   In the late 1960s tariff barriers were the most important impediments to steel trade, a study for 1968 concluding that the effective rate of protection afforded by tariffs was greater than the equivalent non-tariff barriers in Canada, Japan, the United Kingdom and the United States, but not the original EEC[16]. Since then tariff barriers have fallen with

implementation of the Kennedy and Tokyo Rounds and enlargement of the European Community and non-tariff barriers have assumed greater significance. The form of these barriers has, however, differed significantly in the United States and Europe, reflecting structural and institutional factors.

26.   US policy has concentrated on border trade protection. Since 1969 the US market has been restrained by recurrent episodes of protection (Table 5.2), involving non-tariff barriers such as voluntary restraint agreements and, most recently, direct controls on imports. Over time, protection has been extended to a progressively wider range of countries, since as one source of imports is restrained by trade agreement another takes its place until, in turn, the new supplier is brought within the protectionist umbrella. The various non-tariff agreements on steel initially sought to restrict Japanese and European Community producers. The latest round of steel trade negotiations extend to newly industrialising countries such as Brazil, Mexico and South Korea, while continuing to restrain traditional sources of imports.

27.   Despite a sequence of protectionist measures, imports have supplied a growing share of US domestic steel consumption. By 1982 a quarter of the domestic market was supplied from a wide variety of overseas sources. Arguably, the share of imports would have been higher in the absence of trade protection. In 1983 production costs for US bulk carbon steel averaged $570 a tonne shipped, some 20 per cent higher than those of Japan, and 19 per cent above Germany (though the extent to which large increases in imports could occur without an increase in import prices is at least debatable)[17]. In effect, competitive imports have been reduced by trade restraint (at least relative to what they would otherwise have been), but not excluded. Otherwise the domestic steel industry has largely been left to look after itself, though it did benefit from favourable tax treatment in the early 1980s.

28.   In contrast, most European governments have provided direct financial assistance to steel producers, partly to offset their social obligations[18]. So as to prevent competitive subsidisation from irretrievably distorting the EC internal market, the European Community has developed a set of adjustment policies for the steel industry combining trade and industry policy instruments. The aim of Community policy is to reduce excess capacity, eliminate further subsidies and ultimately to restore normal competitive conditions in the European steel market. Towards this end the Community has monitored price setting, output levels and trade flows within the European steel industry. In recent years there has been tight administrative control over prices and outputs coupled with political suasion to reduce production capacity. The intention is to maintain prices at levels above incremental costs so as to support the financial viability of European steel producers. Stringent measures are required to prevent "chiselling" by firms which participate in the price fixing arrangements. Fines are levied on producers which exceed their allotted production quota.

29.   To prevent competition eroding the price fixing and output sharing arrangements, imports from outside the Community have also been controlled. It has at times proved necessary to threaten (with anti-dumping suits), and persuade (through voluntary agreement) external competitors to reduce the quantity of steel entering the Community

Table 5.2

THE CHRONOLOGY OF US STEEL TRADE POLICY

Phase I: The Voluntary Restraint Agreements

February 1966   American Iron and Steel Institute (AISI, the industry's trade association) advocate temporary tariff on steel imports. The first protectionist move. Subsequently AISI switch to advocating quotas.

Late 1967   Senator Hartke's bill proposes imports be limited to 9.6 per cent of US steel market.

Summer 1968   Germany and Japan offer voluntary restrictions on steel exports to USA during Congressional hearings and invite other major foreign producers to join them.

January 1969   Voluntary Restraint Agreement (VRA) setting agreed quotas for bulk steel imports from European Community and Japan comes into effect. Canada and United Kingdom do not join VRA but nevertheless restrict exports to US.

August 1971   Temporary 10 per cent surcharge on all imports into US threatens stability of VRA.

January 1972   VRA extended, with modifications for further 3 years.

May 1975   VRA allowed to lapse.

June 1976   Import quotas imposed on five categories of special steel from Sweden and EEC, initially for three year period, after attempt to negotiate voluntary "orderly marketing agreement" in ninety days fails. Japan concludes voluntary restraint agreement for a special steels on last day of ultimatum.

Phase 2: The Trigger Price Mechanism (TPM)

January 1975-
December 1977   Total of 19 separate anti-dumping complaints submitted to US Treasury Department.

October 1977   Inter-agency task force convened to assess conditions affecting US steel industry and suggest remedial measures.

December 1977   President Carter accepts recommendation of Task Force (Solomon Report 1977) that: "Department of Treasury, in administering the Antidumping Act, set up a system of trigger prices, based on the full costs of production including appropriate capital charges of steel mill products by the most efficient foreign steel producers (currently the Japanese steel industry), which would be used as a basis for monitoring imports of steel in the US and for initiating accelerated antidumping investigations with respect to imports below the trigger prices".

January 1978   Trigger prices for seventeen bulk steel products announced thereby setting defacto minimum prices for bulk steel in US.

February 1980   Import quotas for special steels phased out (bearing steel quota previously dropped June 1977).

Phase 3: The Reinstated Trigger Price Mechanism

March 1980   US Steel Co. alleges steel producers in seven European countries dumping steel below cost. TPM suspended during investigation.

October 1980   Trigger Price Mechanism restored in strengthened form for three to five years and anti-dumping cases dropped. Trigger price based on Japanese costs reinstated. New anti-surge provision prompting investigations in particular product markets whenever US steel industry falls below 87 per cent capacity utilisation and imports reach pre-specified levels. US government agrees package of financial aid for the industry.

Phase 4: Voluntary Export Quotas

January 1982   Anti-dumping and countervailing duty petitions filed by the US steel companies against European, Rumanian and Brazilian steel producers. TPM suspended.

     In order to reduce trade tension European Commission introduces stricter production quotas for EEC steelmakers limiting output for export to US market.

Table 5.2   (cont'd)

August 1982	US Commerce Department rules 38 European steel companies received "illegal" subsidies.
October 1982	Voluntary steel quota arrangement concluded with EEC cutting exports of ten major bulk steel products by 9 per cent. Simultaneous and crucial agreement for limiting sales of EEC tubes and pipes not otherwise precluded under anti-dumping legislation. Threat of penal import duties rescinded.
July 1983	Extra import duties and quotas imposed on European special and stainless steels (not covered by October 1982 agreement) for a four year period. Canada, Japan and EEC subsequently reject overtures to establish an Orderly Marketing Agreement on Special Steels (OMAS).
March 1984	EEC retaliates against US special steel restrictions after talks with USA, first on their withdrawal and then on compensation, break down. Retaliatory quotas imposed on chemicals (including styrene and polyethelene), some sidearms and sportsgoods, and retaliatory tariffs on other chemicals (including methanol and vinyl acetate) and burglar alarms and other anti-theft devices. Retaliatory measures to last for four years.
March 1984	South Africa announces voluntary restraints on a range of steel products customarily exported to US. Exports to be reduced by 22 per cent to 550 000 tonnes.
April 1984	Brazil concedes voluntary curbs on steel exports to the US to run for three years. Agreement immediately cuts Brazil's steel exports to US from 814 000 tonnes in 1983 back to 430 000 tonnes in the year ending April 1985. Decision followed acrimonious eight month long legal trade dispute with the US over alleged dumping and subsidies.
June 1984	US International Trade Commission finds the US steel industry has suffered serious injury in a range of five steel products accounting for 70 per cent of US steel imports. Import injury occurred despite existence of formal and informal export restraints by foreign producers.
July 1984	Following hearings, International Trade Commission recommend five year import quotas covering these 70 per cent of steel products.
August 1984	US Commerce Department recommends formal division of US steel import market between traditional and new exporting nations as follows: Japan 25 %; EC 24 %; Canada 14 %; South Korea 11 %; Brazil 7 %; Mexico 4 %; Africa 3 %.
September 1984	President Reagan rejects International Trade Commission recommendations on quotas in favour of an extended pattern of formal and informal voluntary restraint covering a wider range of countries, to be negotiated within 90 days.
November 1984	US Commerce Department suspends all steel pipe and tube imports from EEC producers after Community proposals to cut shipments from 14.9 per cent to 7.6 per cent share of the US market rejected. The International Trade Commission had earlier failed to find a case for injury to US domestic producers from Community pipe and tube exports.
January 1985	US and EEC finalise an accord limiting Community pipe and tube sales into US market to 7.6 per cent of demand for these products. Import ban lifted.
January 1985	US trade negotiators conclude voluntary restraint agreements with EEC and a range of small producers (Finland, Australia, South Africa and Spain) but agreement still to be finalised with Japan, South Korea, Brazil, Mexico and Argentina.

from outside, and to limit the scope for price competition from imports (through minimum import prices). These controls have either been negotiated by the European Commission, or imposed through national quotas maintained by some Member countries.

30.   Non-EC countries which sign voluntary export restraint agreements with the Community are allowed to sell steel at prices below those prevailing in Community markets, without local producers being allowed to align down to match import prices. In this fashion, importers can usually take up their quota. Foreign producers can sell more than the agreed quantity but at the danger of losing their price concession on any excess quantities. Apart from EFTA and East European producers, the Community also had agreements of this sort in 1984 with South Korea, Japan, Spain and South Africa among others. Nevertheless, some concessionary quotas are redundant under present conditions. The combination of transport costs, external tariffs and low basic prices make the European Community an unattractive market for third countries — for instance, Japan has not taken up its full concession recently. If anything, the external arrangements have tended to ossify the traditional trade flows on which they were based and inhibit entry by newer suppliers in response to market opportunities.

31.   An additional aim of Community policy towards non-EC steel producers is to preserve market stability by spreading exports around Community members and so avoid any bunching of orders. Those who breach this rule and win an undue share of an individual market may face anti-dumping duties. Spain was penalised when its penetration of the German reinforcing-bar market rose from 2 per cent in 1980 to reach 15.4 per cent in 1983. At that time Germany absorbed 90 per cent of Spanish reinforcing bar exports to the Community. In this case the distribution of imports was the cause for concern. It is said that EFTA producers have restricted their exports to particular Community markets for fear of provoking retaliation, even though EFTA steelmakers should, under normal circumstances, have complete and free access to European markets[19]. The impact of implicit restraint is hard to judge as EFTA steelmakers such as Sweden and Austria specialise in products not covered by the Community steel crisis measures.

32.   Viewed overall, it is difficult to gauge the impact of European Community policies towards non-EC producers because the West European steel market is depressed while the strength of the dollar makes the United States far more attractive to third country exporters. Taking two extremes, Antwerp spot prices for a basket of US imports fell as low as half of US list prices for the same products by 1983[20]. More significant is the future impact of European Community voluntary limitation agreements with non-EC producers when the crisis regime is dismantled at the end of 1985. Internal price and output controls are due to finish on the last day of December 1985; yet — on current trends — annual negotiations with non-EC suppliers concerning their sales into Community markets look set to continue.

The impact of policies

33.   The complexity of European policies towards steel makes it difficult to assess their impact. The effect of the crisis measures on trade flows cannot be isolated from their

influence on capacity reduction, output levels and prices. The implications of the European Community crisis regime for competition have been intensively discussed at a theoretical level, but no quantitiative estimates of the policy's overall impacts are available[21]. In contrast, the emphasis of US steel policy on border protection has made it easier to model its impact. Greater transparency, ready availability of data and a tradition of independent policy analysis have helped to stimulate research. As a result, American studies of steel trade policy dominate both in terms of quantity and quality[22]. Any discussion of this issue inevitably concentrates on the United States.

34.   Apart from Crandall[23], all the US studies make two heroic assumptions to simplify their analysis. Firstly, they consider steel as a single product with a single price. Crandall is more painstaking and examines five main categories of bulk steel product separately, excluding special steels which were subject to different trade controls. In the face of quotas, foreign producers can alter their product mix for export to the United States in order to exploit the most profitable market opportunities in a restricted market[24]. Thus, a recent bill introduced into Congress proposed sub-limits on 27 categories of steel product imported from Japan to protect against diversion within a voluntary restraint agreement towards the most profitable items[25]. Studying steel trade in broad product groups goes some way to resolve the difficulties arising from supply shifts induced by trade restraint.

35.   Secondly, most studies assume imported and domestically produced steel are perfect substitutes and, in effect, argue there is a single US steel market with a single demand function[26]. Again, Crandall distinguishes between the market for imported steel and the market for domestically made products. Although there is substitution between the two markets, he shows both supply and demand in the import market are far more responsive to price changes than is the domestic market. The oligopolistic US steel industry maintains more stable and usually higher prices than the competitive fringe of potential importers. "Captive demand" is probably of greater importance to domestic firms than foreign producers. These distinctions between closely related markets are crucial to reliability of estimates of the costs of protection. For this reason, more credence can be attached to Crandall's findings.

... on prices and trade flows

36.   One explicit aim of US trade protection is to raise domestic steel prices on the assumption that increased revenues from "temporary" protection will enable the US steel industry to restructure and invest in order to recover international competitiveness. Estimates of the effect of the "Voluntary Restraint Agreements" (VRA) and "Trigger Price Mechanism" (TPM) on bulk steel prices differ markedly (Table 5.3), reflecting differing assumptions on the elasticity of substitution between domestic and imported steel.

37.   On the unrealistic assumption that domestic and imported steel are perfect substitutes and given oligopolistic pricing behaviour by domestic producers, the VRA leads to an 18 per cent rise in all steel prices above what they would otherwise have been. Conversely, if this assumption is not made, trade restrictions increase prices in the import market to a far greater extent than domestic producer prices. In this case, government

Table 5.3

US STUDIES OF THE IMPACT OF TRADE RESTRICTIONS ON STEEL
AN OVERVIEW

		Prices	Imports (their share of apparent supply)
Counter-factual: Removal of Trade Restrictions GATT Tariff Remains in Place			
MacPhee (1974)	VRA in 1969	No prediction	-26 %
Tackacs (1975)	VRA	All steel prices +15 % to +18 %	n.a.
Crandall (1982)	VRA in 1971/72	Average import prices +6.3 % to +8.3 % average domestic prices +1.2 % to +3.5 %	-15 % to -23 %
FTC (1977)	12 % import quota/$322 ton reference price simulation 1976	+3.5 %	-7.5 %
Crandall (1982)	TPM in 1979	Average import prices +9.1 % to +11.5 % average domestic prices +0.8 % to +1.1 %	-41 %
Counter-factual: Removal of All Trade Restraint			
Jondrow (1978)	VRA plus tariff 1969/73	Import prices +5 % to +26 % no change in domestic prices	-25 % to -58 %
FTC (1977)	12 % import quota/$322 ton reference price and no tariff in 1976	+9 %	-18.5 %

negotiated quotas or prices generate significant rents for foreign exporters but have little impact on domestic producers.

38.   Since domestically produced steel dominates the US market, the overall effect of trade restrictions on prices is small, disguising the fact that much of the additional revenue generated by the measures is captured by foreign steelmakers. Given that imports and domestic production are imperfect substitutes, trade restrictions only have a relatively modest inflationary effect, but impose terms of trade costs on the US economy.

39.   Demand for steel imports is very responsive to domestic prices charged in the US market. Thus, the Federal Trade Commission[27] concludes that steel imports into the United States are highly responsive to differences in the relative price of steel in the United States, Japan and the European Community[28]. Crandall estimates demand elasticities for imports with respect to domestic prices ranging from 3.5 to 14.4[29].

40.   Because import demand is sensitive to relative prices, the TPM was effective in reducing the annual quantities of steel entering the US market as it limited importers' freedom to indulge in price competition against domestic steel. Working through a different mechanism, the VRAs directly limited the quantity of imported steel for sale in the United States and thereby removed an incentive to cut prices. Magee, for instance, argues negotiation of voluntary restraint for steel had an equivalent effect to imposing a tariff on imports of between 17 and 35 per cent (in addition to the MFN tariff already in place)[30].

41.   Crandall suggests that the VRA reduced steel imports by 15 to 23 per cent and the TPM cut them by 40 per cent, figures broadly consistent with MacPhee's rough-and-ready estimate for the VRA of 25 per cent[31]. On the other hand, foreign producers earned much higher margins on steel they sold, leading to a higher total profit on a lower volume of sales. Higher steel prices lead to a transfer of funds from consumers to steelmakers. Crandall estimates that the redistribution towards foreign producers equalled or exceeded that to domestic producers.

42.   However the effectiveness of trade restrictions at curtailing steel imports seems to have declined in recent years. Although Japan and the European Community's share of the US market has remained fairly stable since the late 1970s, substantial growth has occurred in the market shares of imports from Canada and European suppliers outside the Community, and more recently from the newly steel active countries. On the supply side, these trends reflect substantial excess capacity, high levels of cost competitiveness and in some instances provision of export incentives. On the demand side, imports have been pulled in from new suppliers by US recovery, strengthening of dollar exchange rates and constraints on imports from traditional sources. Shifts in the pattern of import supply have led the United States to extend import restrictions to a number of new sources.

43.   These developments highlight the limited usefulness and high potential cost of discriminatory measures. With multiple sources of supply and declining entry barriers, discriminatory measures have little impact on the effective elasticity of foreign supply to the domestic market. The broader pattern of supply creates strong pressures for protection to be extended. This generates uncertainty during the time interval in which

new measures are considered, proposed and negotiated. Moreover, the artificial diversion of output from "more" to "less" restricted sources of supply can involve real economic costs, which are incurred in adjusting output volumes and distribution channels.

... on output, employment and wages

44.   Insofar as the various trade measures against steel were effective in reducing the level of imports into the United States, the cutback was small compared with overall US steel capacity. Crandall suggests the TPM increased the output of domestically produced steel (relative, of course, to what it otherwise would have been) by some 2 to 3 million metric tonnes, while the VRA pushed it up by 3.2 million tonnes, barely enough to load an integrated mill in either case[32]. This means overall capacity utilisation in the US steel industry rose from 74 per cent to, at most, 77 per cent as a result of trigger prices in 1979. In short, trade restrictions are an ineffective way of generating significant additional demand for steel compared to, say, a macroeconomic stimulus working through higher domestic investment or higher consumer durable sales.

45.   The demand for steelworkers is derived from the demand for steel. Since trade restrictions only give a slight boost to domestic steel output, it follows that they have a small effect on employment. Of course, trade protection may keep the oldest and most labour intensive plants in existence. Protection may also have helped generate limited new employment in high productivity mini-mills located away from the traditional sites, although mini-mill development might have proceeded almost as fast in the absence of trade protection. Crandall suggests the TPM maintained between 8,800 and 12,400 steel jobs a year that would otherwise have disappeared — some 2 to 3 per cent of industry employment. Magee's estimates for the VRA are slightly higher.

46.   Protection, combined with oligopolistic price setting, may also affect earnings in the industry. Employee compensation in the US steel industry increased more rapidly than average manufacturing earnings in the period to 1979[33]. Given that productivity was rising more slowly than in the industry's competitors overseas[34], it is unlikely that compensation gains could have been sustained without import controls. Crandall estimates the additional rents accruing to domestic producers from protection amount to approximately $1 000 per worker a year — little more than 3 per cent of average annual compensation. Given plausible assumptions about bilateral bargaining between employers and workers, trade protection would account for no more than a 1 or 2 per cent rise in wages.

47.   More recent estimates by Grossman[35] suggest the dampening effect of trade flows on employment and earnings in the US steel industry strengthened considerably after 1979. Pressure on jobs and wages arose from higher imports drawn in by the appreciation of the dollar and, possibly, by the strong US recovery of 1983 and 1984. Making the strong assumption that collectively bargained earnings in the industry are set so as to maintain employment constant, the model estimated by Grossman suggests each 1 per cent of tariff equivalent quota leads to a slightly less than 2 per cent increase in compensation — clearly a markedly higher result than Crandall's.

48.   The real benefit of trade protection to the workforce is probably not the small "permanent" output, employment and earnings gains. Rather, it is greater temporary job security in a declining but very high wage industry. The US integrated steel industry has long established, highly developed and complex internal labour markets, with well structured promotion and earnings scales[36]. Wages rise sharply with seniority, partly because of unionisation, but also because skills are specific to the job and to the industry. Both employer and worker have a substantial investment in the acquisition of highly specialised skills.

49.   Thus, Jacobson estimates loss of a job in the US steel industry by a prime age male worker is equivalent to a 10-15 per cent reduction in lifetime earnings[37]. Apart from automobiles, this is a considerably greater lifetime income cost from displacement than for other trade-sensitive industries Jacobson studied. The differential partly arises because steel (and automobile) workers have captured part of the above-average profits which once accrued to a highly concentrated and fairly cohesive industry[38]. The steel oligopoly has become less stable in the face of competition from imports and mini-mills. Nevertheless, the relative wages of steel workers remain high and the labour-force have an obvious interest in protecting and restoring the industry's profit potential.

... on profitability and structural adjustment

50.   The main beneficiaries of import protection have been US steel companies and their foreign rivals. While the domestic price rise induced by protection is small, the volume of steel sales affected by higher prices is huge. Since the short-term price elasticity of demand for steel is very low, the transfer of resources to producers can also be huge.

51.   Crandall estimates steel producers received between $371 million and $640 million a year extra in rents on existing assets as a result of trigger prices in 1979. Simulation studies by the FTC of a $322 reference price or quota equivalent to a 12 per cent *ad valorem* duty (not far off what actually took place) suggest an even higher figure for gains to US steel producers of $869 million in 1976. By any standards, this is not a bad return on lobbying.

52.   Estimates of the share of rents going to foreign producers vary widely. Crandall's figure ranges from 43 per cent to 56 per cent, while at the other extreme FTC put the foreign share as low as 12 per cent. Magee estimates that fully two-thirds of the additional revenue from the VRA in 1971 was captured by foreign producers, leaving only $88 million for domestic steelmakers.

53.   Although they vary, these estimates highlight the implicit compensation for foreign steel producers built into trade restrictions. The compensation only reaches the established suppliers (in the form of higher import prices) so long as protection does not simply divert trade among foreign sources. A desire to capture the rents from trade protection helps explain why restricted foreign suppliers have complained about trade diversion and have been anxious to support extension of discriminatory restrictions to newly steel active countries[39].

54.   US steel trade protection was presented as a temporary measure to give the industry a breathing space to restructure and — by investing the rents obtained — to improve its competitiveness. In practice, protection has been renewed and the established producers have put few resources into restructuring. It has been left to the mini-mills to inject new capital into the industry. Aylen has argued there are few signs the US steel industry ever intended to modernise during the 1970s, with the possible exceptions of Inland and Bethlehem Steel[40]. Instead the traditional American steel firms are pursuing a strategy of long-term withdrawal from steelmaking. Rents earned from sustained protection help US steel firms diversify through acquisition and slow down the reduction of their labour force and the rate of plant closure.

55.   In many respects this strategy of phased withdrawal has been highly successful for the companies concerned. The share of steel output produced by the four largest firms only declined from 52 per cent in 1979 to 47 per cent in 1983. Over the same period the whole US steel industry cut capacity by nearly 20 million tonnes and shed about 200 000 workers[41].

56.   Closure of older integrated works has been accompanied by investment in new mini-mill capacity. Three factors have encouraged the growth of mini-mill production in the United States: ready availability of unexploited scrap supplies outside traditional steelmaking areas; rapid technical progress in design and operation of electric arc furnaces and continuous casting machines; and failure of long-established producers to invest in modern bar and rod mills. Evidence for 1980 suggests US mini-mills required barely half the man hours used by their integrated competitors to make a ton of wire rod[42].

57.   Expansion of mini-mill output has been at the expense of foreign producers' market shares as well as the integrated domestic producers. During the 1970s there was a sharp fall in imports' share of the market for bar and wire rod, against an overall trend of rising import penetration for other steel products. The shift towards local supply was accompanied by a drop in domestic prices for rod and bar relative to import prices. Over the period 1966-70, US wire rod prices were 46 per cent above import prices, but, by 1981-2, domestic prices had fallen to equal or undercut the import price[43]. Lower costs meant higher profits. A sample of US mini-mills earned twice the return on equity realised by US manufacturing industry over the ten years up to 1981[44]. A comparable sample of integrated producers show a below average return over the same period.

58.   The US steel industry has therefore been extensively restructured under private ownership by market forces[45]. But despite the changes which have occurred, the US industry's restructuring has been far from complete. In particular, the technology of most integrated US steel firms has fallen well behind their major foreign competitors[46]. Their relative position has worsened over time as other major OECD producers tried to catch up with the technical leaders, Japan and Germany. Though protection has encouraged entry by efficient domestic and foreign owned mini-mills, it has also kept obsolete and poorly located facilities in operation.

59.   Paradoxically, US protection may have strengthened the US industry's foreign rivals, notably in Japan, but more recently also in Europe. Protection has probably

increased the profit margin on Japanese steel sales in the US market by at least 10 per cent. This is around $200 million a year, about half of Japan's annual expenditure (the world's highest) on steel R&D.

60.   Nonetheless, it would be wrong to over-dramatise the costs of US trade protection. At worst, the TPM increased the cost of a US made car by $10. This should be compared with a total cost disadvantage for US small cars of over $1 000[47]. Taken in isolation, steel protection has hardly any identifiable macro-economic effect and is best seen as sectional income maintenance towards an industry with large lobbying power. In fact, it can be argued that protection survives precisely because it has such a slight but pervasive impact on each individual in the US economy. Yet, added up over all consumers, these "slight impacts" amount to considerable rent payments for US shareholders and steelworkers (as well as foreign steelmakers).

61.   It has often been pointed out that it would have been more efficient to give specific subsidies for modernisation to the US steel industry if this was the avowed policy aim[48]. It might be argued the steel industry did not try to overcome political resistance to modernisation subsidies because it did not want to modernise. But, exposure to full international competition during the 1970s might well have made the domestic steel oligopoly less complacent and stable. Those US steel companies that survived would, in this view, have improved their efficiency under the stimulus of competition.

62.   A useful parallel can perhaps be drawn with recent experience in the British bulk steel industry which was internationally uncompetitive by the end of the 1970s. Continued exposure to European competition, and – most importantly – a government determined to reduce subsidies, had dramatic effects on the British Steel Corporation[49]. In the two years subsequent to the 1980 steel strike, labour productivity at the British Steel Corporation rose by 40 per cent and it continued to climb at a slightly slower rate with output per man, matching average European levels by 1983[50]. Rapid progress in cutting manpower was partly due to widespread plant closures, but also helped by bringing working practices into line with modern technology. An energy conservation programme cut energy consumption per tonne of steel by 18 per cent within three years through scrupulous attention to efficient operating practice, but without any major capital expenditure[51]. Product quality, equipment maintenance and reliability, and cost analysis and control have been upgraded in the face of compelling market forces. There is some way to go before the industry closes the gap on best Japanese practice, but driven by overwhelming pressures to return to profitable trading the British Steel Corporation has gone from being a nearly hopeless case to one of the world's most cost competitive steel producers.

Prospects

63.   In the years to come, the OECD steel industry will have to face continuing shifts in demand, in technology, in patterns of capacity utilisation and in relative costs[52]. Even the Japanese firms, which retain an important technological edge, will face adjustment pressures as restructuring in Europe reduces their cost advantage, their home market

stagnates, and industrialisation and self-sufficiency in Asia erodes export sales. Continuing intense competition for open markets will impose further strains on higher cost, less innovative and less adaptive producers.

64.   Protectionist pressures can therefore be expected to persist. This is largely a reflection of the interests of OECD steel producers, and their continuing structural difficulties. But two additional factors are also relevant. The first is a new trend of US and EEC steel trade restraint negotiations feeding on one another. In this fashion, one trading bloc demands the same protection as previously negotiated by the other and as a result, protection tends to accumulate. Secondly, market shares among third country producers are being frozen by the United States and the European Community alike. Since voluntary restraint usually confers rents upon foreign producers as compensation for lower export volumes, foreign suppliers who do well under the existing system have an interest in seeing administered trade perpetuated and extended to any new competitors which threaten stability of existing arrangements. In short, current trade arrangements in steel could become difficult to reverse[53].

65.   In some respects protection in the steel industry has been relatively effective. High entry barriers have contained trade diversion. Overall steel demand is fairly unresponsive to price, so import controls lead to large resource transfers from consumers to producers — domestic and foreign. The returns to lobbying have been high. However, structural change in the industry worldwide is reducing the effectiveness of discriminatory measures. With many sources of supply and widespread excess capacity, trade diversion opportunities are rapidly taken up. Development of "mini-mills" has cut entry barriers for some products, so supply can be expected to become more elastic in the medium term. Large integrated steel companies will find their rents bid away by domestic mini-mill entrants and foreign suppliers which have escaped trade restrictions.

66.   The situation in steel is in this respect analogous to that found in textiles and clothing. Protecting countries come under intense pressure from their domestic industry to increase the scope and coverage of import controls. More severe trade measures impose real economic costs which are ultimately reflected in lower growth potential in importing and exporting countries alike. The steel industry's recent experience suggests that taken alone, protection is not a particularly effective way of encouraging modernisation. The rents it creates may help firms in the industry to diversify by acquisition and so manage the exit process. In effect, trade measures protect a number of firms rather than an industry and its employees. Whether the benefits from doing so justify the costs is clearly a political choice.

NOTES AND REFERENCES

1. Gold: 1982; Aylen: 1982.

2. The importance of market growth in allowing exploitation of scale economies and explaining changes in locational pattern is discussed in Carlsson: 1981 and Hekman: 1978.

3. Gold: 1974; Magaziner and Reich: 1982; Keeling: 1982; Mueller and Kawahito: 1978; Yamawaki: 1982; Barnett & Schorsch: 1983.

4. Metals Intelligence International: 1984; Crandall: 1981, ch.4. Plant construction costs may have been distorted by capital subsidies and export finance on steel plant. However, there is no evidence that the assistance provided to Korean producers is greater than that provided by a number of OECD countries to their steel industry for modernisation investments.

5. Gold: 1982; Economic Commission for Europe: 1979.

6. See Scherer: 1981, pp. 212-220.

7. Crandall: 1981; the same estimate is presented in OECD: 1980. Price data is taken from CRU Metal Monitor: Steel, January: 1984.

8. Gold: 1982; on cutting capital costs see Aylen: 1983.

9. See the discussion of profitability trends in Crandall: 1981 and Genevaz: 1982.

10. Council on Wage and Price Stability: 1977 and Scherer: 1980, pp. 178-80 survey the relevant literature. See also Parsons and Ray: 1975 and De Vany and Frey: 1982 for a more recent discussion.

11. This is the classic result of Gaskins: 1971. See also Caves, Fortunato and Ghemawat: 1984, Jacquemin and Thisse: 1972 and Ono: 1982.

12. Calculated from data in Shepherd and Duchêne: 1983.

13. Marcus and Kirsis: 1984.

14. See especially Padioleau: 1981 for a discussion of the political role of the steel industry.

15. See Cockerill: 1980 and 1984 and the discussion of steel in Shepherd and Duchêne: 1983.

16. McPhee: 1974.

17. Marcus and Kirsis: 1984

18. An estimate of the cost of these obligations and the extent to which they are offset by subsidies is provided in House of Commons, Second Report from the Industry and Trade Committee: 1983, pp. 110-113.

19. Brown: 1984.

20. Metals Intelligence International: 1984b.

21. Martin: 1979; Strange and Tooze: 1981; Tsoukalis and Da Silva Ferreira: 1980; L'Expansion, 18th October 1984, p. 104 cites an industry estimate that EC arrangements regulating steel output increase the price of steel in the Community by around 20 per cent.

22. This is particularly true with respect to studies published by official agencies, and discussing policy choices for steel: see, for example, Federal Trade Commission: 1977; General Accounting Office: 1981; Hanusek: 1984 and Solomon Report: 1978. The quality of the Australian Industries Assistance Commission study of steel policy (Industries Assistance Commission: 1983) should also be noted.

23. Crandall: 1982; see also the earlier piece by Crandall in OECD; 1980.

24. Canto: 1984 argues the VRAs resulted in a decline in the tonnage of imported steel, but foreign producers responded by altering the mix of steel products shipped to the United States. As a result, the value of steel imported by the United States increased substantially thereby reducing effective protection of the most profitable steel products. The VRAs really only protected the least profitable products and did little to significantly improve overall profitability of the domestic steel industry. However, it is hard to establish such direct causal links between trade restrictions and foreign steelmakers product strategy. General demand conditions in the industry and foreign technical leadership in many products may far outweigh considerations of trade policy. The rise of domestic mini-mills producing low value rod and bar products also made these markets less attractive to overseas producers, again biasing Canto's results. Also see Gold: 1982 on pressures underlying moves up-market.

25. Dunne: 1985

26. See, for example, Magee: 1972; Tackacs: 1975; Bright and McKinney: 1984.

27. Federal Trade Commission: 1977.

28. See also Friden: 1972, ch.3.

29. Crandall: 1981, Appendix B.

30. Magee: 1972.

31. MacPhee: 1974; also see Crandall: 1981, Table 7.1 for elasticity estimates.

32. Crandall: 1981, Table 7.2 and p. 107.

33. Bureau of Labor Statistics: 1982 and Crandall: 1981 and, especially, Anderson and Kreinin: 1981 and Barnett and Schorsch: 1982, pp. 66-71.

34. Bureau of Labor Statistics: 1984; Aylen: 1984, Figure 2; Barnett and Schorsch: 1983, Part II.

35. Grossman: 1984, p. 11.

36. Somers: 1980, pp. 151-208.

37. Jacobson: 1979.

38. See also Aho and Bayard: 1982 for a discussion of whether compensation should be provided for a loss of a monopoly element in wage rates.

39. See, for example, Financial Times: 30th November 1983. For evidence on the importance of the "protected" US market for foreign steelmakers see "US demand boosts Thyssen Stahl", Financial Times: 13th December 1984.

40. Aylen: 1982.

41. Crandall: 1984a

42. Barnett and Schorsch: 1983, Chapter 5.

43. Crandall: 1984b, p. 13.

44. Barnett and Schorsch: 1983, Table 4-4.

45. Crandall: 1984a.

46. Aylen: 1980; Aylen: 1982; Oster: 1982.

47. See Chapter 8. The cost impact estimate derives from Crandall: 1981. The fact is that estimates of the deadweight losses induced by US steel trade protection are small, but estimates of the transfer from consumers to domestic and foreign steel producers are dramatic. The resource misallocation arising from protection is small compared with the huge redistributive effect. Trade restrictions barely affect output so there is little resource misallocation in production. The price rise induced by trade restrictions is small, so there is barely any loss of surplus among marginal consumers. But, the volume of steel sales affected by higher prices is huge and so the transfer of resources is likewise huge. Turning again to Crandall's estimates for the TPM, he finds deadweight welfare losses totalling $31 million in 1979. These compare with a staggering $932 milion to $1 201 million transfer from consumers to domestic ($371 to $640 million) and foreign ($519 million) steel producers and US Customs ($42 million). Other studies support this conclusion. The Federal Trade Commission (Table 8A.1) simulation of the effects of imposing a $322 a ton minimum steel price, or an equivalent 12 per cent import quota, in 1976 suggest a deadweight loss of only $14.4 million compared with a baseline including a 5 per cent GATT tariff. Yet these same policies imply a transfer of just under $1 billion away from consumers. In this respect Magee (1972) is very much out on his own with a deadweight loss of $211 million for the VRA in 1971 which is difficult to explain.

48. For example, Adams and Mueller: 1982.

49. Aylen: 1984 surveys BSC's recent experience.

50. Rodger: 1984.

51. Fitzgerald: 1984.

52. Gold: 1982 assesses the role of these various factors.

53. Hufbauer and Rosen: 1984.

106

Chapter 6

TEXTILES AND CLOTHING

1.   Throughout the post-war period, the OECD textile and clothing industries have received exceptionally high levels of tariff and non-tariff protection, culminating in the generalised system of import controls known as the Multi-Fibre Agreement (MFA)[1].

Industry characteristics

2.   Four key features of these industries, increasingly less relevant to textiles than to clothing, have shaped both the pressures for, and the responses to, persistent protection[2]:

- Limited product differentiability, so that competition occurs primarily on a cost basis;
- A cost structure heavily dominated by labour costs, giving a major and durable competitive advantage to low wage countries;
- Weak barriers to entry and exit, reflected in a fragmented industry structure, high rates of firm turnover and the virtual absence of supra-normal profits;
- Wholesalers, retailers and some producers are highly sensitive to new sourcing opportunities.

The protectionist response

3.   As a result of these characteristics, discriminatory restrictions – which in these industries have been the rule rather than the exception – have consistently given rise to trade diversion effects.

4.   One of the earliest major measures of import controls on a discriminatory basis – the US-Japan voluntary export restraint agreement on cotton textiles of January 1957, is illuminating in this respect. The agreement did not prevent the continued growth of total US cotton textile imports, which increased by 60 per cent over the period from 1956/57 to 1960/61, but Japan's share declined from 52 per cent to 30 per cent. The prime beneficiary of these shifts was Hong Kong, whose share rose from less than 1 per cent to 25 per cent, the volume of Hong Kong's total exports increasing over the period by a factor of ten.

5.   From the point of view of the Japanese textile industry, the agreement, though not preferable to a situation of unrestricted trade, nonetheless provided an important opportunity to reduce its reliance on the US market and accelerate the transition from cotton to synthetic fibres — increasing the quality and value of local production, reducing the requirements for imported cotton while strengthening the emerging Japanese chemical industry, and moving out of the products increasingly produced in Hong Kong and other lower-wage countries[3].

6.   Inducements in this direction were built into the quota allocation system. First, since textile restraints were based on quantity rather than price, producers were encouraged to move upmarket. Second, the Japanese government allocated quota shares on the basis of the price exporters charged for textile products, and on the total value of a firm's textile exports, thereby penalising suppliers of low-price, low-quality produce. Moreover, suppliers unable to fill this quota in any one period saw their quotas reduced in subsequent rounds[4].

7.   These inducements were clearly effective, reinforcing those arising from the restriction itself. Between 1956 and 1960, Japan's overall exports of textile products increased by 10 per cent annually. Wool and synthetics accounted for most of this growth: their share in exports to the United States went from 18 per cent in 1956 to 34 per cent in 1960. Cotton textile production — which on a world-wide basis faced mounting competition from synthetics — declined, going from 35 per cent of Japan's textile output in 1958 to 27 per cent four years later. In 1956 the unit value of Japan's exports of cotton textiles to the United States was some 40 per cent below that of equivalent UK produce; this gap was halved some five years later.

8.   This pattern — trade diversion to less restricted sources, while the more restricted sources find new markets and products — has repeated itself systematically in the textile and clothing industries' response to protection[5]. Despite increasing trade restrictions, overall growth in textile and clothing trade exceeded that in all manufacturing throughout the period to 1982. This was largely due to rapid growth in OECD clothing imports; in contrast, textiles trade has stagnated, in some cases — notably the United States — the volume of textile imports actually tending to decline until the recent appreciation of the dollar.

9.   Overall trade growth conceals substantial differences between import markets, as exports barred from highly restrictive countries have moved to countries maintaining a relatively open import regime. The most striking instance of such shifts occurred in 1971-73, when the United States pressed Far East suppliers to restrain exports of man-made fibre and wool products, resulting in a substantial diversion of Far East products to the EC market.

10.   Important shifts have also occurred in patterns of supply, as "less restricted" sources of imports have replaced "more restricted" sources. Thus, in 1971-73, when US restrictions on Far Eastern suppliers led to a 4.8 per cent annual decline in the volume of their exports to the US market, exports to this market from Latin America and other developing countries increased at 15 per cent annually.

11.   In the EC, diversion has occurred from the more restricted Asian exporters to sources with preferential access to the EC market, notably those on the Mediterranean rim (and the very small ACP suppliers). Over the period 1976-1980 the volume of EC textile imports from the Asian NICs increased at an average of 2.2 per cent annually, while the figure for the Mediterranean and ACP suppliers was 9.5 per cent. There has also been diversion from Asian exporters to low-cost sources within the EC, especially Italy, which substantially increased its market share subsequent to the first and third MFA[6].

The impact on prices

12.   Widespread diversion has not prevented prices from being substantially higher than they would have been without import controls. More restricted producers have raised their prices, bringing them closer to production costs in the OECD countries. In items involving a high direct labour input − e.g. women's coats or knit blouses − manufacturing costs in the Asian NICs are around half those in the United States and a third lower than those in the EC; the fact that producers in the United States and the EC can survive is a straightforward indication of the additional costs protection imposes on consumers. Silberston estimates that average UK retail prices of imported and domestically-produced textiles and clothing would be 5 to 10 per cent lower relative to the prices of other goods and services were the MFA abolished[7].

13.   It has been calculated that foreign clothing exporters receive some 15 per cent of the total transfer to producers due to protection in Canada. A recent study for the United Kingdom sets the share going to foreign producers considerably higher, at nearly two-thirds[8]. Even the more conservative Canadian estimate implies an annual transfer from OECD consumers to Asian NIC exporters of at least $2 billion. This is equivalent to around 4 per cent of the total value of NIC exports to the OECD region.

14.   There have also been major changes in relative prices within the textile and clothing group. As producers have moved up-market, prices have increased most for lower-quality fabrics and garments. Protection has also had a disproportionate impact on clothing items having a high number of stitches per length of fabric − a measure of the assembly and hence labour-intensiveness of the product. The British Consumers' Association study of the costs of protection in the UK clothing industry suggests an average increase in UK clothing retail prices due to the MFA of the order of 20 per cent. But on lower quality items such as jeans prices had risen by 30-50 per cent. Prices for children's wear − a highly labour intensive product − had doubled[9].

15.   These changes in relative prices clearly fall most heavily on lower income households in the OECD region. To this must be added the fact that clothing accounts for a larger share of these households' consumption expenditure. Jenkins calculates that protecting the Canadian clothing industry costs lower-income households four times as much as it costs higher-income households[10].

Diminishing scope for diversion

16. Does this mean that the vast system of import controls put in place by the OECD countries has little real impact on output flows, simply shuffling trade around and redistributing income from poorer OECD consumers to those producers against whom the measures were originally aimed? This interpretation holds less and less in recent years.

17. Trade diversion effects have been widespread in the past, but the scope for continued diversion has narrowed. This is mainly due to progressive widening and tightening of the MFA. The marked trend towards more detailed product breakdowns in the bilateral agreements, increasing coverage of exporting sources, and more frequent reviews of quota levels and utilisation rates, has reduced the leeway available for sources to shift among products and markets.

18. As this leeway has been reduced, the system has increasingly functioned to lock importers into their traditional sources of supply. Quotas allocated to the "first wave" NICs were generally frozen in recent years (or even reduced when their bargaining power was weak), but those given to new low-wage suppliers were too small to fundamentally alter the heavy concentration of imports on established suppliers benefiting from large quota rents. The British Consumers' Association notes that ten Far Eastern sources account for 95 per cent of UK quota for "sensitive" clothing products. Hong Kong alone accounted for over 50 per cent of the entire UK quota for the Far East. Similar orders of magnitude appear to hold for other MFA importers. This development contradicts one of the declared aims of the MFA, that is to give preference to small suppliers.

19. The first-wave NICs have tended to become less competitive over time. Wages have increased more rapidly than in the "second-tier" NICs, and productivity increases have not made up the difference[11]. Had it not been for the MFA, they would probably have lost market share more rapidly than they did.

20. In addition to increasingly comprehensive and distorting quantitative restrictions on imports, the OECD countries continue to impose high *ad valorem* tariffs on textile and clothing products. By and large, the reductions in tariffs on textiles and clothing (excluding fibres) negotiated during the Tokyo Round were around one-half those on industrial products as a whole. As a result, post-Tokyo Round tariffs on textiles and clothing are two to three times above the manufacturing average. Moreover, within the textiles and clothing group, there is a clear tendency for tariffs to rise with the stage of processing. Effective rates of protection are therefore higher than nominal rates, notably for clothing. Finally, textiles and clothing are often either excluded from the GSP, or are subject to higher GSP rates or more rigorous quantitative or country limitations than other industrial products[12].

21. Though many of these tariffs are probably redundant for imports from the LDCs, they are clearly important in distorting intra-OECD trade. But in the absence of binding quantitative restrictions, notably in the case of textiles, effective rates of tariff protection

in the order of 20 to 30 per cent or more can be expected to curtail trade and drive a substantial wedge between domestic and world market prices. This presumption is consistent with the evidence. Jenkins finds for Canada that the increase in domestic clothing output due to tariffs was of approximately the same order of magnitude as that due to bilateral quotas[13]. Equally, Pelzman and Bradberry conclude that a 30 per cent reduction in US textile tariffs would reduce domestic textile prices by around 4.5 per cent in real terms and increase the growth rate of textile imports by a quarter. More recently, Pelzman has argued that as far as the textiles industry is concerned, the trade restraining effects of tariffs may dominate those of quantitative restrictions[14].

22.   Finally, structural change, primarily in the textile industry, may have also reduced the scope for diversion. In particular, increases in capital intensity and in minimum efficient scale have raised the sunk costs associated with entry. Greater sunk costs can be presumed to deter "hit and run" behaviour in the face of short-lived diversion opportunities[15]. Reductions in relative labour-intensity in textiles may also have reduced the cost gap separating OECD producers from those in lower-wage countries. Any given level of tariff or restraint on the lowest cost sources will shift a larger share of output to suppliers within OECD customs unions and free trade areas.

23.   The combined trade-suppressing effects of tightening quantitative restrictions, continued high tariffs and structural change can be seen in an econometric model of textiles and clothing trade developed for this study (see Annex). The model estimates import demand and supply equations for textiles and clothing for the United States and the EC over the period 1967-1981. These equations were then used to simulate import behaviour in 1982 and 1983, covering implementation of MFA III.

24.   As with all econometric exercises, the outcomes must be interpreted cautiously. The data sources are diverse and in some cases only partially comparable. More fundamentally, textiles and clothing imports have always been subject to some form of restriction. There is therefore no benchmark of "free trade" against which the impact of protection can be assessed. Bearing these caveats in mind, four main points emerge from the estimates:

- Subsequent to implementation of MFA I, OECD imports of textiles and clothing became almost totally unresponsive to price signals, especially as regards the competitiveness of non-OECD suppliers. Conventional import demand equations which over the preceding period gave excellent fits, ceased to have any explanatory power.
- Again as of 1973, import prices from non-OECD sources tended to align on domestic prices rather than vice versa despite large and persistent cost differentials. In other words, mark-ups on import prices increased.
- Deviations from market equilibrium were particularly great, (a) in the United States relative to the European Community, and (b) in clothing relative to textiles.
- Compression of imports from non-OECD sources in 1982 and 1983 can be estimated at slightly over 10 per cent in volume terms, though the import

figures would be very much larger had 1966-72 behaviour patterns persisted into the late 1970s. On this latter scenario, 1982-83 import volumes from non-OECD sources would be at least twice as great as the observed magnitudes.

The impact on employment

25. Over the period 1973-1982 employment levels in the OECD textile and clothing industries declined at an annual average rate of 4.5 per cent and 3 per cent respectively. In 1953, the textiles and clothing industries together accounted for over 20 per cent of OECD manufacturing employment; by 1980, their share was around 13 per cent (Table 6.1). This steady rundown in employment levels has certainly caused economic hardship, particularly in the textile industry, where workers frequently have few other job options — if they did, it is unlikely they would choose to work in an industry which has consistently paid wages well below the manufacturing average (Table 6.2).

26. In fact, low wages can only persist because the industries draw on a labour force whose occupational and industrial mobility is restricted. Skill levels are under the manufacturing average; the share of women workers is high; the work force is often concentrated in regions or townships with a narrow industrial base and persistent unemployment[16]. Each of these factors makes labour adjustment difficult. The duration of unemployment tends to be higher in congested regional labour markets. Women workers have less continuous employment experience to rely on in getting other jobs. Since the incidence of unemployment is in any case higher among the unskilled, they are more likely to find themselves competing in buyers' markets.

27. Adjustment costs are particularly onerous in periods of slow economic growth. Parsons found that increases in overall US unemployment have a greater adverse impact on the job opportunities of workers laid off from the clothing industry than on the average unemployed person. The variable he focuses on is the monthly rate at which workers displaced from a particular industry find new jobs. An increase in economy-wide unemployment from 4 to 8 per cent reduces this rate by around 8 per cent across all industries; for workers laid off from the clothing industry, it reduces it by over a quarter. Put slightly differently, when overall unemployment is high, the duration of unemployment increases more for displaced clothing industry employees than for the average unemployed person[17].

28. Each of these factors provides a rationale for trying to reduce the adjustment costs borne by workers displaced from the textiles and clothing industries. It may also be viewed as justifying attempts to slow the rate at which displacement occurs. Certainly this has been an important objective of protecting these industries. But whether protection has been effective in this respect is questionable.

29. Even in these industries, imports from developing countries — or more generally, from sources controlled under the MFA — do not account for a large share of domestic consumption. Measured by value, clothing imports from developing countries were some 7 per cent of 1976 apparent consumption in the United States and 10-11 per cent in the

112

Table 6.1

SHARE OF TEXTILES AND CLOTHING IN MANUFACTURING (a) EMPLOYMENT
IN DEVELOPED AND DEVELOPING COUNTRIES, 1953-1980

	Textiles					Clothing				
	1953	1963	1970	1975	1980	1953	1963	1970	1975	1980
MARKET ECONOMIES	17.4	17.3	16.5	15.4	14.8	8.8	9.2	8.4	8.0	8.0
Developed countries	12.1	9.9	9.1	8.4	7.2	8.6	8.0	6.8	6.1	5.7
Developing countries	29.2	28.3	27.8	25.2	24.0	9.2	10.9	11.0	10.7	10.9
North America	7.8	6.3	6.7	6.6	5.7	8.6	8.9	6.9	7.0	6.6
Japan	23.1	16.5	14.2	12.6	10.9	3.0	5.2	4.2	4.6	4.8
E.C. (9)	13.5	9.8	8.7	7.9	6.8	9.4	8.4	7.4	6.2	5.4
Other Western Europe	10.4	8.5	6.8	5.7	5.2	9.8	7.3	6.8	5.3	4.5
Southern Europe	20.0	16.9	15.5	14.8	14.5	9.5	11.1	10.8	10.0	11.0
Asia	34.6	32.9	33.2	29.9	28.5	9.0	10.9	11.6	11.8	11.3
Latin America	20.5	17.9	14.7	14.1	12.2	10.3	11.2	9.0	8.0	8.7
Africa	32.1	32.5	29.3	30.3	-	5.5	9.7	10.3	9.0	-

a) All manufacturing, excluding food, beverages, tobacco, non-ferrous metals and petroleum refineries.

Source: GATT-Textiles and Clothing in the World Economy, 1984.

113

Table 6.2

RELATIVE HOURLY EARNINGS (a) IN THE TEXTILE AND CLOTHING
INDUSTRIES, 1967, 1978 AND 1981

(Index numbers, average for manufacturing each year = 100)

Countries	Textile Industry			Clothing Industry		
	1967	1978	1981	1967	1978	1981
Austria	80.1(e)	74.9	78.4	75.9	64.4	64.0
Belgium	86.4	81.4	82.3	73.6	68.7	68.7
Canada	74.2	72.7	71.4	67.1	70.1	66.4
Denmark	82.5	89.2	87.0	82.5	85.5	83.0
Finland	79.0	77.5	80.1	74.3	72.1	75.0
France	80.6	84.5	83.2	84.0(d)	76.9	77.6
Germany	84.6	83.2	82.3	78.3	74.7	73.8
Italy	82.5	89.6(c)	88.5	74.6	82.1(c)	82.7
Netherlands	94.5	92.9	93.6	68.9	73.6	71.4
Norway	81.7	80.9	83.5	78.9	75.8	79.8
Sweden	82.6	88.5	89.7	78.0	83.8	85.0
Switzerland	80.1	82.7	82.4	71.8	73.1	72.2
United Kingdom(b)	82.0	85.4	81.1	67.4	64.0	63.9
United States	73.0	69.6	69.0	72.0	63.9	62.3

a) Wages for time worked including time rates, piece rates, shift supplements, overtime supplements and regularly paid bonuses and premiums.
b) Figures refer to United Kingdom.
c) Figure refers to 1977.
d) All persons average of FF2.46 in 1967 is below both the male and female averages for clothing. Assuming a misprint, a figure of FF3.46, which is between the male and female averages, is employed.
e) Figure refers to 1969.

Source: Calculated from figures presented on "Wages and Total Labour Costs for Workers, International Survey 1967-1977, 1968-1978 and 1970-1980" Swedish Employers' Confederation, Stockholm, 1979, 1980 and 1981.

EC. This was about twice as high as market penetration rates for textiles narrowly defined[18]. Though import penetration rates have increased somewhat since 1976, notably in clothing, the scope for boosting domestic output by reducing import volumes remains very limited.

30. Moreover, quota restrictions do not always reduce total imports. The problems of trade diversion among restricted sources have been discussed above. To these must be added the effects of diversion within customs unions, notably the EC and EFTA. Import

barriers against non-Member states can increase total output within these areas; but this may (and presumably should) go largely to the benefit of the least-cost internal supplier, such as Italy, Germany and Finland. This is confirmed by the simulations for 1982 and 1983 carried out with the Secretariat's econometric model. These found that while total EC imports from all sources for these years were very close to the expected values (implying little impact of MFA III), imports from non-OECD sources, and notably from the Asian NICs, were well below expected levels, suggesting that substantial trade diversion occurred, to the benefit of the more competitive EC suppliers (presumably Italy) and less restricted non-OECD (presumably Mediterranean) sources.

31.　　Finally, even if domestic output does increase, the impact on employment levels in the industry may not be as great as expected. A distinction needs to be drawn here between the textiles industry on the one hand and the clothing industry on the other.

32.　　The rapidly increasing capital intensity of the textiles industry has drastically reduced its employment potential. The steady rise in the industry's incremental capital output ratio has made each new job increasingly dependent on irreversible capital investment[19]. At least in the short term firms may prefer to supply however much additional output they can with existing plant and labour, but at higher prices. Over the longer term, the accumulated rents from production may stimulate additional investment; yet this goes into plants with higher levels of labour productivity than the plants being scrapped so that overall employment continues to decline.

33.　　Government policies may well have aggravated this trend. Protection can reduce the factor cost of capital relative to labour, because it acts as a signal to the financial markets that the government is willing to socialise part of the industry's investment risks. At the same time, the rents from protection may be reflected in higher wages, pushing up labour costs. To this must be added the effects of investment incentives provided in many countries to help the industry modernise[20]. These will accelerate and further the capital-deepening process.

34.　　Two sets of evidence support this view. The available studies find that – calculated on a simple accounting basis – declines in OECD textiles industry employment have mainly been due to rising labour productivity, and not to changes in net trade balances. For the United Kingdom, for example, labour productivity increases account for over 60 per cent of the 1970-1979 fall in employment. Silberston estimates that productivity increases in the United Kingdom from 1983 to 1992 will lead to a decline of 28 per cent in textile and apparel employment no matter what happens to the MFA[21]. The dominance of productivity effects is even more marked in the United States, where in the absence of offsetting productivity growth, changes in the net trade balance, partly resulting from the depreciation of the dollar, would actually have led to rising employment levels until 1980[22].

35.　　It is not surprising therefore that studies of the direct impact of trade protection on textiles industry employment identify little job-saving effect. A United States study finds that depending on estimating methodology, maintaining the textile tariff at the pre-Tokyo Round MFN level preserved some 2 per cent of industry employment. An alternative estimate, based on a general equilibrium approach, found that no more than 8 per cent of

Graph 6.3

CAPITAL / LABOUR RATIOS IN UK MANUFACTURING, TEXTILES AND CLOTHING *

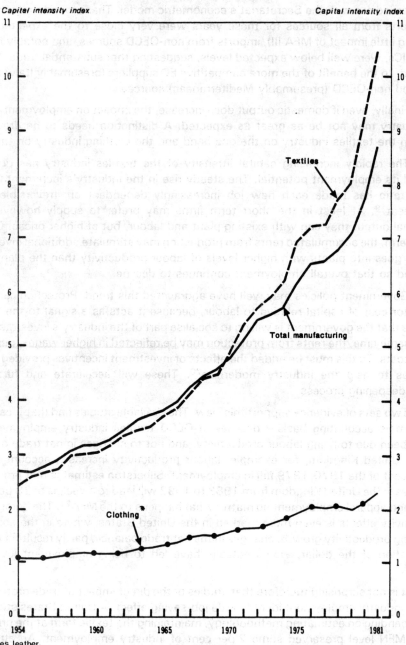

Capital intensity index   *Capital intensity index*

Textiles

Total manufacturing

Clothing

* Includes leather.

Source :   L. Soete, J. Clark, R. Turner - Technology and employment - Textiles and clothing - University of Sussex - 1982.

the industry's 1976 labour force depended on tariffs for their job. For Sweden, it has been estimated that increasing the level of textiles imports under voluntary restraint by 50 per cent would suppress some 3 per cent of industry employment[23].

36. In contrast to the textiles industry, capital-intensity in clothing has remained stable at levels well below the manufacturing average (Graph 6.3). Any net displacement of output from foreign to domestic sources — or vice versa — is therefore reflected in significant shifts in employment levels. The direct impact of changes in net trade is magnified by indirect effects through productivity. Productivity growth in apparel is particularly difficult to measure but seems to be largely the result of greater producer specialisation and organisational innovation in the face of import competition, rather than of exogenous changes in technology. Moreover, the resulting employment adjustments occur relatively rapidly, since little capital investment or scrapping is involved. Limited capital requirements, and generally weak entry barriers, encourage firms to exploit even highly temporary opportunities for expanding output.

37. The Soete, Clark and Turner study of the United Kingdom highlights the dominance of net trade effects in determining clothing industry employment. 75 per cent of the industry's employment decline during the 1970s was due to its loss of international competitiveness; some two-thirds of this could be attributed to rising penetration of imports from LDCs.

38. It follows that measures which effectively reduce imports from developing countries can have a major impact on industry employment. Jenkins estimated in 1980 that Canadian apparel tariffs protected some 7 400 jobs, with bilateral quotas protecting a further 6 000. This represents 7.5 per cent of the industry's labour force. Morkre and Tarr found that 1977 United States tariffs on apparel preserved nearly 90 000 jobs, equivalent to 10 per cent of the industry's employment. Finally, Hamilton finds that a 50 per cent increase in allowable apparel imports under the Swedish VER would reduce employment by 6 per cent — twice as large a job loss as that entailed by a similar increase in textile imports.

39. Nonetheless, the net impact of protection on employment, even in clothing, should not be exaggerated. Silberston estimates that in the absence of the MFA, the UK textile and clothing industry would lose some 10 000 to 50 000 jobs by the 1990s, depending on the exact assumptions used; but these job losses need to be viewed against falls expected to occur anyway of nearly 20 000 a year even with protection. Moreover, "saving" a job by perpetuating the MFA costs the British economy considerably more than the average wage in the textiles and clothing industry. On the basis of simulations with the Cambridge Growth model of the UK economy, Silberston concludes that by the 1990s (when the full effect of abolishing the MFA would be felt) any job losses in textile and clothing would be more than offset by employment gains in other industries which would be more competitive.

40. It should also be noted that whatever jobs are saved through import controls need not go to those whom the measures were originally intended to protect. Thus, major changes have occurred in the regional distribution of clothing industry employment in recent years. These are most marked in the United States, where the share of New

Graph 6.4

**SHARE OF FOREIGN WORKERS IN TOTAL EMPLOYMENT AND IN THE
TEXTILE AND CLOTHING INDUSTRIES**

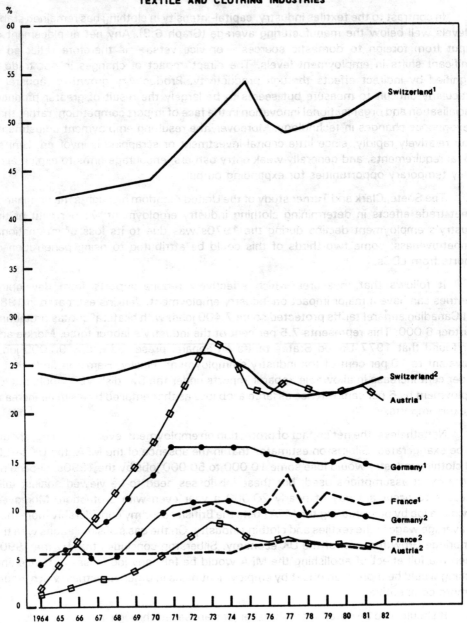

1. Share of foreign workers in the textile and clothing industries.
2. Share of foreign workers in total employment.

Source : OECD.

Table 6.5

COST PROFILE FOR SELECTED CLOTHING PRODUCTS IN US AND ASIAN NICs, 1979

(US $/Dozen)

	Women's Coat US	Women's Coat NIC	Women's Knit Blouse US	Women's Knit Blouse NIC	Men's Dress Shirt US	Men's Dress Shirt NIC	Women's Slacks US	Women's Slacks NIC	Men's Knit Sport Shirt US	Men's Knit Sport Shirt NIC	Men's Casual Slacks US	Men's Casual Slacks NIC	Men's Jeans US	Men's Jeans NIC	Women's Skirt US	Women's Skirt NIC	Men's Briefs US	Men's Briefs NIC
Material cost	40.95	29.59	25.05	20.32	30.19	25.63	26.62	24.20	21.85	21.48	36.08	34.50	42.00	43.92	31.40	29.08	3.41	3.4
Labour (1) cost	25.52	5.65	18.68	3.93	21.78	4.69	14.04	2.91	16.18	4.17	22.56	4.70	15.09	2.95	11.42	2.26	4.95	3.2
Overheads	17.19	8.37	3.71	1.16	4.78	1.42	3.32	1.52	3.19	1.08	5.29	1.95	3.45	1.56	2.88	1.23	3.08	3.0
Total cost of manufacturing	83.68	43.61	47.44	25.41	56.75	31.74	44.03	28.63	41.22	26.73	63.93	41.14	60.54	48.43	45.70	32.57	11.44	9.6
Cost to import (2)		32.76		21.16		20.15		22.33		14.35		28.04		25.96		24.36		6.0
Total cost of goods to US warehouse	83.66	76.37	47.44	46.57	56.75	51.89	44.03	50.96	41.22	41.08	63.93	69.18	60.54	75.40	60.93	66.98	11.44	15.6

1. Includes direct and indirect labour costs.
2. Includes manufacturer's mark-up (partly reflecting quota rents), transport costs and tariffs.

Source: Compiled from Kurt Salmon Associates. Marketing Strategies for US Apparel Producers, 1980, Vol. 1.

England and the Middle Atlantic region in apparel industry has declined by some 25 percentage points since 1960. This reflects the industry's search for the lowest-cost sites within its protected markets.

41.   As a result of these regional shifts, the job gains due to protection have had little positive impact on the employment pools most adversely affected by the industry's long-term decline. The United States figures imply that, even had protection been sufficient to maintain overall employment in 1976 at its 1970 level, regional shifts alone would have reduced employment in the North by 70 per cent. Whatever net job creation there was as a result of protection presumably went entirely to the areas (mostly in the South and South-West) which were in any case benefiting from the regional shifts in economic activity.

42.   Similar shifts, though of smaller magnitude, have occurred in the European countries, with some relocation of employment from traditional textiles/clothing areas to sites closer to fashion centres and large urban markets[24]. However, the principal means of cost reduction for the European industry has been intensified use of migrant labour, notably in the 1960s and early 1970s (see Graph 6.4).

43.   The combined result of shifts in regional and ethnic labour markets has been to reduce wage costs relative to the manufacturing average, most markedly in the United States but also in a number of European countries. Nonetheless, unit labour costs remain very considerably higher in the OECD countries than in their major competitors (Table 6.5). There is therefore little scope in the industry for wage levels to rise towards the norm.

44.   Even under protection, the textiles and especially clothing industries provide job opportunities which can only be described as below the standard set in developed economies — jobs almost invariably filled in peripheral labour markets characterised by low pay, limited training opportunities, little or no job security. Typically, the OECD clothing and textiles industries have a relatively young labour force: probably a third of their current employees were not in the industry at the time of the first MFA. There is a clear equity and efficiency case for assisting these workers to move towards promising and fulfilling employment opportunities[25]; but there can be little case for doing so by attracting them to jobs which are far from meeting these criteria.

Structural adjustment

45.   The OECD textiles and clothing industries have undergone profound structural change over the last two decades. These industries have been shrinking: the number of firms dropped, notably in the countries remaining relatively open to import competition (Table 6.6), bankruptcy rates were high[26], and there was a continuous rundown in employment. Surviving firms have sought to increase their competitiveness through cost-cutting, vertical integration or disintegration, and product differentiation strategies. The strategies followed, and the room for their success has differed greatly both as between the textiles and clothing industries and between countries[27].

Table 6.6

NUMBER OF ENTERPRISES AND ESTABLISHMENTS IN THE TEXTILE
AND CLOTHING INDUSTRIES IN SELECTED COUNTRIES

	Germany (a)		Italy (b)		Japan (a)		United Kingdom (a)	
	Textiles	Clothing	Textiles	Clothing	Textiles	Clothing	Textiles	Clothing
1973	3 269	4 936	3 511	2 228	132 164	31 356	5 744	7 043
1974	3 102	4 652	3 390	2 118	126 974	30 957	6 028	7 623
1975	2 894	4 340	3 322	2 064	131 119	34 835	6 028	7 652
1976	2 765	4 125	3 284	1 984	128 430	34 803	6 046	7 728
1977	2 576	3 049	3 216	1 922	123 661	34 126	6 003	7 669
1978	2 569	2 962	3 173	1 853	124 662	36 987	5 942	7 640
1979	2 510	2 893	3 125	1 814	122 689	36 635	5 868	7 475
1980	2 445	2 824	3 071	1 774	119 788	36 676	5 242	7 402
1981	2 333	2 669	-	-	47 643*	24 049	-	-

a) Establishments.
b) Enterprises.
*) Provisional.

Source: Yearbook of Industrial Statistics, 1980 and 1981, United Nations.

121

46. Firms in the textile industry have pursued three basic adjustment strategies:
  - Cost-cutting through large-scale automation of production processes, reducing labour costs, and internationalisation of activities;
  - Product differentiation, mainly by focusing on products where competition occurs on a non-price basis;
  - Flexibility/fashion orientation, concentrating on market segments where proximity to and/or close links with, centres of fashion and design matter.

These strategies have drawn on a wave of innovations in the textile machinery industry, which has altered the relative cost structure of textile processes and created new, increasingly sophisticated, generations of textile products[28].

47. The *United States* industry has probably gone furthest in a cost cutting direction:
  - A large home market with highly organised and concentrated distribution channels has allowed the industry to reap economies of scale through extensive automation of production, reflected in steadily rising capital intensity.
  - New and more efficient plants have been located in non-unionised, low-wage areas, so that the industry's cost position relative to the manufacturing average has improved.
  - Federal environmental regulations have encouraged the shutting down of older plants, expanding the market available to the more efficient firms.
  - The industry has increased its R&D efforts and has sought to reduce its dependence on the US clothing industry by emphasizing industrial textiles.

48. The *Japanese* industry, having originally penetrated advanced markets with low-cost, low-quality produce, was forced into major restructuring by strong competition from the Asian NICs, the spread of protectionist measures in major export markets, and increasing real wages and currency appreciation. In addition to a substantial rundown in domestic capacity — encouraged from 1956 on by government policies[29] — the industry has concentrated its efforts on the higher value added segments of the market. Aided by the trading companies, Japanese textile firms were amongst the first to internationalise their activities, substituting direct exports from Japan with output produced by joint ventures in low wage developing countries[30].

49. In Europe, *German* and *Swiss* manufacturers have also concentrated on product differentiation strategies, abandoning the more price oriented market segments while focusing on high value added industrial textiles. In both cases, a shift in product composition was imposed on the industry by the concomitance, since the late 1960s, of rising labour costs and currency appreciation. Operating with a relatively open home market, and highly geared to export markets, these manufacturers were forced to adjust some 5 to 10 years earlier than their OECD rivals, so that they were moving into market segments then relatively uncrowded. Moreover, at a time of still rapid growth, adjustment met few political or social obstacles, and was facilitated by:

- Good industrial relations, which allowed manufacturers to generalise shift work earlier than in other European countries, so that high cost equipment became economically viable[31];
- Close links with major industrial users, permitting cooperation in the development of new industrial textiles;
- Proximity to the world's most advanced textile machinery and chemicals suppliers;
- The predominant place of medium-sized firms, large enough to use advanced and high cost equipment and incur the fixed costs involved in exporting, but small enough to be flexible and cohesive.

50.   Starting from a weaker technological base than its Northern competitors, the *Italian* textiles industry has emphasized flexibility in responding to changing fashion trends rather than technical product differentiation *per se*[32]. Enhanced flexibility has been achieved by a shift from the large, vertically integrated production facilities which dominated the Italian industry in the 1960s, to much smaller, highly specialised units, displaying three key characteristics:

- Concentration of similar and interdependent processes in a small number of localities (often only two or three), generally mid-sized towns, with a tradition of artisanal (rather than large-scale industrial) production, providing all firms with important external economies[33];
- A high share of self or family employment remunerated by residual income, so that effective labour costs are highly flexible with respect to changing patterns of competitiveness;
- Exemption from the increasingly tight regulatory constraints being placed on larger firms, notably as regards non-wage labour costs and the hiring and firing of labour.

Initiated in a period when macro-economic circumstances, in particular the devaluation of the Lira[34], favoured labour-intensive exports, and the first MFA created room for trade diversion within the EC, the Italian textile industry has succeeded in consolidating its shift up-market, and is now moving out of the "black economy"[35].

51.   In contrast, *British* and *French* manufacturers, partly as a result of strong pressures from their respective governments, have sought to regain competitiveness through industrial concentration and vertical integration (Graph 6.7)[36]. Underlying this approach has been a search for economies of scale in the basically undifferentiated segments of the market:

- This strategy over-estimated the extent to which costs on standard products could be contained through greater capital intensity and scale economies;
- Rationalisation has been hindered by the conglomeration of firms with distinct production facilities but which could not be integrated without politically unacceptable reductions in employment;
- Large concentrations of employees may have eroded management control over wage costs and work rules;

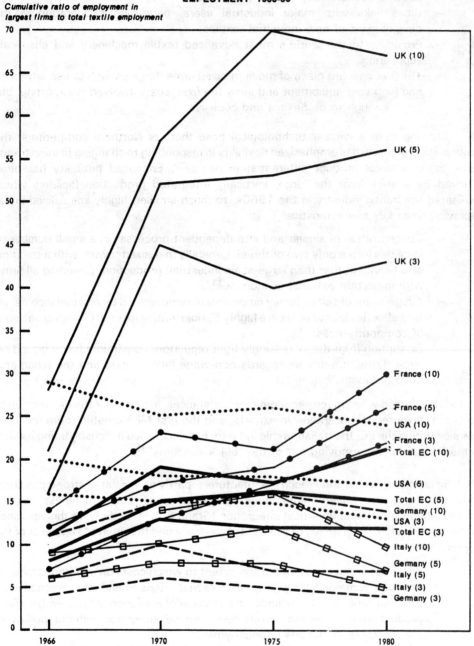

Graph 6.7

SHARE OF 3, 5, AND 10 LARGEST FIRMS IN TEXTILES INDUSTRY EMPLOYMENT 1966-80

Cumulative ratio of employment in largest firms to total textile employment

UK (10)
UK (5)
UK (3)
France (10)
France (5)
USA (10)
France (3)
Total EC (10)
USA (5)
Total EC (5)
Germany (10)
USA (3)
Total EC (3)
Italy (10)
Germany (5)
Italy (5)
Italy (3)
Germany (3)

1966   1970   1975   1980

Source : Textilwirtschaft (Frankfurt) 13 April 1967 ; 11 January 1973 ; 31 December 1981.

124

- The complex and highly politicised management structures resulting from conglomeration can hardly be expected to display flexibility in responding to changing patterns of fashion and levels of demand;
- Having greatly increased capital intensity, British and French firms found themselves with high breakeven points, and are hence particularly vulnerable to the marked variations in demand which characterise the "textiles cycle".

52.   The French and British experience highlights the risks inherent in a cost-cutting strategy centred on scale economies and process automation aimed at the mass market. Textile technology, particularly for standard products, diffuses rapidly worldwide. Capital price distortions in developing countries tend to erode whatever cost advantage OECD producers might derive from greater capital intensity. High breakeven points as a result of automation increase vulnerability in the face of change in competitiveness, since trade flows on standard products can respond devastatingly quickly to shifts in relative prices. The net result, as US producers have found in the face of the appreciation of the dollar, can be to rapidly undermine the market shares acquired through years of restructuring effort.

53.   A corollary is that long-run competitiveness can only be secured in the differentiated, high value-added segments of the market — on which the Japanese, German, Swiss and Italian textiles industries have concentrated. However, the up-market segments account for no more than a third of total demand, so that they can only absorb a small share of the industry's resources. This is particularly so for labour, since these segments typically involve high labour productivity and also draw on more highly skilled occupations than are needed in standard products.

54.   The higher value added segments are also becoming increasingly crowded. OECD country protection, and increased domestic wage costs, has made them more attractive to the Asian NICs, in particular Korea and Taiwan. At the same time, a growing number of OECD governments have identified these segments as offering the greatest survival potential for their domestic industry, and have adopted policies intended to propel them in this direction. Over the medium term, the net result may be to make even this segment unattractive, as the distortions induced by border and non-border interventions compound.

The clothing industry

55.   The opportunities for cost-reduction through capital-labour substitution and scale economies are much more limited in clothing than in textiles. Advances in knitting and in the technology of "non-stitched" products have allowed substantial increases in capital intensity for certain garments, mainly synthetic knitteds and hosiery. However, these account for a small share of the total market and any increase in this share is limited by consumer resistance.

56.   Considerable progress has been made in automating the ancillary parts of the clothing production process, notably cutting and grading. But despite the development of

erasable programmable read-only memory (EPROM) based sewing machines, materials handling constraints limit high-speed automation of the stitching of conventional fabrics, which is the largest single element of value added in clothing. Relative to current performance, automated sewing machines are only cost justified for highly standardized products such as blue jeans[37].

57.   Moreover, the scope for product differentiation in clothing is more limited than the variety of models and designs might suggest. Ultimately, only 20 per cent or so of clothing products are highly "fashion-sensitive", the remainder comprising models which vary little from season to season. Even on fashion-sensitive models, there has been a drastic decline in the time required for imitation with current estimates suggesting lags of less than six months. Quality remains an important competitive factor, but the steady move up-market by producers in the Asian NICs (often relying on imported high quality textiles from the OECD countries) is eroding the advanced countries' advantage in this regard.

58.   OECD producers therefore find themselves competing largely on cost in a highly labour-intensive industry. To the extent to which adjustment under protection has occurred, it has involved three elements: the search for lower labour costs (discussed above); cost-cutting through automation, where this is possible; or, largely as an alternative to automation, increased emphasis on flexibility.

59.   As in textiles, *United States* producers have gone furthest in concentrating on those items where large-scale automation is feasible. They have also made considerable use of outward processing trade (OPT, discussed in Chapter 4 above). Nonetheless, these responses have not been sufficient to restore competitiveness at US sites, particularly in the face of currency appreciation, so that the industry's trade deficit increased to over 8 billion dollars in 1983.

60.   Producers in European countries most exposed to international competition, notably *Germany and Switzerland,* have emphasized product quality and differentiation rather than cost-cutting through large-scale production. Particularly in Germany, this has been complemented by extensive recourse to OPT by manufacturers themselves. Again, the strategies pursued have proved only moderately successful, permitting survival in very limited product segments, while the industry's export positions, and the number of its firms and employees, has declined continuously.

61.   *Italy* is the OECD country which has most successfully modified its competitive position in the industry, with clothing accounting in 1983 for 13.7 per cent of the country's manufactured exports. Clearly, some part of the Italian industry's external competitiveness reflects trade diversion, but it is also due to substantial industrial restructuring. This shares the characteristics of change in the Italian textile industry: local agglomeration and an emphasis on external economies; small, highly adaptive firms, whose labour costs depend at least partly on net income; exemption from the rigidities imposed on larger Italian firms. The industry has also drawn on a long Italian tradition of fashion and design, which has allowed it to capitalise on the diminishing distance between "high fashion" and "everyday wear".

Graph 6.8

RELATIVE PROFITABILITY OF THE TEXTILES AND CLOTHING INDUSTRIES

**Profitability in the textile and clothing industries
as a % of profitability in all manufacturing**

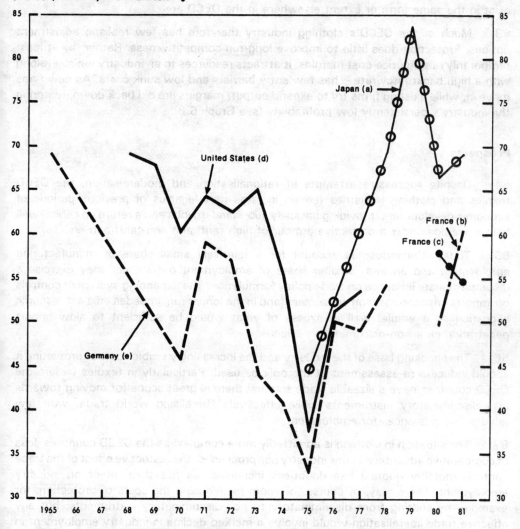

Japan (a)

United States (d)

France (b)

France (c)

Germany (e)

(a)   Japan : textiles, ratio of operating profits to assets.
(b)   France : clothing, pre-tax profits as a % of value added.
(c)   France : textiles, pre-tax profits as a % of value added.
(d)   United States : textile mill products, pre-tax profits as a % of sales.
(e)   Germany : textiles, pre-tax profits as a % of turnover.

62. Despite its obvious success, it is questionable whether the "Italian model" can be transplanted to other OECD countries. Rather than being a sectoral phenomenon specific to the clothing trades it reflects a much broader set of regional, occupational and industrial shifts in the Italian economy during the 1970s, affecting a broad range of labour intensive, mature activities. The economic, political and social preconditions for these shifts have been analysed in detail in other research[38]; suffice it to say that they do not exist in the same form or extent elsewhere in the OECD area.

63. Much of the OECD's clothing industry therefore has few realistic adjustment options. Protection does little to improve long-run competitiveness. Rather, by at least temporarily raising price-cost margins, it attracts resources to an industry which — along with a high bankruptcy rate — has few entry barriers and low sunk costs. As new firms move in, while existing firms try to expand output, margins are bid back down, restoring the industry's persistently low profitability (see Graph 6.8).

Prospects

64. Despite successive attempts at rationalisation and modernisation, the OECD textiles and clothing industries remain in large part legacies of previous periods of economic development, providing basically sub-standard jobs and a return on capital well below average under a protective armour of high tariff and non-tariff barriers.

65. Today, the industries account for a relatively small share of manufacturing employment and an even smaller share of employment overall; yet they exercise a disproportionate influence on trade policy formulation. The expanding system of controls on imports imposes costs on consumers (and in the longer run, impedes efficient resource allocation as a whole) well in excess of what would be sufficient to slow import penetration on a non-discriminatory basis.

66. The shrinking base of the industry and the increasingly visible costs of protecting it should induce a re-assessment of the policies used. Particularly in textiles (where the OECD countries have a sizeable trade surplus) there is great scope for moving towards less discriminatory instruments while effectively liberalising world trade, with few adverse consequences for employment.

67. The situation in clothing is admittedly more complex; as the OECD countries' loss of comparative advantage in this industry has proceeded, the restrictive effect of the trade controls (notably quotas) has doubtless increased, as has their effect on industry employment. There may, of course, be room for reducing the costs of protection, for example, by shifting from discriminatory to non-discriminatory instruments; but any effective trade liberalisation would involve a marked decline in industry employment in many OECD countries.

68. Persistent protection cannot cure the problems of these industries; it merely transfers them from government to successive government. Ultimately, the answer can only lie in policies which effectively promote the movement of resources, and first of all, labour, to more promising and productive uses.

NOTES AND REFERENCES

1. An analysis of the politics of protection in these industries is presented in Aggarwal: 1985.

2. See amongst others, Blackburn: 1982; Cable: 1983; de la Torre: 1978; Donnadieu: 1982; Federtessile: 1980; Mariotti: 1982 and Owen: 1971.

3. Aggarwal: 1985, Chapter 3 analyses this episode of textiles protectionism.

4. Yoffie: 1983, p. 60. For a discussion of exporting country strategies to deal with quotas, see *Far Eastern Economic Review,* 4th September 1981 and Toyne: 1984, pp. 115-123 and pp. 148-169.

5. Aggarwal with Haggard: 1983.

6. See the results on shifts in competitiveness presented in United Nations: 1982.

7. See also Pelzman: 1983 for a literature survey of the costs of protection in textiles and clothing. The cost estimates cited in the text are also consistent with those cited by Jenkins: 1980, Table 3.

8. Jenkins: 1980, Table 4, p. 33. Silberston: 1984, page 43 estimates that foreign producers gain two-thirds of the quota rent.

9. Consumers' Association: 1979; Jenkins: 1980 report broadly similar estimates of quality impacts as does Cable: 1983. Silberston: 1984 estimates that an absence of MFA restraints would lead to a decrease in British retail prices of 5 per cent.

10. Jenkins: 1980, Table 8, p. 43.

11. See OECD: 1979 and Havrylshyn: 1981.

12. See Chapter 1 above.

13. Jenkins: 1980, Table 7, p. 39.

14. Pelzman and Bradberry: 1980 and Pelzman: 1983.

15. For a theoretical explanation see, for example, Bailey and Freidlander: 1982.

16. OECD: 1983 (Textiles and Clothing Industries), pp. 72-78; Aho and Orr: 1979.

17. Parsons: 1980.

18. Keesing and Wolf: 1980, pp. 87-91.

19. Soete, Clark and Turner: 1982.

20. OECD: 1983, pp. 111-115 surveys these policies.

21. Constructed from Silberston: 1984.

22. Krueger: 1980.

23. Hamilton: 1981.

24. EC: *Le Regioni d'Europa,* Tabella D.25 e D.27; OECD: 1983, p. 76.

25. Aho and Bayard: 1982 analyse the case of trade adjustment assistance.

26. Soete, Clark and Turner: 1982, Table 9, p. 42.

27. This section draws on an unpublished paper on "Structural adjustment in the textiles and clothing industries" by V. Grjebine.

28. OECD: 1983, pp. 18-24.

29. Toyne *et al.*, 1984, pp. 234-238 survey the measures taken.

30. Tsurumi: 1976 discusses the internationalisation strategy of the Japanese textiles industry; see also Yoshoka: 1979.

31. Smith: 1974, Chart 10.4, p. 280 highlights the importance of shiftwork in promoting the more rapid diffusion of new weaving technologies in the German textile industry.

32. Federtessile: 1980.

33. Censis: 1984; Fornengo: 1978; Forcellini: 1978; Frey: 1975.

34. Correale and Gaeta: 1983 provide an excellent analysis of the impact of the real exchange rate on Italian textiles and clothing exports.

35. Censis: 1984 is especially interesting in this regard.

36. Knight: 1975 highlights the role of government policy.

37. See Kurt Salmon Associates: 1979 and Rush and Hoffmann: 1984 for cost analysis of automated sewing technologies.

38. See especially Censis: 1982, pp. 22-34, 355-375, 395-402; and G. de Rita "Il paese senza volto", *Mondo Economico,* 21st December 1983, pp. 34-42.

Chapter 7

AUTOMOBILES

1.   Following a prolonged period of relative openness, international trade in automobiles became a source of major political frictions in the 1970s. Reasonably open trade — which had provided a supportive context for realising scale economies, reducing costs and extending consumer choice — was replaced by growing "trade management". While less than 1 per cent of OECD automobile trade (excluding trade within the EC) was affected by discriminatory restrictions in 1973, this share had risen to nearly 50 per cent a decade later.

Industry characteristics and developments

2.   The economic factors underlying trade conflicts in this industry have been extensively documented[1]. Though growth rates of demand for automobiles had been slowing since the latter half of the 1960s, the industry seemed largely immune to recession until 1973. The oil crisis, an increase in the average lifetime of cars, and a rise in the ratio of replacement demand to total demand[2] compressed market growth (Table 7.1) and shifted the pattern of sales towards smaller, more fuel efficient cars, notably in the United States[3]. Combined with increasingly severe environmental, energy use and safety standards, changing consumption patterns placed high demands on the industry and led to an increase in innovation[4] as well as to a large bulge of investment during the latter half of the 1970s .

3.   There were two further complicating forces. The first was the emergence of the Japanese industry as a highly efficient, low cost and aggressive competitor (cost comparisons for the United States and Japan are provided in Table 7.2). High quality, low energy consumption models allowed Japanese companies to greatly increase their sales in the two main OECD markets of North America and Europe, and appropriate what little market growth there was. They also outcompeted established suppliers on third markets, notably in the developing countries (Table 7.3).

4.   Second, the 1979 recession drastically lowered demand for cars, particularly in the United States, where it coincided with the launch of many fuel-efficient models and the necessity of servicing the debt incurred to re-equip production lines and redesign cars.

131

Table 7.1

NEW PASSENGER CAR REGISTRATIONS BY COUNTRY: 1973-1982

(1973 = 100)

	1973	1974	1975	1976	1977	1978	1979	1980	1981	1982
Germany	100	83.3	103.6	113	126	131	129	119	114	102
France	100	87.3	84.9	106.4	109.2	111.3	113.1	107.2	105	116
United Kingdom	100	76.3	71.8	77.3	79.6	95.7	103.2	91.0	89.3	90
Italy	100	88.4	72	81	84	82	96	117	119	115
Sweden	100	115	26	138	106	88	95	85	83	88
All Europe	100	86	88	100	106	108	112	106	103	-
United States	100	76	72	85	95	96	91	77	76	86
Japan	100	77.9	93	83	85	97	103	97	97	104

Table 7.2

CALCULATION OF US AND JAPANESE LABOUR COSTS FOR SUBCOMPACT VEHICLE (a)

Cost category	Share in OEM(d) manufacturing cost (US) (1)	Average hours per vehicle (US) (2)	Estimated OEM employee cost per hour (dollars) (US) (3)	Estimated cost per vehicle (dollars) (US) (4)	Labour content (percentage) (US) (5)	Labour cost per vehicle (dollars) [(4)x(5)] (US) (6)	US - Japan difference (dollars) [(6)x0.575] (7)
Hourly OEM labour (b)	0.24	65	18.00	1 170	100	1 170	673
Salary	0.07	15	23.00	345	100	345	198
Purchased components	0.39	N/A	N/A	1 901	66	1 255	721
Purchased materials	0.14	N/A	N/A	683	25	171	98
Total	-	-	-	4 875 (c)	N/A	2 941	1 690

Note: Totals may not add because of rounding.

a) Calculations assume an exchange rate of 218 yen per dollar.
b) OEM hourly labour includes direct and indirect production worker input.
c) This figure is total manufacturing cost and includes labour, materials and manufacturing overhead of 16 per cent.
d) OEM = original equipment manufacturer.

Source: National Research Council, 1982, p.172.

133

Table 7.3

STRUCTURE OF WORLD AUTOMOBILE TRADE

Destination		Origin								
		EEC		Japan		United States		Other		Total
		Volume 1 000	%	Volume 1 000	%	Volume 1 000	%	Volume 1 000	%	Volume 1 000
EEC	1970	-	-	44.6	30.1	6.4	4.3	96.9	65.5	148.0
	1975	-	-	367	69.0	13.0	2.1	231.9	37.9	611.9
	1980	-	-	743.4	54.6	40.5	3.0	575.0	42.4	1 360.8
Other Europe	1970	647.5	90.6	56.1	7.9	4.9	0.7	5.7	0.8	714.5
	1975	687.1	80.0	118.2	13.7	6.8	0.8	47.3	5.5	859.4
	1980	729.1	71.9	210.6	20.8	13.5	1.3	60.9	6.0	1 014.6
Africa, including Nigeria and South Africa	1970	104.3	85.8	16.5	13.6	0.1	0.1	0.6	0.5	121.5
	1975	94.4	77.7	15.6	12.8	0.2	0.2	3.5	3.1	114.0
	1980	82.3	48.2	71.3	41.7	2.5	1.5	14.8	8.7	170.9
Middle East	1970	74.6	77.2	8.8	9.1	4.5	4.7	8.7	9.0	96.6
	1975	194.3	62.3	59.7	19.2	38.5	12.4	19.0	6.1	311.7
	1980	141.8	31.4	215.1	47.6	50.9	11.3	43.8	9.7	451.5
Far East, excluding Korea and Taiwan	1970	70.7	58.4	41.5	34.3	5.7	4.7	3.1	2.6	121.0
	1975	60.3	37.0	70.9	43.9	15.1	9.3	15.2	9.4	161.5
	1980	59.0	19.5	212.5	70.2	14.0	4.6	17.2	5.7	302.6
Oceania, Australia and New Zealand	1970	119.9	57.6	67.7	32.4	1.0	0.5	20.3	9.7	208.9
	1975	80.1	28.2	185.1	66.3	0.1	-	13.6	5.5	283.6
	1980	25.6	12.4	155.2	75.0	0.4	0.2	25.7	12.4	206.9
North America: United States and Canada	1970	993.9	67.8	404.5	27.6	-	-	67.5	4.6	1 466.9
	1975	627.9	41.9	801.8	53.5	-	-	68.9	4.6	1 497.8
	1980	501.0	21.4	1 986.7	75.8	-	-	73.4	2.8	2 620.2
South America excluding Brazil, Argentina Mexico and Venezuela	1970	39.8	64.9	10.3	16.8	5.0	8.2	6.2	10.1	61.3
	1975	26.6	42.8	24.2	38.9	4.3	6.9	7.1	11.4	62.2
	1980	40.5	30.4	60.7	43.6	12.9	9.7	19.0	14.3	133.2

Table 7.4

REGIONAL COMPARISON OF CHANGES IN FINANCIAL PERFORMANCES FOR
SELECTED MOTOR VEHICLE MANUFACTURERS
(1978 = 100)

	1978	1979	1980	1981	1982
Production					
United States	100	91	69	68	64
OECD-Europe	100	106	111	96	*
Japan	100	106	111	96	104
Employment					
United States	100	99	84	82	74
OECD-Europe	100	106	106	100	*
Japan**	100	101	104	106	109
Revenues					
United States	100	104	87	93	90
OECD-Europe	100	117	135	156	*
Japan**	100	105	124	134	145
Net Income					
United States	100	61	(82)	(25)	10
OECD-Europe	100	118	70	(4)	*
Japan**	100	85	117	111	116
Capital Investments					
United States	100	123	146	160	121
OECD-Europe	100	123	162	178	*
Japan**	100	94	103	172	158
Total long-term debt					
United States	100	95	194	259	270
OECD-Europe	100	100	110	140	*
Japan**	100	91	118	103	188

*   Data for European producers not available for 1982.
**   Except for the two Japanese companies, all of the companies compared
      here have fiscal years that are coincident with calendar years, i.e.
      their fiscal years end on December 31. Nissan's fiscal year ends
      March 31, while Toyota's ends on June 30. The production data are all
      on a calendar year basis. The differing fiscal year definitions affect
      the details, not the substance, of the comparisons.
      Figures in brackets indicate losses.

Source: US Department of Commerce (1983), Table V-7.

The severity of the recession was such as to seriously impede the return to profitability (Table 7.4).

5. A division between winners and losers in adapting to new competitive conditions became increasingly apparent. The major winners — the Japanese industry — found their continued access to export markets increasingly impeded. The United States negotiated a voluntary export restraint agreement with Japan, initially effective within the limit of three years from March 1981. Already subject to strong restraints in France and Italy, and to "prudent marketing" in the United Kingdom, Japan entered into a bilateral arrangement for "forecasting" Japanese car exports to Canada and undertook unilaterally to exercise discretion on the German and Belgian markets. These developments were partly a result of the "demonstration effect" of the US agreement[5]. As agreements expire, they have been renewed, lengthening the "breathing space" provided to the automobile industry of the major importing countries. The recent decision by the US Government to allow its VER with Japan to lapse is a major reversal of this trend.

The impact of policies

Import penetration and domestic output

6. Recent trends in import penetration in the United States, the United Kingdom, France and Italy, shown in Table 7.5, suggest that the VERs were effective in containing Japanese market shares. In the United States, the VER has not been associated with an increase in imports from other countries, with the marginal exception of Sweden and, in 1983-84, the EC luxury car producers. In the EC, however, the stabilisation of Japan's market share coincided with major redistribution of market shares among producers, notably to the benefit of German manufacturers, and, more recently, of Ford's and General Motors' European operations outside Germany.

7. In both regions, the impact of trade restrictions on domestic output has been small relative to that of changes in macroeconomic circumstances. Soras and Stodden have analysed the contribution of different factors to the evolution of US car output over the period 1978-82[6]. New car sales in 1982 were 3.2 million units less than in 1978. Given an estimated elasticity of new car sales to population of 2.76, the increase in US population over this period should have generated an additional 1.1 million car sales; thus actual 1982 sales were 4.3 million below what they could have been, largely because of compressed incomes and rising real interest rates. Set against this shortfall, the 100 000 unit increase (at most) in 1982 domestic output induced by the VER appears small indeed.

8. Nonetheless, the Soras-Stodden model does imply a substantially greater impact of trade restrictions in 1983 and 1984. Changes in the effective dollar exchange rate alone should have increased US automobile imports from Japan by some 4 to 5 per cent over the period April 1981-March 1984. (On one estimate, each ten yen increase in the value of the dollar adds 100 dollars to the Japanese cost advantage on subcompact cars)[7]. To this must be added the import-boosting effect of higher incomes and stronger

136

Table 7.5

IMPORTS AS SHARES OF NEW VEHICLE REGISTRATIONS
BY SELECTED COUNTRY AND IMPORTER (PERCENTAGE)

	1977	1978	1979	1980	1981	1982
UNITED STATES From						
Japan	12.7	13.1	15.3	21.5	21.4	22.4
Germany	4.3	3.7	3.0	3.4	2.70	3.31
France	0.24	0.29	0.32	0.58	0.55	1.45
Italy	0.51	0.68	0.711	0.43	0.20	0.008
Sweden	0.36	0.57	0.63	0.76	0.83	1.19
UNITED KINGDOM From						
Japan	11.37	8.99	10.24	10.7	10.0	10.26
Germany	17.3	16.04	18.49	15.9	17.2	23.74
France	11.7	10.0	12.8	10.3	7.99	8.29
Italy	7.0	6.15	6.0	4.4	2.45	3.55
Sweden	1.57	1.66	2.32	1.97	1.97	1.37
FRANCE From						
Japan	2.19	1.65	2.40	3.18	2.37	2.81
Germany	8.41	8.2	8.86	11.00	14.39	16.67
Italy	4.72	4.65	4.59	5.1	4.70	5.78
Sweden	0.005	0.016	0.027	0.025	0.031	0.056
ITALY From						
Japan	0.06	0.095	0.115	0.069	0.03	0.025
Germany	10.3	13.6	11.55	15.4	14.6	12.8
France	20.6	23.0	22.6	24.9	17.4	17.3
Sweden	0.089	0.014	0.151	0.158	0.168	0.230

demand, bringing the total expected increase in these imports to around 15 per cent. In fact, US imports from Japan remained virtually constant over the period.

Trade composition

9.   In addition to effects on overall trade levels, trade policy instruments alter the composition of trade flows in two important respects. To begin with, if the policies do not apply equally to all product categories within the restricted product groups, substitution can be expected of less or unrestricted for more-restricted product categories.

10.   The Australian market-sharing regime for passenger vehicles, prior to its recent general review, provides a particularly striking instance in this regard[8]. The Industries

Assistance Commission (IAC) has estimated that, in 1981, the tariff equivalent of the assistance provided by the regime was about 70 to 85 per cent. In contrast, light commercial and Four Wheel Drive (4WD) vehicles (which are not covered by quotas) are dutiable at rates ranging from 22.5 to 45 per cent. Their share of the Australian market for motor vehicles has doubled from 10 per cent in 1979 to 20 per cent in 1983. This increase is partly due to changes in tastes, product quality and use patterns; but the IAC estimates that over one-third of the shift may have been induced by differential treatment.

11.   Secondly, VERs encourage the importer to alter the product mix within the restricted product group, so that value added is increased on the limited number of sales permitted. There is some evidence that Japanese suppliers have moved "up-market" in their European car sales, mainly by shifting the range of models on offer[9], but the firmest evidence in this regard comes from the United States.

12.   Hunker has used a complex simulation model of the US automobile market to analyse the impact of different trade policy instruments on product mix and pricing strategies over the period 1980-1995[10]. In addition to carefully distinguishing four size classes, Hunker allows for a range of oligopolistic price setting behaviour in determining relative prices among models. Finally, he assesses the sensitivity of his results to differing estimates of short and long-run supply elasticities for domestic producers and importers.

13.   Starting from a base case of Japanese short-term profit maximisation, Hunker finds that *even in the absence of the VER,* the share of small luxury cars in Japanese exports to the United States would have increased from 40 per cent in 1980 to 55 per cent in 1985 and stabilised thereafter. The VER accentuated the trend, bringing this share up to 63 per cent within five years and to 68 per cent by the end date of the simulation – an increase of 13 percentage points relative to the base case. In contrast, a uniform tariff at an *ad valorem* rate of 20 per cent would have induced an upmarket shift of only 4 percentage points over the base case outcome.

14.   The impact of the VER on product mix is even more pronounced if in the base case the Japanese are presumed to be following a policy of market share expansion, that is continued growth in market share above the short-term profit maximising level. This may result from a greater capacity of Japanese suppliers, operating with lower marginal costs, a relatively low cost of funds and low discount rates, to implement "market capture" strategies – that is, to set prices so as to maximise the volume (at some terminal date) of the increased sales generated by generally high rates of consumer loyalty and repurchase.

15.   Whether the Japanese industry will mainly pursue market share expansion also depends on its capacity to effectively coordinate pricing and output choices. Profit maximisation of course has a higher *present* value for the Japanese than does share expansion. If the Japanese industry is unable to develop patterns of coordination allowing joint profit maximisation, in aggregate it may continue to expand in foreign markets at a higher than profit maximising rate.

16.   Assuming a base case of Japanese expansion, Hunker finds that the share of small luxury cars in the Japanese mix rises from 47 per cent in 1980 to 51 per cent in 1985. Imposing a 20 per cent tariff in this scenario has virtually no impact on product mix – because (with relatively high consumer loyalty) the Japanese suppliers have incentives to absorb the tariff rather than increase prices. In contrast, the VER increases the small luxury car share by a full 12 percentage points over the base case.

Prices

17.   By reducing supply and shifting the product mix towards higher quality items, restrictions affecting imports raise the average price of cars relative to that of other goods and services. The extent of this effect depends on the cost gap between foreign and domestic producers, the substitutability of domestic for imported products, the elasticity of supply of domestic products and the nature of price determination on the protected market.

18.   Feenstra has sought to decompose the observed increase in prices of vehicle imports to the US market into a volume reduction effect on the one hand, and changes in product quality on the other[11]. He uses hedonic regression techniques to estimate the extent of quality change. The pure price effect of the VER is then computed as the difference between the relative change in automobile prices and the rate of quality change. Feenstra finds that two-thirds of the rise in import prices can be attributed to quality improvements. Put slightly differently, the pure price effect of the import restriction is of only 3 per cent, relative to a total rise in import prices (unadjusted for inflation) of nearly 20 per cent – the remaining 17 per cent being due to inflation (10 per cent) and quality improvement (7 per cent).

19.   Feenstra's results are sensitive to a number of assumptions common to most hedonic regression techniques. In particular, it is not apparent whether the regression results identify a shift in the demand or supply curve, nor whether the estimated coefficients reflect average or marginal relations. Hedonic demand functions are particularly difficult to identify under conditions of imperfect competition[12] but these seem to play little role in Feenstra's model. Finally, Feenstra's conclusion that the small pure price effect entails a correspondingly small welfare cost only holds on the restrictive assumption that consumers are indifferent between the pre- and post-VER product mix.

20.   A different perspective on the impact of the US–Japan VER on automobile prices is obtained from Hunker's simulation analysis. When Japanese firms are assumed to be short-run profit maximisers, the VER increases the price of small cars by some 15 per cent, nearly 5 percentage points more than the effect of a corresponding tariff. Since the Japanese are the price-leaders in Hunker's model, increases in import prices translate into approximately similar increases in the price of domestic output.

21.   Hunker also seeks to estimate the price impact of changes in oligopolistic interaction, subsequent to the VER. He assumes that the VER effectively bars a Japanese market share expansion strategy. From being below current-period long-run marginal cost

(the distinguishing feature of an expansion pricing strategy), prices move to the much higher level needed to hold volume constant. For this to be achieved, *after* an expansion strategy has been implemented for some time, prices must rise sufficiently to actually reduce the repurchase rate — that is, to induce some of the consumers previously enticed through low prices to buy a Japanese car not to replace it with another Japanese car. The implied long-run price rise relative to the base case is in the order of 25 per cent.

22.   A recent report by the US International Trade Commission[13] estimates that in 1984 Japanese cars were sold in the United States for $1 300 more, on average, than they would have been in the absence of the VER. The respective increases for 1981, 1982 and 1983 were of the order of $185, $359 and $831 per car. Thus, in a period of buoyant demand, US consumers paid increasingly higher prices as a result of the shortfall in supply. During the same period, increases in the prices of domestically produced cars ranged from approximately $78 in 1981 to almost $660 in 1984, much of this increase apparently due to the VER. Furthermore, the reduced availability and the prevailing higher prices of new Japanese cars led increasing numbers of consumers to turn to the used car market and thereby put upward pressure on the prices of used domestic and Japanese cars.

23.   Price rises of this magnitude are only feasible because of the nature of the US automobile industry. High levels of producer concentration and a long tradition of dominant firm price leadership ensure that increases in import prices are not dissipated through domestic competition[14]. The price umbrella provided by changes in Japanese firms' pricing strategies is therefore readily exploited by domestic firms, who seem relatively able to coordinate pricing (though not styling) decisions.

24.   In contrast, the EC industry, despite extensive rationalisation in the 1960s and early 1970s, remains relatively fragmented. While in 1979 the Herfindahl index for the US industry was 0.5, it was 0.12 for the EC. Though national markets are more concentrated, the rapid growth of intra-European trade has substantially eroded the position of dominant national firms[15]. Moreover, the productivity differentials between European producers are nearly as large as the average gap between Europe and the rest of the world[16]. Particularly in continental Europe, each of these factors has undermined traditional patterns of price leadership, and there is a clear trend towards eliminating intra-EC price differentials[17]. The United Kingdom, at least in the period to 1983, is a marked exception in this regard, with a widening gap between relatively high UK car prices and prices for identical models elsewhere.

25.   More intense internal competition has limited the extent to which EC producers can durably increase prices under a Japanese price umbrella. Moreover, unlike their US counterparts, European producers have not neglected the lower-middle product segments: in fact, the number of distinct European models on offer in these segments doubled from 30 in 1967 to 60 in 1978[18]. As a result, the elasticity of substitution between European and Japanese products exceeds that between US and Japanese products, reducing the price rise needed to ration the Japanese quota. Nonetheless, Japanese costs are — at least in the long run — below the costs of even the more efficient

EC producers, though possibly not at current yen exchange rates[19]. The existence of a pure price effect of protection cannot therefore be ruled out entirely.

26.   In particular, protection may partly explain the persistent price gap between the United Kingdom and the rest of the EC[20]. UK manufacturers moved earlier than their continental competitors to secure a "prudent marketing" agreement from Japanese producers. This reduced the problem of price leadership in the UK market to one of coordination among EC manufacturers. The willingness of the UK authorities to enforce regulations impeding direct imports by final consumers made possible a price discrimination strategy in which the high cost domestic producer, British Leyland, sacrificed market share so as to maintain liquidity. This "end-game" approach[21], typical of declining dominant firms, generates higher margins for the firms which are gradually expanding their market share; but it cannot be sustained when competition is vigorous. Given the Japanese manufacturers' emphasis on rapidly building market share, it is doubtful whether in the absence of protection they would have aligned their prices on the levels set by BL.

Employment and wages

27.   The automobile industry is an important employer in most OECD countries, with its 1980 share of manufacturing employment varying from over 10 per cent in Germany to 4 per cent in the United States. The indirect employment generated by the industry is also important, being in the United Kingdom and France, for example, of about the same order of magnitude as that generated directly[22].

28.   Employment in the industry has fallen in recent years, except in Germany and Japan. Given wage rates well above the manufacturing average, dismissals have presumably involved a large cost to employees in terms of foregone income. Forecasts for the industry suggest a trend of declining employment relative to the 1970s peak[23], but employment losses following the second oil shock may be partially reversed in a more favourable macro-economic environment. Thus recovery in the US industry has led to the number of workers on indefinite lay-off declining from 233 000 in April 1983 to 98 000 in April 1984.

29.   Long-run policies of import substitution have had a major impact on industry employment in some of the smaller net importing countries, notably Canada and Australia[24]. However, the extent to which the protectionist measures adopted since 1979 have significantly or even noticeably increased industry employment is open to doubt.

30.   As already discussed, the output-expanding effect of the restrictions has been very small relative to the effect of macro-economic changes. On one estimate, the output rise induced by US-Japan VER over the period to 1982 increased US employment by no more than 22 000, while the recession was cutting required labour input by more than ten times this figure[25].

31.   Moreover, the producers benefiting from the restrictions, notably in the United States and the United Kingdom, entered the period with considerable scope for

productivity gains and labour-shedding, mainly through closing of obsolete plants[26]. Again, the derived change in employment from trade protection has been very small relative to that due to a move towards best-practice productivity[27].

32.   Protection has also had an at best marginal impact on industry wage levels. At least in the United States, VERs have not prevented the industry from obtaining major concessions from its labour force in terms of earnings and work rules. This may change, as the US recovery increases both the protective effect of the VER and union wage pressure. The current large profits being earned by the industry, partly as a result of the VER, may encourage firms to grant wage rises which — seen in a long-run perspective — the US industry can hardly afford.

Profitability

33.   The price elasticity of demand for cars is relatively low. Price increases as a result of protection therefore lead to little demand compression, and to a large transfer of net income from consumers to producers. The extent of this transfer has been especially well documented in the US case, partly because the price effects of protection have been more marked.

34.   Hunker's analysis is again particularly useful, in that he compares the effects of a range of policy instruments — notably tariffs and VERs — under various assumptions about pricing strategies, cost differentials and supply elasticities. His major results can be summarised as follows:

    —   If, in the base case, Japanese firms are assumed to be short-run profit maximisers, tariffs have virtually no effect on the profitability of the US industry. While quotas do increase the industry's net income, this takes several years to occur. Both quotas and tariffs reduce the net present value of Japanese profits in the US market; but tariffs have an adverse effect nearly three times greater than that of quotas.

    —   When, prior to the restriction, the Japanese firms are pursuing a policy of market share expansion, the VER has a much greater impact on domestic and foreign profitability. Again, the tariff has virtually no effect on domestic net income, though it reduces Japanese net income by 40 per cent. In contrast, the VER not only rapidly increases domestic firms' profitability (and notably that of GM), but also induces a 12 percentage point rise in the net present value of the Japanese industry's profits in the US market.

35.   These simulation results are consistent with analyses pointing to higher margins in the US market on both imported and domestic cars. According to one analysis, earnings in the US market accounted for 50 to 70 per cent of the worldwide profits of Japan's three largest automobile manufacturers. For top-of-the-line cars, the price differential on identical models between the United States and Japan is in the order of 45 per cent — almost entirely because of rent-taking by Japanese exporters[28].

36.   Equally, it has been noted that the substantial cost reductions achieved by US producers have not been passed on to consumers, but rather taken in the form of higher

margins over variable cost[29]. Some part of these margins has presumably gone to cover the high once-off cost of down-sizing cars and converting to front-wheel drive[30]; but a net margin effect of the order of 5 to 10 per cent cannot be ruled out.

Industrial restructuring

37.   Protection, though acting differently in the United States and Europe, has affected the industry's adjustment process at two basic levels:

- It has increased the resources available to domestic firms;
- It has altered the strategies and behaviour of the firms being protected against, and their interaction with domestic suppliers in the importing countries.

38.   There is no evidence that protection has weakened firms' commitment to restructuring. Most automobile manufacturers clearly believe that, through appropriate changes in their strategy and operations, they can compete profitably for world automobile sales. Even in Europe — where a plausible case could be made that some manufacturers are simply not viable — there is surprisingly little questioning of the present number of manufacturers, nor are firms seeking major diversification opportunities unrelated to their car-making activities (FIAT, Ford and Volvo are exceptions in this regard).

39.   Faced with rising international competition, automobile firms have therefore concentrated on restructuring their car-making activities:

- Production facilities have been rationalised and new technologies introduced to increase flexibility both with respect to product mix and output volume.
- Industrial relations and personnel management policies have been reviewed, with major concessions being obtained as regards wage levels and manning practices.
- New procurement and component sourcing policies have changed relations with suppliers, so as to exploit scale economies in development and production, move to lower-cost sources notably overseas, and increase the quality of purchased inputs.
- Product development has been accelerated, both so as to introduce lighter, more energy and materials efficient and safer vehicles, and so as to expand the range of technical features on offer in any size class.
- Finally, relations between firms have changed, with a proliferation of joint ventures and licensing arrangements aimed at pooling technological and marketing skill and exploiting economies of scale and scope at both domestic and international level.

40.   These far-sweeping changes have entailed large investment commitments, incurred in a period of declining net income. *Per se* protection has not had an immediate short-term impact on investment decisions, since these are normally made over a planning period of between five and ten years, and thus cover a period of time longer than that which has elapsed since the imposition of controls. Nonetheless, particularly in the

United States, the increased cash flow generated by higher prices has certainly contributed to improve firms' balance sheets. This should be reflected in the next round of investment decisions[31].

41.   In Europe the largest investment commitments — particularly relative to the number of cars produced — have been made by the manufacturers operating in the luxury car market (Table 7.6). These have presumably benefited less from protection than manufacturers of small and medium-sized cars, whose products compete directly with the Japanese.

42.   In addition to its direct impact on the financing of restructuring efforts, protection has altered firms' strategic options and their implementation. Large cost differentials, the search for manufacturing flexibility and intensified competition have increased the attractiveness of horizontal and vertical cooperation between suppliers. Cooperation is intended to reap economies of scale (notably in components), share fixed development and overhead costs, and — particularly for the US manufacturers — fill out product ranges by selling Japanese-made small cars. Cooperation has also offered the potential for improved coordination of pricing and investment decisions within the industry, and thus of higher price-cost margins.

43.   Cooperative arrangements between firms would clearly have occurred independently of protection, as is evidenced by their spread within the EC. Here — together with

Table 7.6

INVESTMENT PER VEHICLE AT 1975 PRICES CONVERTED INTO US DOLLARS

	1976	1977	1978	1979	1980
United States	201	283	296	352	n.a.
Sweden	585	664	661	658	n.a.
Netherlands	584	688	764	603	n.a.
Japan	171	283	325	279	n.a.
Italy	184	241	294	n.a.	n.a.
United Kingdom	175	253	428	n.a.	n.a.
France	244	305	n.a.	n.a.	n.a.
Germany	309	426	617	814	935

Note: The figures refer to total investment in the road vehicle industry divided by total road vehicle production. Thus, motorcycles, vehicles n.e.s. and commercial vehicles are included. All vehicles are in US $ converted by average exchange rate for that year. Domestic prices were all in constant 1975 prices. The effects of inflation are netted out, but exchange rate effects remain.

rapid growth in intra-industry trade — they have partially substituted for mergers across national boundaries[32]. However, protection has also been important. It has made these arrangements an attractive option — at least in the medium term — for the Japanese suppliers, who set the pace in the industry, and hence transformed cooperation from an ancillary to a central component of corporate strategies.

44.   By selling components, sub-assemblies and kits to their competitors in protected markets, Japanese suppliers:

   —   Obtain a share of the quota rents from protection;
   —   Reduce their own costs by more fully exploiting scale economies, notably in the up-stream stages of production;
   —   Ensure that purchasers in the protected market continue to be exposed to Japanese parts and models, gradually increasing consumer acceptance;
   —   Obtain goodwill from their foreign competitors, increasing the chances that access barriers will be removed.

45.   Combined, these factors have led to a proliferation of joint venture and equity swap arrangements between Japanese suppliers and their foreign competitors, paralleled by a growing international flow of car components and sub-assemblies[33]. Seen in this light, protection has tended to shift international specialization from later to earlier stages in the production process, and notably from trade in fully assembled vehicles (which has now stabilised, at least on an inter-regional basis) to trade in components (which continues to increase rapidly). Flexible manufacturing systems, which reduce the importance of scale economies at the assembly stage of production, may intensify this shift.

46.   Nonetheless, the protectionist measures themselves limit the viability of international joint-ventures as a long-term solution to the industry's problems. The definition of a "domestically" produced vehicle has been open to controversy — notably in the EC with regard to the BL-Honda and Alfa-Romeo-Nissan agreements — creating uncertainties on security of access for Japanese component and CKD exporters. Particularly in the United States, import restrictions have made it difficult for domestic producers to fill out their product lines by importing fully assembled cars from overseas, and especially from Japan. The threat of an extension of import controls to kits or even components must reduce the bargaining power of Japanese suppliers relative to their foreign counterparts, affecting the distribution of quota rents.

47.   Over the longer run, intra-firm agreements in this industry may (as has been the experience of other industries)[34] give way to straightout acquisitions and foreign direct investment, especially from Japan. Recent steps in this direction include a joint venture for a US based assembly facility between General Motors and Toyota, and Nissan's plans to build a large assembly plant in the United Kingdom. These can be expected to generate the "follow-the-leader" response by other Japanese firms which characterises foreign direct investment in oligopolistic industries[35].

48.   Foreign direct investment has of course been the industry's traditional response to import-substituting industrialisation, notably in Latin America and the Commonwealth. While in the past this investment was largely carried out by US firms, these seem to be

currently re-assessing their worldwide involvement, with an at least tactical withdrawal from peripheral markets[36]. The current phase of the industry's history can be seen as one in which this dominant role is transferred to the Japanese companies. Having already acquired the key position on peripheral markets, they are now being forced through protection into direct investment in the markets of the formerly dominant suppliers.

49.   Though creating employment in the host country, foreign direct investment in this industry, particularly when induced by protection, has been associated with large losses in scale economies. Typically, plants in the protecting country have been of sub-optimal scale, produce excessively broad product ranges, and have been too concentrated on assembly activities, with little or no autonomy in terms of design or research. These effects – the long-run efficiency costs of protection – have of course been particularly marked in the smaller countries[37]. But even in Europe, it took thirty or more years of protection for the automobile industry to become competitive relative to the United States, with car prices being considerably higher than those in the United States throughout that period[38]. The efficacy of protection (and even more so, its cost efficiency) in promoting the development of competitive firms in this industry is at least open to question.

Prospects

50.   Today the OECD's trading system in automobiles, set up under the auspices of GATT, stands uneasily poised between the return to a basically liberal trading regime and continued moves towards greater protection.

51.   The initial losers from the process of structural change – namely the United States and some of the weaker European manufacturers – have substantially rationalised their operations, reduced their costs and especially breakeven points, increased flexibility and improved product quality. At the same time, the initial winners, namely the Japanese, have seen their cost advantage narrow, and have been cautioned by protection into taking a more cooperative view of their relations to foreign rivals. Restored oligopolistic equilibrium, together with a more favourable macro-economic environment, should allow a return to normal trading conditions. The recent decision by the US Government to allow the VER with Japan to lapse underscores this assessment.

52.   Optimism must nonetheless be tempered. The unevenness of the macro-economic recovery now underway highlights how great the vulnerability of some of the weaker producers – notably the French and British – remains. A slackening of recovery in the United States could put great pressure on the profitability of some US companies. The longer-term consequences of the move up-market by the Japanese suppliers are still unclear, but the fact remains that it is in the luxury market that profits have traditionally been greatest. Far from easing competitive pressures, the gradual shift of Japanese industry to foreign direct investment – and hence to higher cost locations – may intensify the struggle for market share, as Japanese suppliers seek to maintain total profitability despite a reduction in unit margins.

53.   Many of the industry's fundamental problems therefore persist. Ultimately, the industry must adjust to a lower long-term growth path of demand, at least in the OECD countries. Left to their own devices, the automobile industry's component suppliers have restructured drastically, with many of the smaller firms consolidating or disappearing, and major shifts occurring in patterns of specialization on domestic and international markets. It remains to be seen whether fundamental change along these lines is not needed in the automobile industry itself.

NOTES AND REFERENCES

1.   OECD: 1983 (Long Term Outlook for the World Automobile Industry); Black: 1984.

2.   Prodi and Bianchi: 1981, Table 3, estimate replacement demand as increasing from 52 per cent of OECD registrations in 1970 to 71 per cent in 1980.

3.   Griliches: 1984.

4.   National Academy of Engineering: 1982 and especially Clark: 1981.

5.   See a recent survey by the US International Trade Commission (US ITC: 1985, pp.2-3).

6.   Soras and Stodden: 1983.

7.   Soras and Stodden: 1983, Table 4; and Fortune, 4th March 1985, p.43.

8.   Industries Assistance Commission: 1983 (Passenger and Light Commercial Vehicles – Substitution).

9.   Prodi and Bianchi: 1981 and Financial Times ("Japanese Hit Trouble As They Go Up Market"), 14th September 1982.

10.   Hunker: 1984 represents a considerable step forward over the existing literature in this area, notably Hodder: 1978, both in terms of pricing models and of the range of submarkets distinguished.

11.   Feenstra: 1984.

12.   Rosen: 1974.

13.   US International Trade Commission: 1985.

14.   See Kwoka: 1984 for a recent analysis. See also Pashigian: 1961 and White: 1971.

15.   Adams: 1980. See also Hocking: 1980 for an analysis of intra-EC automobile trade.

16.   Mosconi and Velo: 1982, pp.43-54 and 56-59; Dunnett: 1980, pp.125-6 and 134.

17.   Silva et al., 1982, pp.106-160 provide the best analysis of this process.

18.   Prodi and Bianchi: 1981, p.24.

19.   Mosconi and Velo: 1982, pp.29-31.

20.   Cowling and Sugden: 1984; Ashworth et al., 1982. On the role of the UK authorities see The Economist, September 1981, pp.68-72 and Houtte: 1983.

21.   See the classic study by Worcester: 1957 and Caves, Fortunato and Ghemawat: 1984 and Harrigan: 1980.

22. Armstrong: 1967; Le Monde, 16th October 1984, p.19.

23. Streek and Hoff: 1983.

24. Cronin: 1984 (but contrast Parry: 1981) and Perry: 1981.

25. Feenstra: 1984, p.28.

26. Black: 1984, Table 10, p.38.

27. For example, the three largest US producers have shut about 40 plants, including 10 assembly units, in recent years. The room for further exploiting economies of scale and scope is examined by Friedlaender et al., 1983.

28. Business Week, 7th November 1983, pp.29-30.

29. Wall Street Journal, 21st December 1983.

30. Business Week, 1st March 1982, pp.94-95.

31. Business Week, 21st June 1982, pp.58-63.

32. Black: 1984.

33. United Nations: 1983 provides a comprehensive survey.

34. Franko: 1973; Caves: 1982 examine the limited survival of joint ventures in international business.

35. Knickerbocker: 1973.

36. Maxcy: 1982; United Nations: 1983.

37. Connidis: 1983; Eastman and Stykoit: 1967; Davidson and Stewardson: 1974, pp.147-183.

38. Black: 1981.

Chapter 8

CONSUMER ELECTRONICS:
THE CASE OF COLOUR TELEVISION RECEIVERS

1.   This chapter is devoted to the operation of Orderly Marketing Agreements (OMA) covering trade in colour television receivers. These agreements restricted United States imports first from Japan and later Korea and Taiwan between 1977 and 1980. Although this is a narrowly focused case study, its findings highlight the roles of trade diversion and foreign investment in the response to protection and hence have broader implications for the effects of OMAs and VERs in general.

The Period to 1975

2.   Public colour broadcasting began in the United States in 1954. However, it was only in the early 1960s that a majority of programmes were broadcast in colour. Once colour broadcasting was introduced on a significant scale, the demand for colour television receivers increased rapidly. In 1966, nearly 5 million colour television receivers were sold in the United States; and despite fears of demand saturation, sales continued to increase, passing the 10 million mark in 1978. By 1978, there was at least one colour television receiver in over 75 per cent of households in the United States and an estimated 30 per cent of households had more than one colour television receiver in their home.

3.   United States imports of colour television receivers increased from some 300 000 sets in 1967 to nearly 1.3 million sets in 1971. The growth of US imports – over 90 per cent of which came from Japan – was reflected in their share in apparent consumption of colour television receivers rising from less than 6 per cent in 1967 to 19 per cent in 1970. The level of complete receiver imports remained relatively stable over the five years from 1970, with import penetration fluctuating between 16 and 18 per cent.

4.   The rapid growth of imports was due to a number of factors:

—   First, Japanese manufacturers benefited from significantly lower unit labour costs. Before the currency realignments of the early 1970s, the Japanese cost advantage was probably above 25 per cent.

- Second, Japanese manufacturers introduced product innovations more rapidly than their United States counterparts. In particular, Japanese firms converted their television sets to all-solid-state components some time before US firms did. The result was a significant increase in the reliability of Japanese sets which eased consumer acceptance of imported products.
- Third, Japanese exporters benefited from careful selection of their product market in the United States, largely concentrating on the small to medium size class of sets. US firms considered profit margins on these sets to be lower than those earned on sets 19 inches and over.

5.   In a period of rapid growth in overall sales, US firms were generally willing to tolerate an increase in the volume of imports, especially at the lower value-added end of the market. However, the 1969-1970 downturn in US production of colour receivers drastically altered this situation and led US firms to seek ways to contain the growth of imports. The result was a series of actions which had a major impact on the US colour television receiver industry[1].

6.   The market leaders first engaged in price cutting which quickly put pressure on the smaller US firms. Seven firms either withdrew from the industry or were absorbed by others: by 1975 there were only 12 US producers left[2]. Overall industry profitability slumped, with a decline in the ratio of net operating profits to sales from nearly 9 per cent in 1971 to less than 1.0 per cent four years later.

7.   The surviving firms sought to increase their competitiveness primarily by transferring labour intensive assembly operations to low-wage countries. Components were shipped to free trade zones in Mexico and South East Asia for mounting; and the finished component boards were then re-imported into the United States for final assembly. Production of colour television sub-assemblies by overseas subsidiaries and affiliates of US firms increased from slightly over $10 million in 1971 to nearly $140 million by 1974. US imports of colour sub-assemblies grew rapidly from less than 3 per cent of the value of imports of colour television receivers in 1971 to peak over 16 per cent in 1974.

8.   Greater concentration and geographical shifts in production were associated with significant increases in capital intensity and in labour productivity. Over the period 1967-1975, capital stock at constant prices per employee in the radio and television receiver industry as a whole increased at an average annual rate of 4.2 per cent. This contributed to the growth of apparent labour productivity. Over the period 1971-1974, the number of complete colour receivers shipped per person employed grew at a trend annual rate of 12 per cent.

9.   Since shipments increased over the same period by slightly under 7 per cent, employment in the industry declined from 43 000 in 1971 to 37 000 in 1974. In 1975, shipments decreased by 18 per cent while apparent labour productivity continued to rise; the result was a further decline in employment. It is, however, extremely difficult to assess the social costs arising from this decline as labour turnover in the industry is high. Indeed, attrition accounted for almost all of the net employment decline between 1971 and 1976.

10.   The high level of quits implies that the earnings losses to the displaced individuals were small[3]. These losses were to some extent offset by Trade Adjustment Assistance: over the period from April 1975 to the end of January 1977, 5 775 workers in the television receiver industry received payments under the adjustment assistance programme. However, the decline in employment was concentrated in a small number of locations, mostly in New York State and in Arkansas, with unemployment rates well above the national average, leading to strong local pressures.

11.   The profit squeeze and falling employment led both employers and labour unions to seek import restrictions through a protracted campaign, in which action was sought under a variety of legal provisions.

12.   Though of great interest for the evolution of trade law, these proceedings hardly affected the volume of imports up to 1975. But a favourable ruling obtained in 1976 (though later overturned by the Supreme Court) convinced US manufacturers that legal action against imports can be an effective complement to − if not a substitute for − the more traditional forms of competitive response. The campaign also led Japanese colour TV manufacturers to question the long run viability of a direct export strategy. As a result, a major Japanese producer established a US production facility in 1974 while two others purchased the assets of US firms leaving the industry.

The 1977 Orderly Marketing Agreement

13.   Despite the restructuring undertaken within the US industry, Japanese exports of colour television receivers to the United States increased very rapidly in the second half of 1975 and throughout 1976. Seasonally adjusted, Japan's exports of colour sets to the United States rose from about 44 000 sets in January 1975 to 310 000 in December 1976, raising the annual figures from 1.2 million in 1975 to nearly 3 million in 1976. By the end of 1976, imports from Japan accounted for over a third of US sales.

14.   This upsurge can be explained by: the restructuring in the Japanese television receiver industry, which increased the relative efficiency and the attractiveness of its product; and a decline in Japanese domestic sales, which led producers to intensify their export efforts; the general buoyancy of US sales of colour receivers which encouraged the growth of imports; and a shift in US demand towards the smaller size sets where Japanese suppliers were particularly strong.

15.   During the early 1970s, the wage cost gap between the Japanese and US communications equipment industries narrowed substantially. Whereas, in 1971, United States average weekly earnings in the industry were three times those in Japan, in 1976 they were only 1.7 times the Japanese level. The Japanese colour television receiver industry responded to this by a transfer of certain operations overseas and a large-scale restructuring of production facilities at home. This restructuring involved major changes in components and in the technology used to assemble components into complete sets. As regards component technology, the principal change was the accelerated diffusion of Integrated and Large-Scale Integrated circuits. Integrated componentry permitted a cut

by one-half to two-thirds in the number of components to be assembled. This reduction was accompanied by a major effort to develop and apply automated assembly technology: Axial-lead Automatic Insertion equipment was introduced early in 1975 and was quickly followed by Radial-lead Automatic Insertion[4].

16.   Fewer components and automatic assemblies significantly increased apparent labour productivity in the Japanese industry. In 1972, 175 colour receivers were shipped

Table 8.1

HOURLY LABOUR COSTS OF US AND JAPANESE PRODUCERS IN 1979

		US Producer (1)	
Hourly rates (Wages & Benefits) (in dollars)	Offshore facility	1.04	
	US facility	8.22	
	Weighted average rate	4.44	
Hours needed per set		2.68	
Direct labour cost per set (in dollars)		11.90	
		Japanese Low-Cost Producer	Japanese High-Cost Producer
Hourly rates (Wages & Benefits) (in dollars)	Main facility	8.50	8.50
	Independent sub-assembly	5.95	5.95
	Weighted average rate	8.00	7.40
Hours needed per set		0.85	1.26
Direct labour cost per set (in dollars)		6.80	9.32

1.   US Producer performs sub-assemblies in low-wage country and final assembly in US factory.

Source: Magaziner and Reich, 1982.

per person employed, only 5 per cent more than in the United States. In 1976, the Japanese producers shipped 410 sets per person employed, compared to 204 by the United States. Despite the substantial narrowing in the wage cost gap, the differential in unit labour costs between the Japanese and United States industries increased (Table 8.1)[5].

17.   These technological changes also had a major impact on product quality and reliability. Automatic processes typically require, for their successful operation, a high level of input standardization and quality if costly down-time is to be avoided. The increase in quality levels and testing probably added to costs in the short run but it reduced the probability of set breakdown.

18.   Partly due to demand saturation, demand for colour television receivers stagnated in Japan over the period 1974 to 1976. Capacity utilisation in the industry dropped to about 75 to 80 per cent in 1974 and slightly less in 1975. Relatively low levels of capacity utilisation encouraged Japanese producers to intensify their export efforts, which were assisted by a sharp cyclical increase in United States demand for consumer durables throughout 1976. At the end of that year, colour receiver sales were still below their 1973 peak, but relative to 1975, sales had increased by over 1 million units, equivalent to 15 per cent of the market (Graph 8.2).

19.   However, as capacity utilisation rates in the United States industry did not exceed 60 per cent at any point in 1976, it seems unlikely that the increase in sales met shortfalls in domestic supply. The shift to imported goods was probably due to two inter-related factors: a progressive change in United States consumer perceptions of the attractiveness and reliability of Japanese television receivers; and a change in the composition of United States demand, with a decline in demand for sets 20 inches and over and an increase in demand for sets in the 13 to 19 inch size class.

20.   The United States industry responded to the increases in import penetration primarily by intensifying its efforts to obtain trade restrictions. Appeals were made against unfavourable results to previous anti-dumping actions, and a number of important new actions involving the United States International Trade Commission[6] were launched. The Commission found that the number of colour television receivers being imported into the United States had increased so rapidly as to be "a substantial cause of serious injury" to the domestic industry. The industry therefore qualified for import relief as provided for under Section 201(b) of the Trade Act of 1974. Consequently, the Commissioners recommended that tariffs on colour television receivers be increased, from 5 to 25 per cent during the first year, decreasing to 20, 15, and 10 per cent in the following years of the relief programme[7].

21.   Though the United States Government accepted the determination that imports were causing substantial injury to the domestic industry, it was unwilling to accept the International Trade Commission's recommendation on tariff increases. In the Government's view, a substantial increase in tariffs would be inflationary, would injure the minor exporting countries, and could lead to expensive compensation claims both from these countries and from Japan[8]. As an alternative, the United States Government sought to

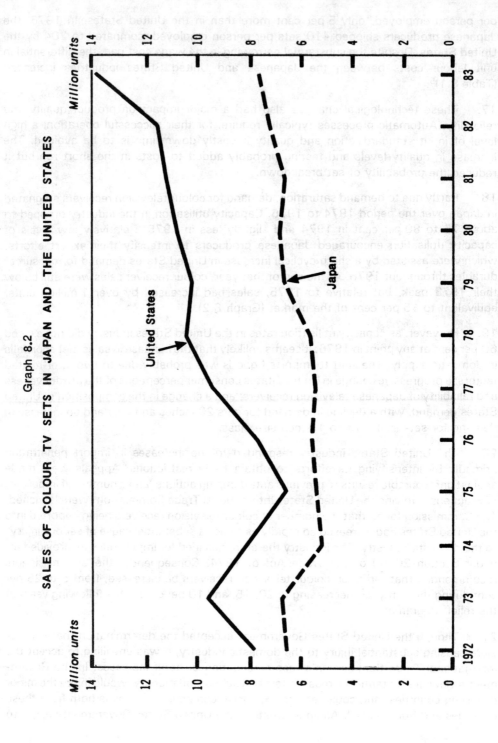

Graph 8.2

SALES OF COLOUR TV SETS IN JAPAN AND THE UNITED STATES

Million units

United States

Japan

Million units

154

negotiate directly with the Japanese Government a voluntary export restraint agreement. The result of these negotiations was an "Orderly Marketing Agreement" (OMA) for the colour television receiver industry.

22.   Under the Agreement, Japan's exports of complete receivers to the United States were to be limited to 1.56 million units for each of the three years from 1st July 1977. This was 1.3 million units less than Japan had exported to the United States in 1976. In addition, exports of incomplete colour television receivers – defined, in the OMA, as receivers assembled to substantially full extent – were limited to 190 thousand units in each year[9]. On the assumption that Japan continued to account for around 80 per cent of US imports, these limits would have reduced total US imports of colour receivers by nearly 1 million units in the first year; on reasonable projections about demand growth, this implied a fall in import penetration from over 35 to around 20 per cent.

The impact on trade

23.   Despite the Agreement, US imports of colour television receivers did not decline. Imports were lower in 1977 and 1978 than they had been in 1976; but in 1978, the first full year of operation of the agreement, imports were nearly a quarter of a million sets higher than in 1977[10]. Econometric analysis carried out by the secretariat suggests that thanks to the increasing availability of imports from countries other than Japan, the Orderly Marketing Agreement did not significantly affect the US import demand or supply function for colour receivers. It was the *pattern* of imports that changed rather than their *level*.

24.   In 1976, Japan accounted for 90 per cent of US imports of complete colour television receivers, in 1977 for 80 per cent, but in 1978 for only 50 per cent. At the same time, the share of the South East Asian producing countries increased. In the third quarter of 1977, imports from Korea and Taiwan accounted for around 15 per cent of US imports of complete colour television receivers; by the fourth quarter of 1978, their share had risen to 50 per cent. Thus, the relative stability of import prices in the nine months from second quarter 1978, combined with a rise in colour receiver sales, resulted in a significant increase in import volumes.

25.   Given that over 1978 as a whole, the share of imports in apparent consumption was at 27 per cent, only 1 per cent lower than in 1977, US manufacturers regarded imports from South East Asia as a major threat to their long-run viability. In fact, the net revenue position of the US industry had deteriorated substantially, despite the OMA: the dollar value of total sales was 15 per cent greater in 1978 than in 1976, but net operating profits were 54 per cent smaller. Faced with declining net revenues, and a net loss – before tax – of approximately $1.6 million on industry sales of over $3 billion, the major firms in the industry increased their prices, particularly in the third quarter of 1978, and sought an extension of import controls.

Extension of the OMA

26.   Early in 1978, industry groups had contacted the office of the Special Representative for Trade Negotiations — who was charged with monitoring the effectiveness of the Orderly Marketing Agreement — to complain about mounting imports from Korea and Taiwan. After investigating these complaints, the Special Representative determined: "... that imports of colour television receivers and certain sub-assemblies thereof have increased in such quantities so as to disrupt the effectiveness of the orderly marketing agreement with Japan"[11].

27.   As a result, restrictions on imports through Orderly Marketing Agreements were extended to Korea and Taiwan. These agreements, running from 1st February, 1979 to 30th June, 1980 restricted imports to 500 000 complete and 918 000 incomplete sets from Taiwan and 289 000 complete and incomplete sets from Korea. The quarterly upper limit on complete sets was equal to 70 per cent of last quarter 1978 imports from Taiwan, but to only 34 per cent of last quarter 1978 imports from Korea. As a consequence, average total quarterly imports declined from about 700 000 to 350 000 sets between 1978 and 1979 and import penetration dropped from 27 to 15 per cent.

28.   As import competition subsided, prices increased. Foreign producers, faced with restrictions, raised export prices closer to market clearing levels. As is apparent from Graph 8.3, while Japanese domestic prices for colour television receivers continued to decline, the colour television receiver export price index (in Yen) increased by 17 per cent in the first nine months of 1979, compared with a 1 per cent increase in 1978 and a 10 per cent decline in 1977. Competitive pressures on domestic producers eased, allowing them to consolidate the price rises announced in the third quarter 1978 and to further increase prices in several screen size categories.

29.   As to the combined impact of the import restrictions and the increase in import prices, econometric evidence suggests:

-       The extension of the OMA led to a significant increase in the mark-up in US import prices over wholesale prices in the exporting countries. On average, US import unit values were 4 to 8 per cent higher in 1979 than they would have been had the restrictions not been in force.
-       On average, US wholesale prices for colour receivers were 4 to 5 per cent higher in 1979 than expected on the basis of 1975 to 1978 behaviour relationships. This increase in wholesale prices appears to have been fully passed on to consumers.
-       Actual total imports of sets in the first three quarters of 1979 were fully 45 per cent lower than predicted. The behavioural shifts in price and output determination induced by the extension of the OMA (and notably the expansion of output of Japanese-owned plants in the United States) led to trade effects far greater than those needed to price ration the quota.

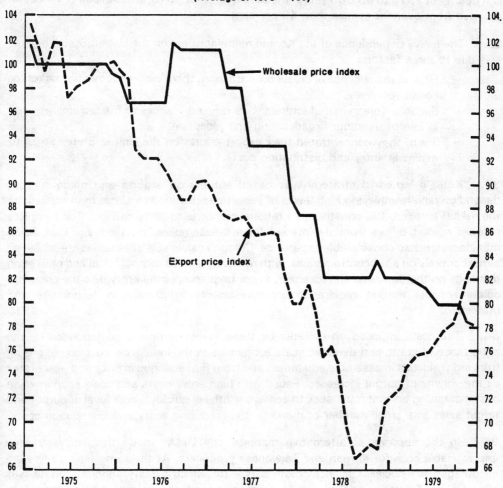

Graph 8.3

JAPAN : WHOLESALE AND EXPORT PRICE INDICES FOR COLOUR TELEVISION RECEIVERS
(Average of 1975 = 100)

Wholesale price index

Export price index

The impact on foreign producers

30. The extension of trade restrictions created considerable difficulties for foreign producers competing in the United States market. The Korean manufacturers found themselves virtually excluded from their major export market, the Taiwanese found their growth opportunities — particularly in the complete set area — curtailed, while the major Japanese manufacturers were also forced to reappraise their long-term strategy.

157

31.   For Korea, the upper limit on quarterly complete set exports to the United States was equivalent to less than 20 per cent of South Korea's anticipated 1979 output. The reduction in exports led to a fall in monthly output from an average of 82 000 sets in the last quarter of 1978 to 45 000 sets in the third quarter of 1979, while capacity utilisation dropped from over 90 to less than 40 per cent.

32.   The heavy dependence of the Korean manufacturers on the United States market was due to three factors:

—   First, in the absence of colour broadcasting, there was no domestic market for colour receivers;
—   Second, Korean manufacturers were refused licences to the technology used in European colour broadcasting and reception;
—   Third, they concentrated their export efforts on the United States so as to minimise entry and distribution costs.

33.   Korea's industrial strategy was based entirely on exports and made success depend on rapidly achieving high levels of import penetration in a single market. Despite the risks it entailed, this constituted a rational response to entry barriers. The complete receiver market differs from the market for sub-assemblies, in which the East Asian manufacturers had considerable experience. Colour receiver sub-assemblies are produced almost entirely on a subcontract basis, with relatively limited technological and marketing demands on the domestic entrepreneur. In contrast, successful entry into the complete colour receiver market requires major investments in production technology and marketing.

34.   The costs imposed on entrants by these investments are compounded by the importance of static and dynamic scale economies in the industry's cost curve, arising from indivisibilities in assembly equipment and from the reduction in error and reject rates as the volume of output increases. Faced with high entry costs and scale economies, a cost-minimising entrant must seek to achieve relatively quickly a high level of output and target sales at a small number of markets, thus reducing entry and distribution costs.

35.   In the absence of alternative markets, the OMAs made this entry strategy impracticable both for Korean and Taiwanese producers. At the same time, they were encouraged to specialise in incomplete sets — for which a fairly generous quota was allocated to Taiwan — and of sub-assemblies, on which no import limits were set. However, specialisation in these products would do little to enhance or even fully utilise these producers' technological and marketing capabilities, while making them increasingly vulnerable to competition from other lower wage countries.

36.   By contrast, the Japanese producers had, by the early 1970s, consolidated their entry into overseas colour receiver markets: their marketing and distribution channels were well established, their brand image secure. However, the 1977 and 1978 appreciation of the Yen undermined the competitive advantage they had gained in the 1975 and 1976 restructuring, and the OMA seemed to permanently rule out any return to the early 1976 level of exports to the United States.

37.   Drawing on their increased profitability due largely to rents in the North American market, the Japanese manufacturers responded to this challenge at three inter-related levels:

-    First, they intensified their research and development efforts, while concentrating production in Japan on the most technologically advanced products and processes;
-    Second, they transferred part of their production facilities to sites in South East Asia;

Table 8.4

19" COLOUR TELEVISION COST COMPARISONS, 1979

(In dollars)

	United States producer	Japanese sets produced in Japan		Japanese sets produced in United States	
		Low-Cost Producer	High-Cost Producer	Low-Cost Producer	High-Cost Producer
Purchased materials					
Picture tube	62	57	58	66	66
Other	89	62	71	67	74
Total materials	151	119	129	133	140
Labour and variable overheads	32	24	29	23	28
Overheads (excluding marketing and distribution)	41	31	37	29	36
Quality cost penalty	-	-	-	-	-
Sub-total	224	174	195	188	207
Freight, duty, insurance	6	25	25	6	6
Total cost before marketing and distribution	230	199	220	194	213
Advantage	0	31	10	36	17

Source: Magaziner and Reich, 1982.

159

— Third, they purchased and extended production facilities in the United States itself, replacing direct exports by local production.

Thanks to a careful strategy of technological transfer, they maintained at their US locations the cost advantage relative to American firms from which they had previously benefited in Japan (Table 8.4).

38. From 1976 on, the Japanese producers' research and development efforts had three main objectives:

— To simplify further and automate the colour receiver production process;
— To accelerate the development of video-tape and video-disc technology;
— To bring substantially new technologies — such as flat screen and high definition television and pulse code modulation audio — to the development stage.

39. As production technology advanced, the composition of output at Japanese plants changed. In essence, the Japanese producers of consumer electronics have pursued a modified product-cycle strategy, concentrating domestic production on the processes most difficult to transfer abroad, and with the highest growth rates and lowest price elasticities of demand (Graph 8.5). As the television technology reached maturity, output

Graph 8.5

OUTPUT STRUCTURE OF CONSUMER ELECTRONICS IN JAPAN

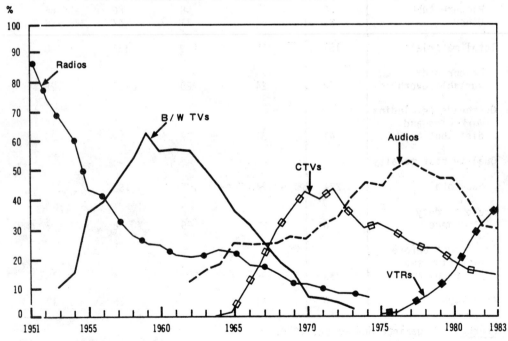

Source : Ministry of International Trade and Industry.

160

Graph 8.6

OUTPUT GROWTH COLOUR TV SETS AND HOME VTRs, JAPAN 1965-1983

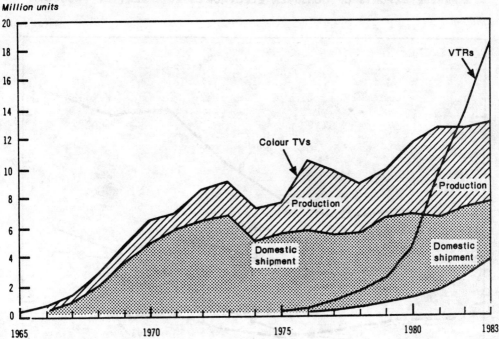

Million units

of colour receivers in Japan therefore declined. In the fourth quarter of 1976, nearly 3 million complete sets were produced. By the fourth quarter of 1977, output was down to 2.4 million. However, a growing volume of resources was transferred to video production: monthly output of video-tape recorders increased from less than 30 000 in December 1976 to over 250 000 three years later (Graph 8.6).

40.   This change in the composition of output was reflected in the changing composition of trade. In 1976, exports of video-tape recorders were a minute fraction of exports of colour receivers. By the end of 1979, the number of video-tape recorders exported was equal to 70 per cent of the number of colour receiver exports. More strikingly, Japanese firms exported 25 per cent more video-tape recorders to the U.S. than colour television receivers (Graph 8.7).

41.   The decline in domestic output and exports of colour television receivers was compensated for by increases in output at Japanese-owned plants overseas. Already by the early 1970s, Japanese firms had transferred the production of monochrome receivers to facilities in Taiwan and elsewhere in South-East Asia. The Yen appreciation and the 1977 OMA made the transfer of colour receiver production even more attractive. Japanese firms may have accounted for as much as 70 to 80 per cent of Taiwan's peak output of complete colour receivers and 40 to 50 per cent of Korea's.

Graph 8.7

JAPANESE EXPORTS OF CONSUMER ELECTRONICS EQUIPMENT BY PRODUCT

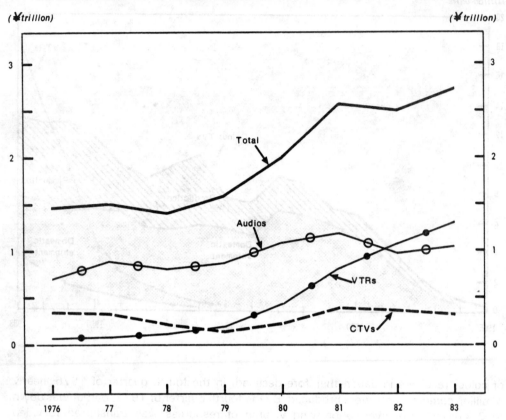

Source : Ministry of Finance, Japan.

42.   The transfer was impeded by United States import restraints. Already in early 1978, pressure was put on the Taiwanese Government to restrict exports of complete colour receivers to the United States from Japanese subsidiaries and affiliate firms operating in that country. In May 1978 – more than seven months before the extension of the 1977 agreement – these firms received "export guidance" from the Taiwanese authorities to keep their exports to the United States at or below 1977 levels. As a result, Japanese subsidiaries operating in Taiwan were subject to restrictions even more severe than those contained in the December 1978 OMA. At the same time, the extension of trade restrictions to Korea made it difficult to use that country as a production base for exports to the United States market[12].

43.   With the generalisation of import controls, it became apparent to the Japanese producers that any country used as a production base for large scale exports of colour

162

receivers to the United States would rapidly find itself subject to trade restrictions. Given the significant scale economies involved in colour receiver production, the risks associated with direct investment in colour receiver facilities outside the United States became excessively high. To maintain their share in the United States market, Japanese producers had to develop production facilities on site.

44.   Japan's colour receiver manufacturers had been investing in United States production facilities since the early 1970s in response to the threat of restrictions. The intensification of the United States industry's campaign after 1976 accelerated the shift to local production: by end 1977, Japanese firms were producing 1.75 million sets a year in the United States; by end 1979, this had increased to over 2.5 million, equivalent to 25 per cent of United States apparent consumption.

The adjustment process in the US industry

45.   Throughout the 1970s, the US colour television receiver industry suffered from two fundamental weaknesses: inadequate expenditure on research and development and extremely low level investments in new machinery and equipment[13]. By the late 1970s, the US firms lagged behind their principal competitors both in product and in process innovation.

46.   Only once market acceptance was proven were US firms willing to incur the higher costs entailed by introducing new features on existing products. A similar attitude was adopted to the development of new products. Thus, United States firms had pioneered video technology, producing the first broadcast quality video-tape recorder in 1956 and the first broadcast colour video-tape recorder in 1958. However, they lost the initiative in the 1960s and played little part in the successful commercialisation of video-tape technology in the mid-1970s.

47.   The process innovation performance of the US industry was even weaker. In the early 1970s, one United States firm made a commercially unsuccessful attempt to automate the component insertion process. After the failure of this attempt, United States firms devoted few resources to process innovation.

48.   US firms therefore entered the period of import restrictions with an ageing capital stock, a substantial technological lag, and a competitive strategy centred on reducing product prices through the transfer of labour-intensive processes to low wage countries. The evidence does not suggest that the introduction of trade restrictions substantially altered this situation. To a large extent this may be explained by the fact that the trade restrictions did not improve the industry's overall financial position.

49.   In 1978, profit margins were compressed by imports from South-East Asia, and in 1979, by the rapid growth of low-cost high-quality output at Japanese-owned plants in the United States. In 1978, the industry had registered a relatively small before-tax-loss. Despite increases in prices in late 1978 and early 1979, the United States industry's net loss increased to $25 million in 1979[14]. This loss might, of course, have been greater had the restrictions not been in effect; but what little evidence there is suggests that even

within the United States industry, the principal gainers from the restrictions were not the domestically-owned firms.

50.   Since colour sub-assemblies and printed circuit boards were excluded from the OMAs, United States firms have tried to improve their profitability by accelerating the transfer of their labour-intensive operations to low-wage countries. However, this strategy was clearly ineffective even in reducing the cost differential relative to Japan (Table 8.1); and, if anything, it tended to undermine the quality of the United States firms' products[15].

51.   The result of offshore assembly was a further increase in apparent labour productivity in the United States industry. Between 1977 and 1979, the number of colour receivers shipped per worker increased at an annual rate of 11 per cent. However, since shipments increased at an annual average rate of only 6 per cent, employment in the industry continued to decline, passing from 29 000 in 1977 to 26 700 in 1979 and 21 000 in 1981.

52.   The decline in employment would have been greater had the restrictions in imports not been in effect. Without import restrictions, domestic shipments would probably have been at least 0.5 million sets smaller; on the assumption that productivity continued to increase at its trend value, 1979 employment in the industry would have been 1 000 to 1 500 less than actually observed. "Saving" each of these jobs cost United States consumers over $60 000 a year (on the conservative assumption that the price of a $200 set increased by $5).

53.   It is worth noting, moreover, that a considerable part of this employment gain was due to the creation of job opportunities by Japanese firms in areas where colour receivers had not previously been assembled, while employment at already existing plants continued to decline. The extent to which the restrictions improved employment prospects for those workers already in the industry is therefore open to question.

Prospects

54.   The restrictions on colour television receiver imports into the United States were lifted in 1982. This makes the colour television receiver industry one of the few which has benefitted from genuinely *temporary* protection in recent years, and some analysis of the factors which allowed protection to be dismantled appears warranted.

55.   It is doubtless true that the trade restrictions neither strengthened the long-run competitiveness of United States firms in this product nor significantly improved the industry's employment situation. Faced with a continued deterioration in its net earnings position, the industry did not finance necessary expenditures on research and development and on new machinery and equipment. Rather, United States firms sought to reduce product costs by accelerating the transfer of labour-intensive operations to low wage countries. The larger, already diversified firms, notably GE and RCA reduced their dependence on consumer electronics. Zenith, the least diversified of the national brand

manufacturers and the major advocate of protection, sought new growth areas in the electronics industry, mainly in the sale of computer terminals and micro-computers.

56.   Both of these responses limited the viability of a long-run protection strategy. To secure protection, firms had to coalesce with labour unions but these were naturally opposed to offshore assembly. Indefinite protection would have created strong pressures for restrictions to be imposed on sub-assemblies and kits, not to mention fully assembled receivers produced on a subcontract basis in Mexico. Equally, diversification out of consumer electronics diminished the importance of receiver sales to the major firms, with even Zenith no longer relying so heavily on this product.

57.   At the same time, heavy investment in the United States by Japanese firms (on any reckoning, the major gainers from protection) made the restrictions largely irrelevent. It was clear, and was explicitly stated by the major Japanese suppliers, that it was their intention to serve the US market mainly from US sites, regardless of whether or not the restrictions were lifted. This proved to be the case, with little import growth immediately subsequent to the dismantling of trade controls. Though import growth accelerated after the sharp appreciation of the dollar, protection had succeeded in at least partially replacing an inefficient, domestically-owned oligopoly with a more efficient, foreign-owned oligopoly.

58.   This highlights the difference between measures which protect domestic producers and measures which protect domestically-owned producers. Where a substantial technological gap separates domestically-owned firms from their principal foreign competitors, the principal impact of restrictions may be to encourage an inflow of foreign direct investment. Given the market power conferred upon foreign-owned firms by their technological lead, the gains to domestically-owned producers can be slight, while domestic consumers suffer from higher prices.

59.   Vigorous inter-group competition among foreign firms would, under normal competitive circumstances, make market power difficult to exploit. OMAs and Voluntary Export Restraint, however, intervene by changing the institutional framework within which this competition occurs, since industry co-operation is needed to allocate shares in the fixed volume of exports. As a result, the restricted producers are put in a position to pursue a strategy of joint profit maximisation.

60.   A parallel may be seen with the recent Voluntary Export Restraint agreement on video-tape recorders between the European Commission and Japan. Here too, the Japanese producers appear particularly well placed to capture the rents — by increasing their export prices, by investing in European production facilities and from the sale of licenses on VTR technology to European firms. But while the Unites States OMA left the increase in prices to the vagaries of the market, the EC Agreement explicitly stipulates a minimum increase in prices, at a rate which, according to an estimate for one major EC country, is equivalent to the price effect of a 130 per cent *ad valorem* tariff[16].

61.   Even if the Japanese producers did not want to exploit their market position (and the present over-capacity in the Japanese VTR industry would, under other circumstances, have made it difficult for them to do so) the Agreement would force them into it.

Here too, the restricted producers will presumably use the rents to invest in the "products of the future": digital and high resolution television, PCM audio and so on. In a few years, these investments will lead to new generations of products, yet further undermining those producers whom the restrictions were intended to protect.

NOTES AND REFERENCES

1. Throughout this paper, the US colour television receiver industry is defined as including *all* firms producing colour receivers in the United States, regardless of their country of ownership. In contrast, the terms US firms and US manufacturers refer only to US owned firms.

2. In 1971 there were 19. Concentration levels in the industry probably increased but no data on this subject is available. Data for the radio and television receiver industry as a whole does not suggest a significant increase in concentration levels over the period 1967 to 1975.

3. In a detailed longitudinal study of the earnings losses from displacement, Jacobson and Thomason: 1979 examined the earnings losses to males aged 23 to 53 who lost jobs in the television receiver industry over the period 1962 to 1966. They found that these workers lost approximately 0.7 per cent of their expected earnings in the two years following displacement; but that their earnings over the subsequent four years were 7 per cent higher than they would have been, had they remained in the industry. More generally, Jacobson and Thomason found that earnings losses from displacements were low where industry turnover rates were high. However, they also found that earnings losses increased in labour markets with above average unemployment rates or with a relatively small number of job opportunities and that losses were typically greater for women than for men.

4. Ikeda: 1979: "The Subcontracting System in the Japanese Electronic Industry"; Engineering Industries of Japan, No. 19, May; pages 43 to 71.

5. In 1972, unit labour costs — calculated using wages for production workers in the radio and television receiver industry as a whole — were approximately three times higher in the United States than in Japan; in 1976 they were 3.5 times higher.

6. In January 1976, a major United States producer filed a complaint to the Commission alleging that colour television sets exported to the United States were being unfairly subsidized by the Japanese Government. Though this action was unsuccessful, it appears to have been an element in the Commission's decision to initiate an investigation on allegations covering some 14 unfair trade practices; these included practices contrary to anti-dumping, countervailing duty and anti-trust laws. Finally, in September 1976, the major US television producers, together with 11 labour unions covering employers in the television receiver industry, filed an escape clause action under the terms of the quotas on the grounds that Japanese competition was causing serious injury to the United States industry.

7. The Commission also investigated the monochrome receiver industry but was unable to reach a majority decision as to whether or not "serious injury" was being caused by imports. Since the Commission was evenly divided on this subject, the President — pursuant to section 330(d) of the Tariff Act of 1930 — determined that no injury was being caused.

8. These factors are outlined in: *Import Relief for the United States Colour Television Industry: Communication from the President of the United States,* United States House of Representatives document No. 95-163 of 19th May, 1977.

9. Sub-assemblies considered less than "incomplete receivers" (TSUSA 685.2066) and printed circuit boards with components attached thereto (TSUSA 685.2067) were excluded from the OMA, primarily so as to prevent injury to United States firms which incorporated these into their final products.

10. The very high level of imports in the last quarter of 1976 was partly due to fears of import restrictions. It was widely believed at the time that tariff levels on imports would be substantially increased. Importers of colour receivers sought to maximize their windfall profits from the tariff change by anticipating orders. Stocks of imported receivers therefore increased rapidly: at the end of 1975 inventories of imported receivers were equivalent to approximately one months's imports; by the end of 1976, despite a near trebling in monthly import levels, they were equivalent to over one and a half months of current imports. Once the restrictions entered into effect, demand for inventories declined. This reduced import levels, as did the subsequent rundown in stocks.

11. *Colour Television Receiver Imports;* Presidential Proclamation 4634 of 26th January, 1979, paragraph 4. See also *Federal Register* of 29th January, 1979.

12. Shortly after the extension of the OMA, Matsushita withdrew from its joint venture for producing receivers in Korea; see *Japan Economic Journal,* 1st April, 1980.

13. Over the period from 1973 to 1978, the US producers of colour television receivers spent an average of 3.1 per cent of their annual sales revenue on R&D. This compares with 13 per cent for the entire United States communications equipment and electronic components industry. The contrast with the Japanese producers of colour television receivers was also marked: these producers — whose total sales were very much larger — devoted approximately 5 per cent of their sales revenue to R&D. Over the same period, expenditure by the United States owned firms on new machinery and equipment for their domestic production facilities was probably less than 1 per cent of sales; the equivalent figure for the electrical industry as a whole was over 4 per cent.

14. It is worth noting, however, that the reported profit and loss data may be affected by intra-firm transfer pricing. In particular, sub-assembly prices charged by overseas affiliates may be artificially high.

15. Over the period 1974 to 1976, 8 per cent of the industry's expenditure on new machinery and equipment was for facilities overseas; for 1977 to 1979, this share jumped to over 19 per cent. At the same time, Unites States imports of sub-assemblies and incomplete receivers increased rapidly. By the end of 1979, these imports had more than doubled with respect to their 1977 level, while imports of complete receivers had been halved. The increase in sub-assembly imports was due both to the transfer oveaseas of sub-assembly operations by US firms and to imports of sub-assemblies by Japanese firms, the latter accounting for perhaps one-third of the total.

16. Messerlin: 1983.

Part III

PROTECTIONISM AND INTERDEPENDENCE

The growing interdependence of the world economy makes the evolution of trade policies critically important. Protection is therefore a major factor in the development of economic relations and the business climate. This not only holds true for the North-South context, but also for North-North and South-South relations. Chapter 9 highlights the North-South dimension of the issue of protectionism, bringing together information on the level and composition of trade flows and the effects on economic growth, debt service and the shaping of development strategies. Chapter 10 analyses the factors determining the "demand" for (and resistance to) protection in the light of costs and benefits of trade to economic and social actors, and of the "supply" of protection by the political system in response to the pressures of sectional interest groups.

Chapter 9

PROTECTIONISM AND DEVELOPING COUNTRIES

1.   Restrictive measures also affect the protecting country through their impact on the income levels, financial solvency and hence capacity to import of the countries against which the measures are taken. The magnitude of these effects depends on the degree of openness of the various economies. As interdependence has grown throughout the post-war period, so has the importance of the developing countries as trading partners of the OECD economies. This trend has strengthened since the early 1970s:

- First, the share of all LDCs in industrial countries' total exports rose from 17 per cent in 1973 to about one quarter in the early 1980s. Though subject to sharp cyclical variations, the industrial countries' export surplus in manufactures with non-oil LDCs (and, of course, with OPEC) remains very high, providing an important outlet for industrial activity in the OECD area.

- Second, the industrial countries absorbed nearly two-thirds of the non-oil LDCs' exports of manufactures and a steadily rising share of their total exports. For a growing number of LDCs, demand conditions in and access to industrial country markets for manufactures have become more important in determining their export earnings than has demand for their primary commodities.

2.   The slowdown of OECD growth in the late 1970s and early 1980s was accompanied by a slackening in the expansion of LDC exports of manufactures and a perceptible strengthening of pressures for protection in many OECD countries. Not surprisingly, the empirical studies reviewed in this report, many of which refer to that period, are impregnated by pessimism as regards the export prospects of LDCs and the role of OECD protectionism. This mood of pessimism was enhanced by two further factors. First, there was the strong 1981-82 recession which culminated in the LDC debt crisis. This led to doubts about the economic viability of major debtors — also major trading partners of the OECD — confronted with weak export markets and a threatening protectionist backlash. Second, there were fears that a circular process may be unfolding, whereby growing retrenchment and protectionism in LDCs would add to widespread uncertainty in the world economy and magnify the economic feedback effects throughout the multilateral trading system.

3.   The exceptionally fast recovery in the United States, preceded and accompanied by the continued appreciation of the dollar, has created an entirely new situation. The one-sided concentration of the growth of demand on the United States has been highly beneficial to LDC exporters of manufactures, while exporters of primary products would have been better off if the recovery had been more evenly spread. Despite the adverse effects of persistent high real interest rates, the acuteness of the debt crisis diminished somewhat with the rise in LDC export earnings. Indeed, it may well be that the clearer perception of the nexus between LDC export earnings and debt servicing capability has helped to bolster resistence to protectionism in several OECD countries.

The evolution of protection and North-South trade

4.   As shown in Chapter 1, despite tariff reductions, barriers confronting LDC exports of manufactures to the industrialised economies remain above those applying to intra-OECD exports. Tariff escalation persists, and tariffs have been falling more slowly on manufactured goods exported by LDCs[1]. Weighted average MFN tariffs facing LDC manufactured exports (7.9 per cent) are higher than on OECD exports (5.8 per cent). This differential widened after the Tokyo-Round, mainly because duties were not substantially reduced on footwear, leather goods, textiles and apparel. Given product exclusions and limitations, GSP schemes have only been moderately effective in reducing the gap.

5.   Non-tariff barriers facing major LDC export products have also spread and tightened in recent years. The second renewal of the MFA in 1982 affected more developing countries and more of their items than the previous arrangement. In other areas, such as steel, consumer electronics and footwear, new quantitative restrictions have been introduced or existing ones strengthened. Requests for protective measures against low-cost imports have mushroomed and although only few have resulted in actual actions, the mere threat of further restrictions has an adverse impact on the trading and investment climate.

6.   Nonetheless, in the period 1973-83 non-oil LDCs expanded their share of OECD manufactured imports rapidly. After registering a real annual growth rate of nearly 10 per cent up to 1979, manufactured imports from non-oil developing countries slackened off over the following two to three years. They rebounded, however, in 1982-83 at a rate of 16.3 per cent, pushing up their share of total OECD manufactured imports to about 14 per cent by 1984. From 1982 onwards real growth in OECD GDP was associated with a proportionately much higher intake of LDC manufactured imports than in the previous periods (Table 9.1).

7.   An above-average proportion of the rise in imports of non-oil LDC manufactures was shipped to the United States, which by 1983 had increased its share in total OECD manufactured imports to well over half. It can be estimated on the basis of recent figures on manufactured imports from the major East-Asian NICs (Table 9.2) that this share rose to about 60 per cent in 1984. The reasons for this recent upward trend are to be found chiefly in the appreciation of the dollar and, since 1982, the strong recovery of domestic

Table 9.1

OECD IMPORTS OF MANUFACTURES FROM NON-OIL LDCs, 1973-83

	US (1)			Japan			Rest of OECD			Total				Annual rate of change in real OECD GDP
	Value in $US billion	% Share A	% Share B	Value in $US billion	% Share A	% Share B	Value in $US billion	% Share A(3)	% Share B	Value in $US billion	% Share A	Volume of Index 1973=100	Imports(2) Rate of Change	
1973	7.1	17.2	41.2	2.4	25.3	13.7	7.8	4.3	45.1	17.2	7.4	100		6.1
1974	9.5	18.7	42.5	2.7	22.9	12.1	10.2	4.5	45.4	22.5	7.7	107	7.0	0.6
1975	8.8	18.4	40.5	2.1	21.6	9.7	10.9	4.5	49.8	21.8	7.3	92	-13.6	0.3
1976	12.8	21.0	42.6	2.9	25.8	9.8	14.3	5.2	47.7	30.1	8.6	126	36.5	4.9
1977	15.5	21.4	43.5	3.0	24.5	8.5	17.1	5.5	48.1	35.6	8.9	134	6.5	3.9
1978	22.5	22.8	47.8	4.2	26.3	9.0	20.4	5.4	43.2	47.1	9.6	159	18.6	4.0
1979	26.1	23.8	43.4	6.2	28.4	10.3	27.9	5.9	46.3	60.2	10.0	175	9.9	3.1
1980	30.2		43.3	6.1	25.5	8.7	33.5	6.3	48.0	69.8	10.3	187	7.0	1.2
1981	35.4	25.5	47.4	6.8	27.3	9.1	32.4	6.6	43.4	74.6	11.3	200	6.8	2.1
1982	37.9	26.7	49.8	6.5	26.7	8.6	31.7	6.7	41.6	76.2	11.8	230	14.8	-0.5
1983	46.4	29.1	54.4	6.3	24.5	7.4	32.6	6.8	38.2	85.6	12.8	269	17.2	2.6

A. % share in the region's total imports of manufactures
B. % share in total OECD imports of manufactures from non-oil LDCs

1. F.o.b.
2. Values deflated by the export price index of manufactures.
3. Share A for EEC:

	Including intra EEC trade	Excluding intra EEC trade
1973	4.7	14.5
1974	4.7	14.4
1975	5.0	14.9
1976	5.6	16.4
1977	5.9	16.9
1978	5.8	16.5
1979	6.3	18.0
1980	6.8	18.5
1981	7.1	18.2
1982	7.0	18.3
1983	7.1	18.2

Table 9.2

TOTAL OECD IMPORTS FROM FIVE MAJOR EAST-ASIAN NICs 1979-84
$ US billion

	1979	1980	1981	1982	1983	1984 (a)
Singapore	5.1	7.0	6.6	6.6	6.9	8.6
Korea	10.8	11.1	12.5	12.7	14.6	18.1
Taiwan	11.9	13.8	15.2	15.6	18.4	23.7
Hong Kong	10.2	12.3	12.6	12.2	13.3	15.5
Malaysia	8.3	9.2	7.7	7.2	7.7	10.1
Total	46.2	53.4	54.6	54.2	60.8	75.9
of which imported by US	17.6	20.4	23.0	24.1	29.7	39.8
Annual rate of change (%) in real terms (b)						
Total		6.3	2.2	11.6	17.5	29.4
US		6.4	14.0	14.3	28.8	42.1

a)   For 1984, based on data for the first three quarters.

b)   Volume of imports: values deflated by the export price index of manufactures.

Source: OECD Foreign Trade Statistics.

demand. By contrast, in the other OECD countries as a whole the value of manufactured imports from non-oil LDCs did not increase at all between 1980 and 1983.

8.   OECD exports of manufactures to non-oil LDCs grew in real terms by some 40 per cent between 1977 and 1981, bringing the non-oil LDCs' deficit in manufactures trade with the OECD to an all-time peak of nearly $110 billion or more than 60 per cent of imports. With the falling dollar and relatively weak domestic demand, the United States increased its share in the OECD total during this period to over 27 per cent. 1982 and 1983 witnessed a slight decrease in the volume of total OECD manufactured exports to non-oil LDCs. In these two years the US sustained a substantial reduction in its share of the total, and saw its export surplus in manufactures turn into a deficit. Japan increased its share and maintained its export surplus, while the rest of the OECD continued to lose ground (Table 9.3).

9.   There is no unambiguous method for assessing the influence of various factors on the overall level of LDC exports of manufactures, let alone measuring them. In the short

173

Table 9.3

OECD EXPORTS OF MANUFACTURES TO NON-OIL LDCs, 1973-83

	US			Japan			Rest of OECD			Total				Annual rate of change in real GDP of non-oil LDCs
	Value in $US billion	% share A	% share B	Value in $US billion	% share A	% Share B	Value in $US billion	% share A	% share B	Value in $US billion	% share A	Index 1973=100	Rate of change	
1973	11.1	26.1	21.5	13.6	39.7	26.5	26.7	13.1	52.0	51.4	18.3	100		6.3
1974	17.3	28.6	22.4	21.1	41.2	27.3	38.8	14.6	50.3	77.2	20.5	123	23.2	5.9
1975	19.2	28.4	22.9	20.9	39.9	24.9	43.8	15.1	52.2	83.9	20.5	119	-3.3	4.9
1976	19.6	26.4	23.4	22.4	35.2	26.7	41.9	13.0	49.9	83.9	18.3	117	-1.3	5.2
1977	19.9	26.8	21.2	26.5	34.5	28.1	47.8	13.3	50.7	94.2	18.1	119	1.3	5.3
1978	24.3	26.9	20.9	33.0	35.5	28.4	59.1	13.3	50.8	116.4	18.6	132	10.6	4.5
1979	34.1	30.3	23.7	35.7	36.6	24.9	73.7	13.9	51.4	143.6	19.2	140	6.1	4.7
1980	45.7	33.3	26.3	44.5	36.3	25.6	83.8	14.7	48.2	174.0	20.2	156	11.7	5.4
1981	49.0	32.9	27.1	49.7	34.2	27.4	82.4	13.8	45.5	181.2	21.2	162	4.1	2.7
1982	41.9	31.3	26.1	42.8	32.3	26.7	75.8		47.2	160.5	19.6	161	-0.4	0.6
1983	37.2	29.3	24.4	45.6	32.5	29.9	69.6	12.9	45.7	152.5	18.9	159	-1.0	0.7 (1)

A. % share in the region's total exports of manufactures.
B. % share in total OECD exports of manufactures to non-oil LDCs.

1. Estimate.
2. Values deflated by the export price index of manufactures.

174

run, apart from the effect of restrictive trade policies, the level of exports is influenced by a variety of factors: notably demand in importing countries, relative prices – partly influenced by exchange rate developments – and supply conditions in exporting countries.

10.   The figures quoted above suggest that, at the aggregate level, economic growth or, more precisely, demand in the OECD countries has been by far the most powerful factor. As regards changes in relative prices, they had a very powerful influence in determining the direction of LDC exports. One has to assume, however, that for all the manufactures where competition is largely on the basis of price, the major LDC exporters have maintained their competitive edge more or less unchanged, explaining the steady rise in import penetration.

11.   In addition, there is some circumstantial evidence that supply constraints, caused by the very success of the export drive, but partly also related to the pressure of domestic demand, pushed up relative prices and held down exports in some major NICs around 1978-80. In Singapore, the government raised real wages between 1978 and 1981 by 10 per cent a year to push entrepreneurs up-market and drive out marginal low labour productivity firms that were unable to make the move. Real wage increases, reflecting labour shortages and a catch-up on productivity gains, were having the same impact in Korea up to the mid-1970s. It is, however, not possible to separate these supply factors from the tightening of restrictive measures in the OECD on some traditional export products, notably textiles and clothing, in explaining the slight slowdown in LDC import penetration during this period.

The impact of protection on LDC trade

12.   Though aggregate demand and supply are clearly the primary factors determining the level of LDC manufactured exports, this does not mean that persistent protection has no influence on trade flows or that liberalisation would make no difference to them.

13.   A number of studies indicate that in the absence of, or at least with fewer restrictions, imports from developing countries would certainly have been higher. In some product categories the orders of magnitude involved are substantial:

   — One study on the textiles and clothing sector has calculated that if income elasticity of demand in developed countries for imports from developing countries had remained the same as between 1968 and 1976, then clothing imports from developing countries would have been around 90 per cent (or $10 billion) higher in 1980 than they were, and textiles imports a quarter more (or $1.25 billion)[2].

   — Another approach has been to use data on price elasticities of demand and supply, to estimate the effects of removing existing tariff and non-tariff restrictions. The World Bank estimated in 1977 that if all existing barriers were removed for manufactures, LDC exports would be almost 30 per cent higher by 1985 than an extrapolated trend figure[3]; UNCTAD estimated 25 per cent more over the same period[4]. A separate study of about the same time

Table 9.4

DIVERSIFICATION OF EXPORT STRUCTURE IN SELECTED DEVELOPING COUNTRIES

-- Percentage share of selected commodity groups in total merchandise exports --

		Manufactured goods	Machinery and equipment	Textiles, fibres, yarn and clothing	Metals and metal manufactures	Transport equipment	Other Manufactured goods	Diversification Index (1) 1970, 1980
Brazil	1970	9.66	3.55	8.51	4.10	0.53	4.71	0.718
	1975	23.31	10.34	6.41	2.98	3.44	10.83	0.555
	1981	34.75	18.09	4.29	6.05	8.06	12.45	
Hong Kong	1970	95.25	11.78	44.33	3.45	0.56	82.56	0.781
	1975	96.72	14.57	52.63	2.91	0.25	81.28	0.759
	1982	96.25	17.27	40.77	2.75	0.18	78.03	
India	1970	45.13	4.72	26.68	8.96	1.78	38.07	0.653
	1975	42.18	7.29	19.31	9.37	2.45	32.22	0.675
	1979	56.12	6.88	23.04	5.96	2.42	46.20	
Korea	1970	74.91	7.22	41.11	3.34	0.98	66.33	0.736
	1975	76.81	13.82	36.28	7.07	3.62	61.52	0.642
	1981	81.30	22.09	30.04	14.27	9.67	56.00	
Pakistan	1970	57.18	0.49	74.64	0.23	0.04	55.89	0.823
	1975	54.28	0.64	55.62	0.53	0.03	52.50	0.779
	1981	51.10	9.72	52.67	0.56	0.43	49.58	
Singapore	1970	26.71	10.95	5.62	2.40	2.97	13.03	0.606
	1975	39.91	22.69	4.85	3.17	4.18	13.49	0.570
	1982	46.90	25.52	3.98	4.38	3.30	12.18	

1. Absolute deviation of the country commodity shares from world structure, as follows

$$S_j = \sum_i \frac{|h_{ij} - h_i|}{2}$$

where h_{ij} = share of commodity i in total exports of country j;
h_i = share of commodity i in total world exports.

The lower the index, the higher the degree of diversification.

Source: UNCTAD Handbook of International Trade and Development Statistics, 1983.

suggested that exports of manufactures by LDCs in 1974 would have been 16 per cent greater if tariffs were reduced by 60 per cent (and textile quotas relaxed to permit these additional flows)[5].

— An estimate of the increased value of exports accruing to developing countries from a cut of 50 per cent in OECD tariff and non-tariff restrictions on food imports suggested an 11 per cent increase even ignoring the effects of tariff escalation on processed items (the distributional effects are however complex because changed world food prices have a different effect on LDC net importers and net exporters of food products)[6] Separate estimates have indicated potentially very large increases in exports from a liberalisation of trade in processed products[7].

14. Nonetheless, by far the most important effect of protectionist policies has been to accelerate the product and geographical diversification of LDC exports of manufactures. The more advanced NICs have been particularly successful in diversifying out of industries most affected by restrictive trade measures: into other labour intensive industries; into unrestrained subproduct areas within industries where protection exists; into new geographical markets; and — more important — into industries which are less-labour intensive and more intensive in the use of skill, especially engineering skills and/or capital (Table 9.4).

15. The evidence on the impact of protection on the geographical pattern of LDC exports can be summarised as follows:

— During the late 1970s, the five top export earning NICs most exposed to protectionist measures by industrial nations (Hong Kong, Taiwan, Korea, Singapore, Brazil) diverted a large share of their exports to non-OECD countries[8]. Moreover, it would appear that in recent years, the sharp rise in LDC exports to the booming US market was concentrated on the less restricted product categories (e.g. engineering products, electronic components, etc). This may also explain the exceptionally good export performance of the NICs, which benefited from their know-how and well-established contacts in the US market.

— Another development helping to maintain export growth has been the deliberate shifting of certain production activities out of the NICs particularly restrained by protectionist measures into less restricted low labour cost countries. For instance, several NICs have established production facilities in even lower-wage countries (e.g. Malaysia, Philippines, Thailand) partly to circumvent quotas under the MFA and GSP schemes. There is also evidence that mounting risks in international trade and investment — of which protection is but one — are contributing to a rapid expansion of offshore subcontracting initiated by NIC firms[9].

— In the 1970s middle income countries with substantial manufacturing sectors[10] that turned towards export-oriented growth have been able to capture market shares from the more inward-looking LDCs[11] and expand their exports of manufactures at a very fast rate (Table 9.5). These countries have also been less hampered by protectionist measures than the NICs.

Table 9.5

AGGREGATE GROWTH RATES OF MANUFACTURED EXPORTS
BY LDC GROUP, 1965-80

	Country Group 1	Country Group 2	Country Group 3	Country Group 4	All countries
% Share of total manufactured exports (a) of sample countries					
1965	72.6	4.7	20.4	2.5	100.0
1973	81.6	5.9	9.9	2.6	100.0
1980	82.6	8.6	6.6	2.2	100.0
% Annual growth rates of total manufactured exports of countries in each category					
1965-70	16.2	12.9	4.9	16.8	14.1
1970-73	20.1	31.4	7.8	17.0	19.1
1973-77	7.9	11.7	5.1	8.8	7.9
1977-80	10.2	18.8	-0.7	2.7	9.8
1965-73	17.6	19.5	6.0	16.8	15.9
1973-80	8.9	14.7	2.6	6.2	8.7

Notes:

Country Group 1 = Argentina, Brazil, Greece, Hong Kong, Israel, Korea, Mexico, Portugal, Singapore, South Africa, Taiwan, Yugoslavia.

Country Group 2 = Chile, Colombia, Malaysia, Morocco, Peru, Philippines, Thailand, Tunisia, Turkey.

Country Group 3 = Bangladesh, Egypt, India, Indonesia, Pakistan, Sri Lanka.

Country Group 4 = Costa Rica, Dominican Republic, El Salvador, Guatemala, Honduras, Jamaica, Jordan, Nicaragua, Paraguay, Uruguay.

a) Manufactured goods are those classified under SITC categories 5-8 excluding 68 (non-ferrous metals).

Source: Hughes and Newbery.

16.   The quota rents created by OECD trade restrictions and accruing partly to established LDC exporters had two unintended and unexpected effects:

- On the one hand, by helping to compensate established producers for volume losses, they facilitated in some cases the financing of investments in other product lines and hence diversification. This happened notably in Korea where the profits on clothing exports were used for investments upstream, in particular in synthetic fibres.
- On the other hand, it also happened that resources were locked into activities which have been kept artificially more profitable by large producer rents. This may well have impeded diversification in small scale textile and clothing industries in some Asian NICs.

17.   On the whole, the experience of the last ten years shows that LDC exporters of manufactures have displayed remarkable flexibility and ingenuity in adjusting the commodity composition and geographical pattern of their trade flows in order to take maximum advantage of demand conditions in major markets while minimising the adverse impact of protection. This applies essentially to established LDC exporters, who not only took advantage of the specific nature of the protectionist instruments used, but also joined forces with OECD producers to keep out independent newcomers.

The implications of continuing protectionism

18.   The recent experience does not preclude the possibility that, under different circumstances, continuing protectionism or its accentuation could have a serious damaging impact on LDC exports. This in turn would have serious repercussions on the debt problem, on the economic performance of industrial countries and on the whole fabric of international economic relations.

Continuing protectionism and LDC exports

19.   Projections made by the World Bank in 1982 indicated a possible range of 4.7 per cent to 11.4 per cent in the annual real growth of LDC manufactured exports in the 1980s, following 14.0 per cent in the 1970s[12]. Alternative assumptions concerning protection account for part of the difference between high and low estimates, together with those made on growth in industrial countries. Similar projections made five years earlier had a range of 10.2 per cent to 14.2 per cent. This suggests that since then uncertainty about growth prospects and trade regimes in industrial countries had increased.

20.   As shown above, even the upper range of these projections proved to be too pessimistic so far. However, recent developments have created a highly unstable situation in which LDC exporters of manufactures critically depend on access to a single, though admittedly large, market. Hence in the event that US growth subsides and/or the exceptionally large trade deficit is reduced by compressing US imports in some other way, LDC exporters may find themselves in a precarious position where the stance of trade policies in various OECD countries could play a crucial role.

21. If access to OECD markets were to diminish, the impact on the various developing countries and products would be uneven. Given the flexibility that the more advanced NICs have demonstrated over recent years, they may have less reason to be concerned about protection in industrialised economies, even though prima facie they seem to be the chief target. The main casualties of protection are likely to be in the second and third generation of manufacturing exporters, including populous countries such as India, Bangladesh and Indonesia.

22. There are three main reasons for this.

— First, as some of these countries become more reliant on manufactured exports, further advances on industrial countries' markets will require additional skills, capital and technological capacity, all of which will be more difficult and costly to acquire than 10 or 15 years ago.

— Second, in some sectors, such as textiles and clothing, established exporting countries may be more interested in preserving market shares than pressing for overall liberalisation. As a result, the capacity of trade patterns to evolve on the basis of comparative advantage is undermined, making access more difficult for new suppliers. This is only partly offset by some discrimination in the MFA (and other restrictions) in favour of new suppliers, as long as they remain very small.

— Third, as the more advanced NICs diversify into other product groups, the second-tier LDCs — still frequently inexperienced in the export of manufactures — should normally move up to take their place. But they then find themselves entangled in a mesh of trade restrictions, and especially quotas, which bite all the harder as these countries try to expand exports quickly from a relatively small base. These countries are also handicapped by a lack of flexibility in their economies. They are frequently plagued by widespread domestic distortions caused by their own protectionism and subsidy practices.

Implications for the international debt situation

23. A continued healthy expansion of manufactured exports is becoming increasingly vital to LDCs. It constitutes an important link in the chain of maintaining their own demand for imports (notably for investment goods and other manufactures), servicing their external debt, and sustaining investment.

24. Debt service ratios for developing countries moved erratically during the 1970s, around 15-16 per cent, but increased sharply to 24.4 per cent in 1982 as interest rates rose and export earnings slowed down. Had developing countries been able to achieve in 1980-82 only half the average annual growth rate in export earnings they recorded in the 1970s, their 1982 debt service ratio would have been more than 4 percentage points lower[13]. The subsequent decline in the ratio to about 21-22 per cent in 1984 resulted almost entirely from the upsurge in export earnings. This highlights the interdependence of trade and financial performance.

Table 9.6

IMPORTS FROM MAJOR LDC DEBTORS TO THE OECD SUBJECT TO ACCESS BARRIERS, 1982

($US billion and percentages)

	Brazil	Mexico	Argentina	Chile	Korea	Indonesia	Philippines	Yugoslavia	All
Manufactured imports affected by non-tariff barriers (1) ($US billion)	1.8	0.4	0.2	0.01	6.8	0.2	0.6	0.8	10.8
-- As % of total OECD manufactured imports from that country	42.9	8.2	22.2	14.3	58.1	40.0	30.0	34.8	40.6
Agricultural imports (2) affected by non-tariff barriers ($US billion)	3.2	1.4	2.0		0.9	0.6	1.4	0.3	10.4
-- As % of total OECD agricultural imports from that country	51.6	73.7	100.0	95.0	98.0	54.5	93.3	68.2	74.8
Manufactured and agricultural imports affected by non-tariff barriers (1)(2) as % of total OECD imports from that country	35.7	8.0	55.0	21.0	58.3	4.3	41.7	31.4	25.3

1. Textiles, clothing, iron and steel, footwear, consumer electronics.

2. Meat, cereals, sugar, fish, vegetables and fruit, animal feeds, tobacco, vegetable oils.

Source: Cable: Protection and Interdependence, updated by Secretariat calculations.

25.   Given the high indebtedness and the small (or even negative) inflow of resources into most developing countries, export earnings will in future be a major determinant of their ability to invest. As capital itself becomes more of a constraint, there will be a much higher premium on its efficient use. The capacity to allocate investment on the basis of undistorted price signals, and secure access to world markets, is particularly important in this context.

26.   Clearly not all LDCs constrained by OECD protection have serious external debt problems (e.g. Taiwan, Singapore and Hong Kong)[14]. But particularly for those that do, the ability to expand export earnings depends critically on the extent to which their exports are concentrated in a few sectors which are seriously hampered or threatened by trade restrictions. In the case of eight major debtor countries in 1982, 25 per cent of their total OECD exports and over 40 per cent of their manufactured OECD exports were affected by non tariff barriers (Table 9.6).

27.   For five of these countries, Brazil, Argentina, Korea, the Philippines and Yugoslavia, a substantial rise in exports of restricted products (both manufactures and agricultural products) would make a major contribution to alleviating their problems of debt servicing, which totalled $28.7 billion in 1983. There is no detailed evidence yet, to what extent the recent increase in these countries' export earnings has taken place in the restricted categories.

28.   It should be noted in this context that the healthy growth of export earnings since 1982 has encouraged many heavily indebted LDCs to carry on the painful process of adjustment, without a wholesale shift to retrenchment. The process has not yet been completed and will require continued efforts by debtors and by creditors. The application of differential trade policies to debtors would not, however, prove an effective remedy, as it would lead to further distortions of the multilateral trading system.

Increased protection and economic performance

29.   An increase in protection beyond present levels would in all probability be very costly not only to the developing countries but also to the industrial economies.

30.   First, significant economic efficiency losses and feedback effects would be involved. Very little work has been done to trace and quantify the international interactions arising from a possible tightening of trade restrictions. One study merits particular attention. Calculations have been carried out with the Brussels world model to assess the implications of a gradual increase in protection (import licences, quotas, VERs) equivalent to a 15 percentage point rise in tariffs. The model forecasts a significant reduction by 1995 of GDP both in developing and developed countries. Middle income oil-importing LDCs, it is projected, would sustain a loss in GDP of 3.4 per cent, i.e. hardly more than the 3.3 per cent decrease the industrial countries would suffer, chiefly as a result of the self-inflicted effects of their own protective measures[15].

31.   Second, a further rise in the level of protection imposed by industrial countries might tip the scales towards a crucial shift in policy stance in developing countries:

- As an increasing number of product categories and developing countries are affected by restrictive trade measures, the scope for product diversification, geographical relocation of production and penetration of new markets could decline markedly at a time when demand conditions on these markets become less favourable.
- As a result there is a greater risk, particularly among the second and third generation NICs, of a shift to export pessimism and policies of inward-looking, import-replacing industrialisation.
- Finally, in such a context, the credibility of the developed countries' requests for a gradual dismantling of protection in developing countries is undermined.

32. So far, increasing protection has had more effect on the commodity composition and geographical patterns of LDC exports than on the aggregate level of their export earnings. The future balance of impacts will depend on whether trade relations are conducted basically in a framework of free trade with few exceptions, or in a framework in which free trade itself is the exception.

NOTES AND REFERENCES

1. In the Tokyo Round, as in the Kennedy Round, average tariff reductions on LDC imports were smaller than the average for all imports. Weighted tariff averages on total imports of semi and finished manufactures fell by 30 per cent in the United States, 28 per cent in the EEC and 46 per cent in Japan. Tariffs on imports from LDCs decreased by only 24 per cent, 25 per cent and 32 per cent respectively. See Balassa and Balassa: 1984.

2. Cable: 1981.

3. World Bank, mimeo, 1977.

4. UNCTAD, unpublished.

5. Cable: "Protection and Interdependence", mimeo, 1984.

6. Valdes and Zeitz: 1980.

7. Birnberg: 1979.

8. Hughes and Newbery: 1984.

9. Cavanagh and Machel: 1983.

10. Group 2 in Table 9.5 consisting of Chile, Columbia, Malaysia, Morocco, Peru, Philippines, Thailand, Tunisia, Turkey.

11. Group 3 consists of Bangladesh, Egypt, India, Indonesia, Pakistan, Sri Lanka.

12. World Development Report, 1982.

13. World Development Report, 1983.

14. Conversely, a number of LDCs are heavily indebted but largely unaffected by OECD protection, notably some of the oil exporting countries.

15. World Bank Development Report, 1983.

Chapter 10

THE POLITICS AND ECONOMICS OF PROTECTION

1.   Ultimately trade policy is a matter of politics. Whether protectionism spreads depends on the domestic and international political process. Are the protectionist measures adopted in recent years simply the result of sluggish growth and high unemployment? Or are they symptomatic of diminished resilience of the multilateral trading system?

2.   Trade policy decisions by governments are the result of two sets of factors: pressures coming from the domestic interest groups whose well-being is affected by trade; and government trade objectives, determined in part by the country's broader international interests and obligations. In turn, international trade agreements, and the obligations they give rise to, reflect the advantages of international policy coordination. But their successful development and implementation depends in large part on the distribution of international power among actors.

3.   This implies that changes in domestic and international trade policy can be analysed as a function of four factors:

- The costs and benefits of trade flows for domestic political actors, which shapes the demand for and resistance to protection;
- Governments' objectives and ability to cope with protectionist pressures, which sets the supply of protection;
- The perceived need and advantages of international agreements in satisfying government objectives, which sets the demand for international action;
- International constraints, which impede or facilitate the development of international accords.

The domestic politics of protection

4.   The slowing of economic growth subsequent to 1973/74 did not reduce the increasing interpenetration of markets. Particularly in manufactures, trade expanded more rapidly (or declined less) than real output in every year except 1975. This was reflected in an increase of the ratio of exports and imports to domestic output and supplies at current prices in the major OECD economies.

184

5. Growing interdependence has not, however, been a frictionless process. Rather, three interrelated factors have generated greater demands for protection. First, major shifts in the structure and dynamics of the OECD's trading relations have increased the need for adjustment. Second, the costs of adjustment have been aggravated by slower, more unstable growth, which puts downward pressure on profits, wages and employment in a number of industrial sectors. In this context, exchange rate volatility has often had a ratchet effect on protection. Third, pervasive rigidities — reflected since the late 1960s in the declining ability of OECD economies to adapt to rapid change — have encouraged interest groups to seek insulation from market forces.

Structural shifts in trade

6. Two features marked trade expansion in the twenty years prior to 1973: trade in manufactures was primarily among the developed countries and notably within regional trading blocks, in particular the EEC and EFTA; and intra-industry trade grew in significance. Since the oil crisis, shifts in the centres of dynamism in the world economy have altered this pattern.

7. Supply within the OECD region has become increasingly competitive and multipolar. This is partly due to the continuing "catch-up" of the Western European economies with that of the United States. However, the dominant factor has been the trend rise of Japan as a major exporter both to the OECD and to third markets. This trend — already evident in the latter half of the 1960s — accelerated sharply after 1978 (Graph 10.1).

8. Unlike the United States earlier, Japan has translated its technological and cost advantage mainly into exports, rather than direct foreign investment — seeming to reduce the benefits to other countries from this advantage, particularly in terms of employment. The competitive impact of these exports has also been magnified by their concentration in a small number of industries, and by the low levels of interpenetration between Japan's industries and those of its trading partners, either through intra-industry trade or through foreign direct investment into Japan. Invulnerable to retaliation on their home market, Japanese firms have tended to act as aggressive outsiders in oligopolistic industries, seeking long-run market share rather than high short-term margins[1].

9. The dominant place of intra-OECD trade and investment flows has also been eroded, as non-OECD countries became increasingly important suppliers to the OECD region and to each other. At the same time, the developing countries have become important markets for OECD exports and host (and home) countries for foreign direct investment. This has been the result of two factors: first, the resource transfer implicit in the increase in the real price of oil bolstered the share of energy in the value of world trade and created a vast OPEC market for agricultural and manufactured exports; and second, the resilience in the 1970s of economic growth in many oil-importing developing countries expanded their demand for imports.

10. The OECD countries have therefore faced a dual challenge: to adjust to the greater import competition coming from the more dynamic LDCs; and to seize the new export and

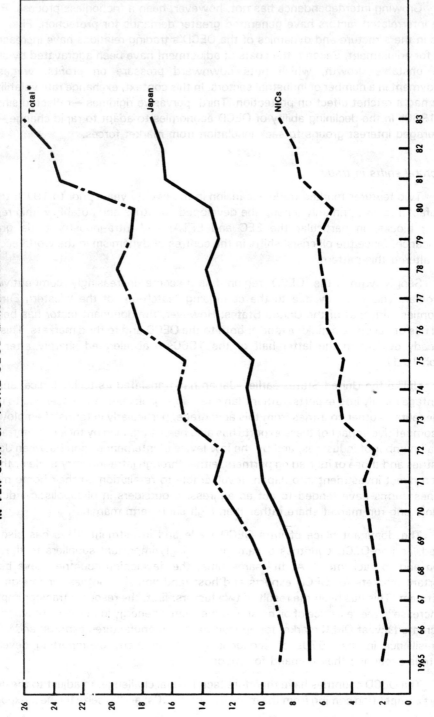

Graph 10.1.

OECD IMPORTS OF MANUFACTURES FROM JAPAN AND THE NICs
IN PER CENT OF TOTAL OECD MANUFACTURED IMPORTS

Total*

Japan

NICs

* Japan, Singapore, Hong Kong, Korea, Taiwan, Mexico, Brazil.

Source : OECD, Foreign Trade Statistics.

investment opportunities this same process has created. The structural features of this challenge have accentuated the competitive pressures to which it gives rise:

- The NICs' exports of manufactures are concentrated on a limited number of product categories, within which the ratio of exports to imports is high. Exports in these categories are more than balanced by imports of other manufactures, principally investment goods, but the level of intra-industry trade is low[2].
- Though increasingly sophisticated, NIC exports are mainly in products characterised by low product differentiation and intense price competition. In their attempts to penetrate new markets, NIC producers naturally tend to rely on price advantage rather than on advertising and extensive distribution networks.

11.   The characteristics of the new markets created for OECD producers by rising incomes in the LDCs have also generated intense competitive pressures:

- Both in OPEC and NIC markets, the lack of well-established suppliers has generally meant that customer loyalty, "switching costs"[3] and other entry barriers are weak. A broad range of OECD producers can therefore compete for contracts.
- In a vast potential market, producers are willing to incur short-run losses for the sake of gaining an entrenched market position and a continuing flow-on of sales. Moreover, the huge size of individual contracts, especially for turnkey plants and public infrastructures, has tended to focus rivalry on a relatively small number of individual contests, each of which is seen as having major consequences for the firms concerned.
- Lastly, the competitive pressures bearing on OECD suppliers have been heightened by the rapid expansion into OPEC markets of producers from the NICs and by the fact that both public and private purchasers in these importing countries are increasingly sophisticated in their sourcing of imports[4].

Adjustment in a recessionary context

12.   The adjustment pressures arising from shifting trade patterns have been aggravated by slower growth and greater instability in the international economy[5]. Slower growth itself exacerbates international competition. As domestic markets grow less rapidly, companies naturally seek new outlets overseas. They have been encouraged in this by their national governments, for balance of payments as well as employment motivations. More generally, the slower growth of world markets has made even relatively small shifts in the structure of international trade more difficult to absorb, increasing the importance of flexibility as a determinant of competitiveness.

13.   Adjustment pressures have been accentuated by:

- Increased variability in real exchange rates, apparent exchange rate misalignments and rapid changes in the strength of domestic demand (and hence capacity utilisation)[6].

187

— The convergence of OECD countries' technology levels (and in particular of the United States' and Japan's), the growing share of high-technology products in world trade, the shortening of technology diffusion lags and, probably, of product life cycles, may have made technology-based competitive advantages more precarious than in the past.

14. As a result, export markets for manufactures have become increasingly unstable, with a substantial rise in the yearly variance of countries' market shares. Moreover, the pressure of competing imports — in addition to being in absolute terms greater — has become more unpredictable, with a frequent threat of import "surges", that is, sudden large changes in import penetration[7].

15. Adverse trends in factor incomes have made these shifts in competitiveness more difficult to absorb. From the late 1960s, profit margins and rates of return have tended to decline in the main OECD countries, reflecting a slowing of productivity and output growth, wage resistance and adverse distributional shifts. This accelerating decline was only stopped and reversed in the early 1980s.

16. Though evidence is available for only a limited number of countries, cross-section analysis shows that the decline in margins has been particularly sharp in the concentrated industries most open to import competition[8]. At the same time, good export performance — measured by the ratio of exports to shipments — appears not to have had any positive impact on margins, suggesting that the profitability of export sales has been low and possibly declining[9]. Overall, the more exposed parts of the traded goods industries appear to have faced the greatest constraints in passing on increases in costs.

17. Paralleling these impacts of trade on the return to capital are impacts on labour. In assessing the latter, what must be examined are the earnings losses (or gains) due to changes in international competition. These changes in earnings arise from trade related shifts in

i) employment levels,
ii) the earnings of those displaced from employment and
iii) the earnings of those who retain their jobs.

18. With respect to employment levels, there has certainly been a prima facie relationship at an industry level between import penetration and the scale of employment losses. Despite the growth of intra-industry trade, employment has tended to decline more rapidly in the industries with above average import penetration[10].

19. Disparities in labour force composition mean that greater export volumes — though doubtless creating jobs — have not been perceived as offsetting the employment effect of increased imports:

— Though the share of intra-industry trade has continued to increase in Europe, a considerable part of the labour force remains in industries very asymmetrically affected by import and export activity[11].
— Particularly in trade with the developing countries, increased imports tend to be concentrated in the consumer goods industries (and some intermediate

Table 10.2

LABOUR CONTENT OF IMPORTS AS A MULTIPLE OF THE LABOUR CONTENT
OF EXPORTS FOR SELECTED OECD COUNTRIES, 1980 (a)

	Trade with		
	OECD countries	Developing countries	State trading countries (b)
Germany	1.06	1.31	1.15
France	1.02	1.32	1.23
Italy	0.88	1.15	1.09
United Kingdom	0.98	1.19	1.07
Netherlands	1.05	1.16	1.18
Belgium	1.06	1.28	1.28
USA	0.94	1.41	1.13
Japan	1.08	1.38	0.96

a)   Per \$US billion of imports and exports at 1977 prices and sectoral
labour productivities of the respective OECD country. The trade
figures cover SITC 5-8 excluding ores, metals and mineral products,
broken down according to the commodity structure in the individual
years. The calculation of the labour content only considers direct
requirements.
b)   In Europe.

Source   Calculated on the basis of background material to A. Sapir and
D. Schumacher (1984).

products) while increased exports are largely generated by the industries
producing investment goods[12].
- More generally, the labour intensity of imports and exports is different,
particularly in trade with the developing countries (Table 10.2). Predictably,
the skill content of imports into the main OECD economies is lower than the
skill content of exports. This gap in skill composition may have even increased
over time, as the importance to the advanced OECD economies of low-skill
labour-intensive exports diminishes[13].
- The geographical distribution of the labour force in import-competing and
export-oriented industries differs substantially in a number of OECD countries.
This is particularly clear in the United States, where a more far-reaching shift
in the regional structure of industry is underway; and in the mature industries
in Europe, especially steel, shipbuilding, textiles, clothing and footwear, which
tend to be highly geographically concentrated.

20. Turning to the effect of earnings losses as a result of displacement, if labour displaced from one industry could readily find work in another at equal conditions of employment, the costs of displacement would be low, even if the numbers affected were high. This implies that the overall costs of unemployment to displaced workers will be greater (i) the longer the duration of their unemployment; and (ii) the greater the reduction in their earnings as a result of changing jobs:

- During the 1970s and early 1980s, the mean duration of unemployment increased sharply in the OECD region, as did the incidence of long-term unemployment.

- While this in itself would have raised the costs of displacement, the mean duration of unemployment has tended to increase more for employees in import competing industries than overall, at least in the United States (the only country for which systematic evidence is available)[14]. This presumably reflects the greater regional concentration and cyclical sensitivity of some of the import competing industries.

21. The evidence regarding changes in earnings subsequent to displacement is much less clear:

- Throughout the 1960s and early 1970s, the import competing labour force was mainly concentrated in the textiles, clothing and footwear and light manufacturing industries, where wage levels are relatively low and turnover rates high. If workers displaced from these industries ultimately find jobs in better-paying industries, their lifetime earnings losses may be low[15].

- By contrast, the prospects for employees in the industries more recently affected by the combined impact of trade flows and adverse macro-economic developments, such as steel and automobiles are not encouraging. They benefit from a monopoly rent element in their wage levels (which in a number of countries are well above the manufacturing average), and from the accumulation of sector and firm specific human capital, reflected in relatively low levels of voluntary quits and highly differentiated internal earnings structures. As a result, displacement from these industries has substantial adverse impacts on employees' expected lifetime earnings[16].

22. Finally, through their impact on wage-setting behaviour, changes in trade patterns may also affect workers who remain employed. In particular, greater import penetration may constrain real wage increases in the industries most exposed to foreign competition; while employees in industries increasing their export sales may benefit from higher levels of labour demand. Little research has been carried out on these questions. Nonetheless, two points can be made:

- Over the period 1971-1979 unit labour costs increased less rapidly in the industries most exposed to import competition than in manufacturing as a whole, in Canada, Sweden and the United Kingdom, (but not in the United States shielded by currency depreciation)[17], as increases in labour productivity in these industries have not been passed on into higher wages.

- There was not a significant difference in rates of increase in unit labour costs between export oriented industries and those primarily serving domestic markets[18], again suggesting that the compensatory effect of exports may have been very limited.

23.   The overall implications of these data seem consistent with the post-1979 experience. In particular, growing recognition of the intensity of international competition contributed to increased wage moderation from late 1981 on and — especially in the United States — to the spread of concession bargaining. This in turn may have played a part in changing "wage leader" patterns of inter-industry wage determination, reducing the trend-setter role of the more highly unionised import-competing sectors[19].

24.   In summary, international competition has had a significant impact on sectoral factor incomes in the OECD:

— The destabilisation of some mature oligopolies (both on domestic and export markets) as a result of the entry of new competitors has contributed to compress profit margins in concentrated industries.

— There has been a stronger association between import penetration and employment losses in industry, while the cost of unemployment to those displaced has increased. Moreover, import competition may have affected those who remained employed through its impact on wage setting.

Diminished flexibility

25.   Though facing sharply changing conditions, OECD economies have exhibited diminished flexibility over most of the 1960s and 1970s, mainly as a result of growing government involvement in the economy, changes in the organisation of production, and in the functioning of labour markets[20]. With respect to the role of government in the economy:

— Direct controls on factor markets, such as those bearing on access to bank credit or on the sale of securities, can distort factor price signals and impede rapid adjustment[21];

— "Social" regulation, involving health, safety and environmental standards, may raise the costs of adapting products and processes to new technological opportunities[22];

— Public enterprises, which accounted in the 1970s for an increasing share of industrial output in many European countries, may privilege social and political, rather than economic, considerations in their decision-making[23].

26.   Particularly in Europe, the average size of plants, levels of capital intensity, and the share of fixed costs in total costs, increased substantially, at least until the early 1970s[24]. At the same time, work organisation and skills were affected by the spread of mass production techniques, with greater emphasis being placed on task standardization and simplification. This had two implications:

— Break-even points tended to increase, heightening the importance of long planning horizons and raising vulnerability to shifts in demand and comparative advantage;

- Changes in product design and mix became more costly, as they involved modifications to intricate and interdependent systems of specialised machinery[25].

27. Labour markets may also have become less effective in reallocating human resources among areas of activity. There is surprisingly little solid empirical work in this area, but a number of factors can be identified:

- Increasingly sophisticated production technologies have required greater investment in human capital, much of it specific to particular industries or occupations.
- Changes in collective bargaining, notably the indexation of contracts, may have eroded the efficacy of wage differentials as signals for industrial and occupational labour mobility.
- Constraints on hiring and firing procedures increase the "quasi-fixed" element of labour costs, and can slow labour turnover.
- Rising home ownership, increases in average school leaving age, and a greater prevalence of two income households, may all have reduced geographical mobility at a time when the outflow of labour from agriculture was practically completed and immigration was curbed.

28. In sum, structural shifts in trade, a slowdown in the world economy and volatile exchange rates have put increasing pressure on import competing industries. Yet the diminished flexibility of OECD economies has prevented rapid adaptation and encouraged affected groups to press for protection. The result has been a marked increase in demand for controls on imports.

The supply of protection: Government response to pressure

29. Changes in the size and distribution of the costs and benefits of trade create a "potential demand" for protection. Whether this leads to protectionist measures will depend on the capacity of the groups affected by trade to express this demand through the political system, and on the receptiveness of decision-makers to sectoral interests. In very general terms, two tendencies can be identified:

- The permeability of political systems to sectional demands has increased.
- The range of policy options governments have for dealing with these demands has diminished.

Interest group pressure

30. Specific interest groups play an increasing role in public decision making. The growing size and importance of the public sector in the OECD economies has itself been a factor in this regard, as a wider range of resource allocation decisions involve a political element. Economic and social actors have therefore acquired new incentives to become politically organised, as the frequency and density of their contacts with government rises.

192

31.   Faced with intensifying trade competition, a growing number of specific interest groups increasingly find it worthwhile to organise independently to press for protection. This has had two inter-related implications[26]:

-    Interest representation has become increasingly fragmented. Specific sectional or sectoral interest groups have become stronger relative to their parent organisations — that is broadly-based, economy-wide employers' associations and trade unions. This trend has been most pronounced in countries with historically weak central organisations.

-    Interest group access to the political system occurs on an increasingly issue-specific basis — that is, demands are placed on governments to meet specific needs and concerns of particular groups.

32.   The bargaining agenda between governments and interest groups tends to be influenced by these changes in the structure of interest representation. Three features distinguish central organisations relative to sectional interest groups: first, they are more likely to be aware of the macro-economic implications of their behaviour. Second, the interests of any particular section, for example the import-competing industries, are more likely to be balanced out by those of other sections before they enter the political system. Third, this balancing can be done at fairly low costs since it occurs within an established and ongoing organisational framework. As a result, their negotiating agenda will focus on economy-wide issues of income distribution and social welfare.

33.   In contrast, sectional interest groups are likely to take macro-economic performance as independent of their behaviour. Their members will generally benefit less from an improvement in the economy as a whole — and have less scope for securing such an improvement — than from a policy targeted to their individual needs. Since the balancing of sectional interests in countries without strong central organisation occurs through the political system itself, this creates greater scope for "log-rolling", that is for votes to be traded across interest group lines on the basis of differing intensities of preference[27]. The counterbalancing of sectional interests may involve high costs — since complicated trade-offs must be made, ad hoc bargaining procedures established, and ways of preventing opportunism identified[28]. The distribution of a given total income, rather than increasing the "size of the pie", may dominate the negotiating agenda of governments.

34.   Within this negotiating agenda, the spread of narrowly organised sectoral interests favours those seeking protection at the expense of those whom protection would harm. Protection from imports imposes direct costs on consumers, through its price effects, and indirect costs on export-oriented industries and regions through its effects on exchange rates and domestic input prices. Generally, producer interests — including those of exporters — can be organised more effectively than can the diffuse and heterogeneous mass of consumers. As a result, the organised interests of exporters have been, and remain, a dominant and powerful force opposing any reversion to generalised import controls and promoting broadly-based trade liberalisation.

35.   However, protectionist measures taken on a highly sector specific basis will have only a very small adverse impact on any single export-oriented firm, particularly in a

context of continuing reductions in overall tariff levels. Moreover, for any single export oriented firm, impeding such protectionist measures would have a strong "public good" aspect, since the firm in question would obtain only a small share of the resulting expansion in social income. In this environment it becomes very difficult to establish and maintain coalitions opposed to protection:

- A large number of relatively minor policy decisions must be monitored and opposed.
- While the costs each of these decisions imposes on coalition members are small, real trade-offs will have to be provided if the decisions are to be prevented.
- Finally, there are few opportunities in the policy process for reviewing and revising the operation of trade policy as a whole.

36. It is consequently not surprising that export-oriented interests have preferred to lobby for policies which directly promote exports rather than against protectionist policies which reduce them indirectly.

The receptiveness of government

37. Changes in interest group organisation have substantially modified the environment of trade policy. As trade flows come to affect a rising share of economic actors, and as actors are increasingly organised to advance their sectional interests, the conduct of trade policy becomes more politicised. The scope for technocratic decision-making diminishes, though the issues to be dealt with are more complex.

38. Faced with sectional pressures, governments can be viewed as using a portfolio of policy instruments to maintain a target level of political consensus, both because consensus is a societal goal in itself, and so as to increase their chances of re-election. Two important constraints bear on this process:

- The sensitivity of electoral performance to sectoral income maintenance;
- The range of instruments in the policy portfolio, the costs and benefits of each instrument, and the trade-offs between instruments.

39. There is some evidence that electoral patterns have become more unstable, as voters respond more rapidly to perceptions of the government's failure in meeting their requirements[29]. Higher levels of education, urbanisation, social mobility, the changing role of religion as a social force, and the growing participation of women in the labour force, have all reduced the extent to which voters' choices are made on the basis of class, regional or religious loyalty. In turn, greater electoral volatility means that governments resisting sectional interests cannot count for their re-election on inertia in political choices. The maintenance of support among powerful electoral groups therefore acquires higher priority.

40. The range of instruments governments can use to retain electoral support is partly conditioned by political and ideological traditions. In some countries, such as the United States, the economic ideology prevalent among decision-makers is one of meeting economic objectives through vigorous inter-firm competition. As a result, anti-trust

considerations have played an important role in shaping government-industry relations. The philosophy of avoiding direct intervention in production through subsidies or other forms of visible financial assistance leads affected import competing groups to primarily seek government help through trade protection. In other countries, such as France or Japan, government policy makers may try to pursue industrial policy objectives by combining intervention in trade and production. The underlying premise is usually that these interventions can promote adjustment processes more efficiently and at lower cost than pure trade intervention.

41.   A second factor affecting choices within the policy portfolio is the cost-effectiveness of the various instruments. In the post-war period, governments have primarily sought to maintain electoral support through growth-enhancing macro-economic policies and broadly-based welfare and income redistribution schemes. The efficacy of these policy instruments has declined drastically. In a more integrated world economy, the international constraints bearing on each government's policy choices have become increasingly tight. External constraints and internal rigidities have made it impossible to achieve and maintain full employment solely by stimulating aggregate demand. Budgetary considerations limit the further growth of transfer payments through the welfare system. Regional policies, while possibly having some effect on the location of industries in periods of expansion, have had less impact as fewer decisions are made to open new plants.

42.   This has increased the political attractiveness of narrowly focused protectionist measures as an instrument of consensus maintenance. Such measures:

— provide implicit subsidies that can be easily modulated according to the political importance of sectional interests.
— are highly visible to the groups to which they are targeted while their costs are typically thinly spread.
— do not require matching increases in taxation to maintain budgetary balance.

43.   The "new" forms of protection are particularly attractive in these respects. VERs and OMAs impose a tax on imports far less visible than that imposed by tariffs. Anti-dumping and countervailing duty measures are clearly legitimate instruments of policy; but they can confer the aura of "fairness" to actions with a protectionist motivation. The administered nature of these instruments removes them from public scrutiny, further disarming their potential opponents.

44.   In turn, the granting of protection to particular sectors — in the form of import restrictions or subsidies — generates a momentum in the political system as a whole. The visibility of the protection accorded to one interest group incites other groups to seek it; protection gains legitimacy from its repeated use; and equity considerations make it difficult to refuse comparable treatment to groups in comparable situations.

45.   Yet policy makers realise that protection is hardly an ideal instrument of economic policy, particularly when it passes a fairly small threshold share of economic activity. The conviction persists that a liberal trading regime is ultimately in each country's best

interest. More fundamentally, the threat of international retaliation, and the consequences of a generalised reversion to protection, have provided an excellent argument for resisting the mounting pressure of sectional interest groups.

46. But as protection is accorded to a growing range of groups, the precedent of previous action progressively weakens this argument. Governments seeking to re-affirm their international obligations with respect to a particular sector find both their own transgressions in other sectors and those of foreign governments being cited as arguments for protection. From being an obstacle to protectionist measures, the international system can become a transmitter of the pressures for them.

The international dimension

47. Inevitably, controls on imports affect income levels not only in the country which adopts them, but also in the exporting countries facing restraints. Moreover, a rational option for a country adversely affected by foreign trade restrictions may be to itself restrict imports. Both countries may be worse off with bilateral import restrictions than with bilateral free trade. But they may still each believe that they are better off than by unilaterally adopting free trade while the other country continues to restrict. This interdependence in policy choices — a version of the well known "prisoner's dilemma" — creates a need for international cooperation, which can be pursued on a bilateral or a multilateral basis.

48. An important feature of the early post-war period was the shift to multilateral instruments in the framing of trade policy. In particular, the principles, norms, rules and procedures embodied in the GATT provided a framework for the liberalisation of world trade on an MFN basis, while creating a multilateral framework for regional integration. The factors underlying this successful shift from bilateralism to multilateralism, and the subsequent evolution of this balance, can be analysed by focusing on the incentives and constraints which countries face in negotiating such international regimes[30]:

The incentives for developing international arrangements

49. Countries face three basic incentives for pursuing trade cooperation on a multilateral rather than bilateral basis. The first arises from the scale effects of international agreements:

- Most multilateral economic agreements — and particularly those liberalising trade — have the character of quasi-public goods. Though non-participants may be excluded from the direct benefits, they will eventually gain some share of the benefits of liberalisation, especially when it is carried out on a large scale. The greater the range of participants, the more willing countries will be to make concessions.
- When there are economies of scale in production, the total benefits of liberalisation to participants may increase more than proportionally with the range of trade affected. This feature will be of particular importance to smaller countries.

196

50.   Second, multilateralism may be more cost-effective than purely bilateral approaches in securing agreement:

- An internationally accepted multilateral framework of rules and procedures reduces the "transactions costs" countries incur in negotiating and implementing multiple bilateral bargains.
- Through multilateral agreements, the effects of all concessions can be aggregated, whereby each country achieves its objectives at the lowest cost in terms of concessions.
- The indefinite duration of the regimes means that a balance of benefits can be achieved over time; even if a country does not gain today from observing the established rules, it can assume that it will do so tomorrow.
- Low cost procedures can be established for monitoring compliance and exchanging information, and special arrangements made for consultation, dispute settlement and compensation.

51.   Third, governments may favour multilateral agreements to control other actors – both domestic interest groups and other countries[31]:

- By binding themselves to international agreements countries can pursue their objectives with respect to other governments by appealing to "neutral" rules and procedures which apply to all, rather than through the exercise of direct pressure on trading partners. Small countries who rely heavily on trade are particularly supportive of such rules since they provide a stable environment for commerce.
- Pressures from domestic interest groups can be partially contained by appealing to a country's international obligations as embodied in arrangements to which they are a party.

The constraints on developing international arrangements

52.   While countries may have numerous incentives to develop or abide by multilateral agreements, creating these arrangements and adapting them to a changing context can involve substantial political costs. Countries must be enticed to commit themselves to agreements which are vulnerable to abuse by other participants. If a country participates, it may have to renounce some of its autonomy in coping with domestic pressures. Conversely, the country may be able to appropriate some of the benefits of other countries' participation without itself participating or even observing the broad rules.

53.   Historically, the capability of the international system to overcome these costs has depended on the distribution of economic and political power. The presence in the world system of a strong country, accounting for a substantial share of power resources, has played a crucial role for three reasons[32]:

- When there is a clearly dominant power in the world system, smaller countries stand to gain from multilateral rule setting. These rules protect them from arbitrary and divisive action and allow them to coalesce in the bargaining process.

- The dominant power still derives large benefits from the multilateral regime. This is both because of its economic strength and of its large relative size. It can "internalise" a greater share of the external benefits generated by the trade system.
- Given these benefits, the dominant power is in a position to compensate mid-sized countries for participating in the trade regime, both through concessions and by linking trade issues with broader economic and political concerns.

Changes in international arrangements

54.   Combined, the above factors explain the successful development of the GATT, the primary thrust of which has been to promote trade liberalisation. Yet unlike earlier bilateral attempts at free-trade diplomacy, the rules and procedures of the GATT have always envisaged the possibility that, under given circumstances, a country may temporarily restrict its imports. Recourse to import controls should not, therefore, be seen as prima facie evidence of a weakening in the multilateral trade regime.

55.   In effect, contrary to the expectations of some analysts, the GATT has maintained its resilience, as evident from the new Codes agreed to in the Tokyo Round. Many of the factors which explain the success and stability of the multilateral trade regime persist. Multilateral arrangements are still seen as reducing organisation and information costs in negotiating bilateral agreements and as providing an indispensible framework for the orderly and predictable conduct of world trade.

56.   Nonetheless, the inference of some weakening in the GATT can be drawn from two aspects of the recent evolution of trade policy:

- The growing range of products subject to import restrictions, and the fact that restrictions are increasingly applied in a bilateral framework contrary to the letter and/or the spirit of the GATT, notably as regards discrimination and compensation;
- The difficulties experienced in extending the multilateral rules and procedures of the GATT to other areas of activity (services, agriculture) and adapting them to sudden changes in the position of trading partners (safeguards).

57.   Three important changes underlie this weakening of the GATT and the declining incentives and constraints to maintain multilateralism[33]. First, the expanding number of participants in international trade negotiations, and the growing diversity of their interests, points of view and technical capabilities, has reduced the efficacy of multilateral fora. The widening agenda of multilateral negotiations fragments each participating country's power resources, rather than allowing their effective deployment in the bargaining process. There is a danger that bilateral bargains, where agendas can be more clearly defined, and issue-linkages more systematically exploited, appear as an increasingly attractive alternative to multilateralism.

58.   Second, in many instances, the trade conflicts to be dealt with have in any case not been perceived as multilateral in nature, but as arising primarily from new sources of

supply and/or a few very dynamic competitors. Far from increasing the returns to negotiation, it was felt that trying to solve these conflicts through multilateral instruments would have imposed costs on a broad range of "innocent bystanders", that is, countries not viewed as responsible for market disruption.

59. Finally, the political will necessary to reinforce the multilateral system, and restore its liberalising dynamic, may have weakened, despite the successes registered in the Tokyo Round. In a context of sluggish growth, and in a more multi-polar world, with a more equal distribution of power resources than prevailed in the 1950s and 1960s, it has been difficult to secure and implement international consensus for bringing the management of conflict back into the established multilateral structures.

60. In seeking to preserve those parts of the multilateral trading system which create large mutual benefits, trade policy-makers have therefore tended to segregate the major problem areas out of the multilateral system of conflict resolution. Moreover, they have increasingly resorted to bilateral instruments — such as VERs and OMAs — which provide for bargaining flexibility, and where the agreement itself automatically gives some advantages to the restricted suppliers. However, this has compromised the legitimacy and perceived usefulness of the multilateral system itself.

The outlook for policy

61. Trade policy makers have therefore had to face four interacting sources of pressure. Domestically, structural change has increased the direct costs of adjustment to economic actors while the capacity of these actors to express their grievances through the political system has increased. Internationally, the incentives for maintaining multilateral arrangements have been weakened and the credibility of international commitments undermined.

62. In part, the bunching of structural changes in the 1970s, occurring in a context of prolonged recession, had a traumatic character to which the more mature economies have responded through a painful process of adjustment. Though the nature of this ongoing process has differed from country to country, three common characteristics can be identified:

- Even within the traditional manufacturing sector, changes in corporate strategy, production technology and the functioning of internal labour markets are substantially enhancing firms' flexibility in dealing with changing patterns of competitiveness[34].
- Firms most adversely affected by protectionism, and notably the Japanese suppliers, increasingly take the threat of protectionist measures into account in framing their international strategies. As a result, they are more careful to preserve oligopolistic equilibria, or at least to provide powerful actors in the importing country with tangible benefits from changes in the distribution of market power.
- The structure of activity in the advanced economies has changed. There has been a sustained run-down of employment and productive capacity in

industries facing severe adjustment difficulties — textiles and clothing, steel, shipbuilding and so on. This has been accompanied by an accelerated transfer of resources into high-technology manufacturing and services, though to a differing extent in the various Member countries.

63. As structural adjustment proceeds, the trade conflicts arising from greater multipolarity and interdependence should diminish. However, much will depend on the outcome of the present disinflationary process. In a sustained and more balanced recovery, which improves the macro-economic context of world trade, it should be much easier to absorb the pervasive changes in competitive advantage which characterise a dynamic economy.

64. More fundamentally, the process may alter the challenges which the OECD countries must face, particularly in their relations with the developing economies. Continued high real interest rates may reduce the viability of certain of these economies' industrialisation strategies, slowing their growth and leading them to revise their approaches to trade and investment. Whether they can retain their dynamism as both exporters to and importers from the OECD countries remains to be seen. In this changing economic context, the problems of debt and of financial relations may dominate those of trade — though the interaction of these problems will remain strong.

65. Despite an improved macro-economic and trade context, powerful pressure groups will continue to seek protection from international competition. Whether the resistance of the trade policy system to sectional pressures can be increased will be a major factor in determining the future of the multilateral trading system[35]. Improved evaluation and knowledge of the costs and benefits of protection can clearly play an important role in this regard.

66. Even in a more favourable trade and domestic policy environment, the system of multilateral cooperation cannot be expected to right itself automatically[36]. Nonetheless, there are reasons for optimism. In particular, new actors have emerged with an interest in maintaining and extending an open trading regime. These include parts of the high technology and service industries, and the financial institutions based in the OECD area with the greatest stakes in the economic viability of the indebted developing countries. Consumer organisations are also increasingly active in opposing protectionist measures. Much will rest on the capacity of these actors to mobilise in defence of their interests, and the willingness of national governments to place the interests of future-oriented activities at the top of the multilateral agenda.

NOTES AND REFERENCES

1. According to Secretariat calculations from OECD trade data, the Grubel-Lloyd index of intra-industry trade for Japan was in 1980 20 points lower than that for the United States and nearly 40 points lower than that for the EC countries. Moreover, in marked contrast to other OECD countries, the value of this index declined in the 1970s. On the product concentration of Japan's exports see Messerlin: 1984. The low level of FDI in Japanese manufacturing is discussed in OECD: 1979 (Penetration of Multinational Enterprises in Manufacturing Industry). Finally, Imai and Sakuma: 1984; Caves and Uekusa: 1976 and Tsurumi: 1976 examine the fragility of oligopolistic coordination among Japanese firms and their emphasis on market-share expansion.

2. Havrylshyn: 1982 and 1983.

3. "Switching Costs" are the once-off costs purchasers incur in changing supplier.

4. Wilkinson: 1983 finds, for example, that former colonial ties are an increasingly poor predictor of sourcing patterns for LDC imports.

5. OECD: 1979 (Facing the Future), pp.133-160; Michalski: 1979.

6. See, for example, Helleiner: 1981.

7. A rough calculation made by the Secretariat using 4-digit SITC data shows the year-on-year variance of export shares for manufactures increasing by approximately half in the period 1974-1981 relative to 1965-1971. Similar calculations also show that the number of 3-digit ISIC categories experiencing a rise in import penetration of 10 percentage points or more in one year tended to increase in most of the developed OECD economies during the 1970s, almost doubling, for example, for the United States.

8. Encaoua: 1983.

9. Encaoua: 1983; Jacquemin: 1982; Jacquemin et al., 1980.

10. In France, for example, 60 per cent of the 1973 manufacturing labour force was employed in industries which over the period 1973-1980 experienced both an above-average increase in import penetration and an absolute decline in employment levels. This was three times the proportion for the period 1959-73. A similar increase occurred in the United Kingdom and − though to a lesser extent − in Germany.

11. In France, for example, some 35 per cent of 1979-80 manufacturing employment was in industries with import penetration 50 per cent higher or 50 per cent lower than the manufacturing average.

12. Schumacher: 1982 and 1983; Berthelot and de Bandt: 1982.

13. Vellas: 1981; Aho and Orr: 1979; de Grauwe et al., 1979; Schumacher: 1982 and 1983.

14. Parsons: 1980.

15. Jacobson and Thomason: 1979; Aho and Bayard: 1982.

16. Jacobson: 1977; Jacobson and Thomason: 1979, pp.15-18.

17. Encaoua: 1983, Statistical Annex.

18. See the similar result found by Jarret: 1980.

19. Kochan and Piore: 1983.

20. OECD: 1979 (Facing the Future), pp.161-186; Michalski: 1979.

201

21. See, for example, Barth, Corden and Tassy: 1980.

22. Litan and Nordhaus: 1983, pp.8-34.

23. In 1977, for example, state-owned enterprises accounted for 22 per cent of European plastics capacity, but for nearly 50 per cent of capacity augmenting investments — at a time when the industry was clearly suffering from over-capacity. See Morandi and Pantini: 1982, pp.166-183 on the role of public enterprise in slowing the adjustment process in the European chemical industry.

24. George and Ward: 1975.

25. The automobile industry is, of course, a prime example of this trend (see National Academy of Engineering: 1982). Note, however, that changing design and production technologies tended to increase manufacturing flexibility as of the mid-1970s; see Ergas: 1984 for a survey.

26. It is worth noting that the view presented here contrasts with that which is becoming conventional in the "political economy of protection" (e.g. Anderson and Baldwin: 1981; Bhagwati: 1982; Hartle: 1983; Pugel: 1984; Waelbroeck and Messerlin: 1983). This latter view draws on simple models of political behaviour stemming from Mancur Olson's early work (see Barry: 1970 for a survey), stressing the demand for protection in terms of interest group formation. However, it fails to explain why the demand for protection should vary over time or to adequately explain the supply of protection. The approach taken here focuses on the changing capacity of sectional interest groups to organise and express their demands; there is an extensive literature in this regard, of which the most relevant items are: Berger: 1981; Crouch: 1983; Dahl: 1982; Olson: 1983; Lesourne: 1976; Shonfield: 1982. See also Richardson and Jordan: 1979 and Skidelsky: 1984 on the UK; on the US see Fedele: 1981. Ahearn and Reifman: 1983; Baldwin: 1982 ("The Changing Nature of US Trade Policy since World War II") and 1983; Cohen: 1981; Cohen and Metzer: 1982 (esp. pp.65-90) and Pastor: 1982.

27. Frey: 1984; Demsetz: 1982.

28. Some interesting game-theoretical results on this are derived in Johansen: 1979 and 1982.

29. Korpi: 1984; see also the discussion of "governability" in Berger: 1981.

30. Keohane: 1982. This discussion draws heavily on the theory of international regimes; see, among others, Keohane and Nye: 1977; Krasner: 1982 and 1983.

31. Aggarwal: 1985

32. The "hegemonic stability" approach to explaining the framework and conduct of trade policy is elaborated in Gardiner: 1965; Imlah: 1958; Kindleberger: 1978; (Kindleberger: 1951 placed much more emphasis on the domestic policy process as a factor affecting the sustainability of liberal trade); Gilpin: 1981; McKeown: 1983; and Stein: 1982 and 1984.

33. The sources of weakening of the multilateral trade regime are examined by Cowhey and Long: 1983; Lipson: 1980; Keohane in Holsti: 1980, pp.131-162; Ruggie: 1982; and Strange: 1979 and 1981. An interesting parallel can be drawn to the League of Nations: 1942 discussion of the causes of the breakdown of liberal trade in the interwar years.

34. See Ergas: 1984 for a survey.

35. However, the scope for improving the process of trade policy formulation and implementation should not be over-estimated. The Australian experience with the Industries

Assistance Commission is particularly illuminating in this regard. See Glezer: 1982; see also Trade Policy Research Centre: 1983.

36. The broader structural changes underway in the world distribution of economic and political power certainly induce many observers to pessimism in this regard. See, for example, Reich: 1983 or Diebold: 1984. However, as Pastor: 1982 notes, economists' views of the resilience of the multilateral trading system are highly cyclical; Diebold: 1952, for instance, was very pessimistic as to the future prospects for the GATT.

TABLES AND GRAPHS

Econometric Annex to Chapter 6

TEXTILES AND CLOTHING

This Annex presents a simple model of European Community and United States international trade in the textiles and clothing industries. The aim is to use this model to examine the impact of changes in trade regimes on import flows. The structure of the paper is as follows:

Section I — outlines the major features of the underlying analysis

Section II — reports estimation results covering the period 1967-1981

Section III — presents simulations of expected trade flows in textiles and clothing for 1982-83

I. Analysis and Model Structure

1. Demand functions for imports (D^m) and domestic (D^d) as:

$$D^m = ap^m + a'p^d + c(Z) \tag{1}$$

$$D^d = ap^d + b'p^m + d(Z) \tag{2}$$

with $a < o$, $a' \geqslant o$, $b' \geqslant o$ and if there is imperfect substitutability between domestic and imported goods, $a' < |a|$, $b' < |a|$.

Equally, the simplified supply block can be written:

$$\int^m = \alpha p^m + e(Z) \tag{3}$$

$$\int^d = Bp^d + p(Z) \tag{4}$$

with $\alpha > B$ by assumption.

2. Introducing an import quota q, we write:

$$q \leqslant ap^{-m} + a'p^d + c(Z) < D_e^m + a'p_e^d + c(Z) \tag{5}$$

where the subscript e refers to equilibrium conditions in the absence of the quota.

3. Solving equations (1) — (5) for domestic and imports prices and differentiating we obtain:

$$_d\overline{p}^m = \frac{1}{a} \, d\overline{q} - \frac{a'}{a} \, _dp^d = (\frac{B - a}{aB - \alpha^2 + a'b'}) \, d\overline{q} = K_1 \, d\overline{q}$$

$$_dp^d = \frac{1}{(B - a)} \frac{b'}{a} \, d\overline{q} - \frac{a'b'}{a} \, _dp^d$$

$$= (\frac{b'}{aB - a^2 + a'b'}) \, d\overline{q} = K_2 d\overline{q}$$

with $K_1, K_2 \leqslant 0$.

4.   This implies that domestic prices will increase if the quota is binding, under all but two conditions. First, if there is no substitutability between domestic and imported goods, $b' = 0$ hence $K_2 = 0$. Second, if domestic supply is infinitely elastic, we have:

$$_dq^d = (\frac{Bb'}{aB - a^2 + a'b'}) \, dq$$

$$\lim_{(B \to \infty)} \frac{_dq^d}{d\overline{q}} = \frac{b'}{a} \quad \text{et} \quad \lim_{(B \to \infty)} \frac{_dp^d}{d\overline{q}} = 0.$$

II.   Model Estimation

5.   Table 1 presents the results of estimation of demand functions for textiles and clothing imports.

6.   The striking feature of these results is the excellence of fit in the pre-1973 period; followed by the breakdown of the relation between import prices and volumes from 1973 on — the period of spreading protectionism in the textiles and clothing industry.

7.   For example, the simple correlation coefficient between United States textiles and clothing imports (in volume terms) and the relative price of imports to domestic textiles and clothing products moved as follows:

    1965-1972 $r = 0.91$
    1973-1983 $r = 0.39$

That is, subsequent to 1972, increases in the price competitiveness of imports no longer led to increases in import volumes. This result is common to all the equations estimated.

8.   The assumption underlying OLS demand function estimation — that the variability of the supply function exceeds that of the demand function — may seem plausible in a highly competitive industry, with weak entry and exit barriers. Nonetheless, the robustness of the results to the estimation procedure (and, in particular, to simultaneous equation bias) was tested using three stage least squares. The model estimated was as follows:

Table 1

DEMAND FUNCTIONS

Dependent variable	Period	Coefficients			F	R^2	
		Competitiveness	Income	Constant			
QMT	65-72	31.6 (7.001)	0.18 (0.161)	-4223.8 (775.9)	99.12	0.975	UNITED STATES
QMT	73-83	25.46 (5.71)	0.24 (0.12)	-3516.2 (1597.6)	9.9	0.712	
QMH	66-72	8.11 (2.79)	0.0067 (0.0005)	-5373.8 (484.1)	153.9	0.987	
QMH	73-83	10.2 (6.74)	0.0076 (0.0013)	-6915.3 (2210.9)	60.3	0.937	
QWTC	65-75	$0.25 \ 10^3$ (320.5)	0.113 (0.09)	-52439.6 (11645.6)		0.94	EUROPEAN COMMUNITY
QWTC	72-83	-0.223 (0.813)	0.748 (0.719)	0.7472 (0.1757)		0.09	
QCT	67-83	1.05 (0.829)	$4.25 \ 10^{-4}$ ($105 \ 10^{-4}$)	-331.4 (167.5)	36.6	0.84	UNITED STATES
QCT	72-83	1.04 (1.06)	$4.73 \ 10^{-4}$ ($1.33 \ 10^{-4}$)	-384.8 (208.4)	11.8	0.72	
QCH	67-83	9.53 (5.7)	$1.74 \ 10^3$ ($2.323 \ 10^{-4}$)	-1535.6 (388.2)	216.4	0.97	
QCH	72-83	6.9 (7.9)	$1.76 \ 10^3$ ($3 \ 10^{-4}$)	-1504 (481.1)	67.2	0.93	
QCPC	65-75	214.8 (365.2)	0.121 (0.0107)	-0.563 (.13)	65.7	0.94	EUROPEAN COMMUNITY
QCTC	72-83	-611.7 (693.2)	0.015 (0.08)	0.67 (2)	1.714	0.27	
QNTC	72-83	6484 (3620)	00207 (0.0053)	265123 (1.36 388)		0.33	
QNTC	65-72	-129 (8064)	0051 (0.051)	46481.3 (65836.5)	41.85	0.93	

208

$$D^m = a \left(\frac{pd}{p^m}\right) + bR + \tilde{u} + c_1 \tag{6}$$

$$\int^m = \alpha \left(\frac{pd}{Pm}\right) + BW + \tilde{v} + C_2 \tag{7}$$

$$D^m = \int^m \tag{8}$$

(Variable names are listed in Table 4). The results, reported in the Table for the EEC, did not differ from those obtained by OLS techniques.

9.   The breakdown in the price-volume relation suggests a systematic departure from competitive market clearing in the post-1972 period. This can be tested using a disequilibrium version of the model defined by equations (6) – (7), making price the only endogenous variable:

$$D = ap + bR + u \tag{9}$$

$$S = \alpha p + BW + v \tag{10}$$

$$Q = \bar{Q} \text{ (and not } D = S) \tag{11}$$

This can be estimated using a price adjustment equation:

$$P_t - P_{t-1} = \lambda (D_t - S_t) \tag{12}$$

Solving equations (9) and (10) for an equilibrium price and rewriting the difference equation yields:

$$P_t = \frac{1}{1 + \lambda(\alpha - a)} P_t - 1 + \frac{\lambda(\alpha - a)}{1 + \lambda(\alpha - a)} p_t^e + n_E$$

This can be written:

$$P_t = \gamma P_{t-1} + (1 - \gamma) p_t^e \tag{13}$$

with, in equilibrium: $= \lambda = \infty$ so ($\gamma = o$)

From equations (6) – (8) we can write:

$$p_t^e = \frac{1}{\alpha - a} (b - R_t - BW_t) + \delta_t \tag{14}$$

By substitution of (14) into (13) market-clearing can be tested for. P_t is projected on the space (P_t-1, R_t, W_t) and the significance is examined of (i) the relation as a whole, and (ii) the lagged variable. (A market clearing equilibrium will yield $\gamma = o$).

10.   The results are presented in Table 2. In all the equations, the post-1972 period is characterised by substantially higher significance of the equation as a whole, confirmed by analysis of co-variance on the residuals. Moreover, the results suggest that the departures from equilibrium have been considerably greater in the United States than in the European Community. This may be due to differences in the external trade regime. It may also reflect a higher elasticity of substitution between imported and domestic goods for the European Community as a whole, and a higher elasticity of supply in the European Community market.

11.   Moreover, the results suggest that the post-1972 departures from market clearing are larger and more systematic for clothing than for textiles.

Table 2

PRICE EQUATIONS

Dependent variable	Period	Coefficients				F	R^2
		P_{t-1}	R_t	W_t	Constant		
PRMT	73-83	0.71 (0.42)	3.8 (1.33)	-2.6 (2.1)	-9.14 (1.3)	10.45	0.82
PRMT	66-73	-0.12 (0.55)	-2.11 16^{-6} (1.45 10^{-6})	1.32 10^2 (8.13 10^{-3})	1.63 (0.98)	0.91	0.4
PRMH	73-83	0.864 (0.075)	1.6 10^{-6} (2.45 10^{-7})	-9.2 10^4 (3.7 10^{-4})	-1.24 (0.21)	583.04	0.996
PRMT	66-73	1.49 (0.52)	1.47 10^{-6} (201 10^{-6})	-4.04 10^3 (1.2 10^2)	-1.4 -1.4	13.98	0.913
PWTC	72-83	0.22 (0.37)	-0.16 10^{-5} (0.70 10^{-6})	0.52 (0.022 10^{-1})	-0.59 (0.79)	22.4	0.89
PWTC	66-73	0.581 (0.62)	-0.37 10^{-5} (0.23 10^{-6})	0.45 (0.22 10^{-1})	0.13 (1.63)	H statistic not given as imaginary	
PNTC	73-83	0.99 (0.21)	0.33 10^{-5} (0.17 10^{-5})	-0.18 10^{-1} (0.82 10^{-2})	-0.92 (0.96)	16.6	0.87
PCTC	72-83	-2.45 (0.24)	-1.22 10^{-5} (0.53 10^{-6})	0.074 (0.014)	-0.23 (0.68)	53.2	0.95
PCT	67-83	0.26 (0.122)	-7.3 10^{-4} (4.7 10^{-4})	16.86 (2.9)	-114.4 (289.1)	191.2	0.98
PCT	72-83	0.33 (0.175)	5.45 10^{-4} (8.06 10^{-4})	15.23 (4.13)	-218.1 (602.2)	70.1	0.96
PCH	67-83	0.34 (0.155)	-9.8 10^{-4} (1.54 10^{-3})	29.6 (6.79)	4.4 (941.14)	137.5	0.97
PCH	72-83	0.7 (0.21)	-2.82 10^{-3} (2.1 10^{-3})	22.7 (7.9)	1627.6 (1532)	55	0.95

UNITED STATES

EUROPEAN COMMUNITY

UNITED STATES

12.   Finally, the relations between domestic and import prices in the post-1972 period can be tested. The critical question is whether domestic producers are price leaders, with importers marking up prices to domestic costs; or whether import prices set the market price level in the quota equilibrium. The second hypothesis is clearly less plausible in a market subject to binding quotas and with a large domestic-import cost differential.

13.   The approach adopted is the Granger-Newbold causality test, based on cross-spectral analysis of residuals in a seemingly simultaneous model. Though such analyses are only robust when there is a large number of observations, the results obtained consistently reject the hypothesis that importers are price setters. In other words, importers move their prices towards those of high cost domestic suppliers.

III.   Simulations of 1982 and 1983 Behaviour

14.   The equations, estimated for the period to 1981, can be used to simulate import volumes for 1982 and 1983, that is, the period of renewal and implementation of the third MFA. Prices are determined by simulations on the equations of Table 2. These are then used to determine import volume. The results are presented in Table 3. They can be summarised as follows:

—   For the United States, observed import volumes are 11 per cent below simulated volumes. Almost all of this shortfall is in clothing, with textile imports revealing little systematic variation from projected levels.

—   For the European Community, though imports from all sources are only marginally below projections, imports from all non-OECD sources are down 3 per cent and from Asian sources by 8 per cent. This implies that major reallocations of trade flows (that is, trade diversion) occurred during this period.

15.   It should be noted that these estimates are highly conservative, in that the shortfall between projected and realised values is much greater when the simulations are based solely on 1966-72 behavioural patterns. Had United States and European Community import demand equations remained stable in the 1970s, 1982-83 imports from non-OECD sources would be approximately twice as large as they were, assuming also stability in the supply function over this output range.

Table 3

SIMULATIONS OF IMPORT VOLUMES, 1982 AND 1983

	Shortfall of observed volume over projection (percentage)
QMUS	11 per cent
QWTC	0.5 per cent
QCTC	8 per cent

Table 4

VARIABLE NAMES

QMUS -- Import quantity, United States, textiles and clothing, all sources.

QMH   -- Import quantity, United States, clothing, all sources.

QMT   -- Import quantity, United States, textiles, all sources.

QCT   -- Import quantity, United States, textiles, Asian NICS (Hong Kong, Korea, Taiwan, Singapore).

QCH   -- Import quantity, United States, clothing, Asian NICS (Hong Kong, Korea, Taiwan, Singapore).

QWTC -- Import quantity, European Community, textiles and clothing, all sources.

QNTC -- Import quantity, European Community, textiles and clothing, non-OECD sources.

QCTC -- Import quantity, European Community, textiles and clothing, Asian NICS.

PRMUS -- Import price, United States, textiles and clothing, all sources.

PRMT -- Import price, United States, textiles, all sources.

PRMH -- Import price, United States, textiles, all sources.

PCT   -- Import price, United States, textiles, Asian NICS.

PCH   -- Import price, United States, clothing, Asian NICS.

PWTC -- Import price, European Community, textiles and clothing, all sources.

PNTC -- Import price, European Community, textiles and clothing, non-OECD sources.

---

16.   Bearing these caveats in mind, four main points emerge from the estimates:

   — Subsequent to implementation of MFA 1, OECD imports of textiles and clothing became almost totally unresponsive to price signals, especially as regards the competitiveness of non-OECD suppliers. Conventional import demand equations, which over the preceding period gave excellent fits, ceased to have any explanatory power.

   — Again, as of 1973 import prices from non-OECD sources tended to align on domestic prices, rather than vice versa, despite large and persistent cost differentials. In other words, mark-ups on import prices increased.

- Deviations from market equilibrium were particularly great, (a) in the United States relative to the European Community, and (b) in clothing relative to textiles.
- Compression of imports from non-OECD sources in 1982 and 1983 can be estimated at slightly over 10 per cent in volume terms, though the import figures would be very much larger had 1966-72 behaviour patterns persisted into the late 1970s. On this latter scenario, 1982-83 import volumes from non-OECD sources would be at least twice as great as the observed magnitude.

213

Econometric Annex to Chapter 8

CONSUMER ELECTRONICS: THE CASE OF COLOUR TELEVISION RECEIVERS

This Annex presents the broad outlines of the model used to obtain the econometric results cited in Chapter 8. The aim of this model is to provide estimates of the impact of trade restrictions on:

- the volume of United States imports of colour television receivers;
- United States import and producer prices for colour receivers.

The Annex proceeds as follows: Section I summarises the structure of the model and presents the main estimation results. Section II discusses the within range predictive capacity of the model. Section III presents the major results about the impact of trade restrictions.

I.   The Structure of the Model

1.   The structure of the model, briefly outlined, is as follows (variable names are in parentheses, endogenous variables are starred, full estimation results are presented in Table 5):

Equation
number

- *US sales* of colour television receivers (U. Sales*) are determined by the stock of colour television receivers in use (U. Stock), the moving average of producer prices for colour receivers (U.PP1.A*) and consumer durable expenditure in the previous
(1)   period (U.Dur(-1)).

- The volume of *US imports* of colour receivers (U.Imp*) is determined by the level of sales (U.Sales*), the price of imported relative to domestically produced receivers (Rel.pr*) and expectations of consumer durable expenditure for the three months following the import period (U.Dur.Pr).
(2)

- *Expectations of consumer durable expenditure* (U.Dur.Pr) are proxied in the following manner: in each month x, importers are assumed to estimate a regression relationship between constant price consumer durable expenditure in month x and in months x-1, x-2 and x-12, for each month from January 1955 to x. The estimated coefficients are then recomputed using an 11-th order autocorrelation function. Final values of the regression coefficients, together with the coefficients of the auto-correlation function, are used to compute expected expenditure in months x+1 to x+3. The arithmetic mean of these expected values is defined as the expectation in period x of next period expenditure[1].

214

Table 5

PRINCIPAL ESTIMATION RESULTS

Equation
number

(1) LN(U.Sales) = - 2.7 + 0.2 LN(U.Dur(-1))

SE   3.2   0.16

              + 0.28 (Ln(U.Stock) - 2.1 Ln (U.PP1.A)

              0.07   0.6

SEE = 0.05 $\overline{R}^2$ = .92   D.W. = 1.7

Estimation period: Q2 1975 to Q3 1979. Estimation method: 2SLS.

(2) Ln(U.Imp)= -85.6 -3.3 LN (Rel.pr) + 3.6 Ln (U.Dur.Pr) + 1.7 LN (U.Sales)

SE   11.3 0.4   0.5   0.1

SEE = 0.01 $\overline{R}^2$ = .96   D.W. = 1.9

Estimation period: Q1 1975 to Q4 1978. Estimation method: 2SLS.

(3) Ln (J.Exp) = -45 + 0.5 Ln (U.Sales) + 2.1 Ln (U.Dur.Pr)

SE   10.1   0.08   0.47

              -2.8 Ln (J.Rel.pr)   -2.2 Ln (J.Rel.pr(-1))

              0.9   0.9

SEE = 0.2 $\overline{R}^2$ = .83   D.W. = 2.5

Estimation period: February 1975 to December 1978. Estimation
method: 2SLS.

(4) U.PP1 = 1.18 + 0.24 E -07 [(U.Sales - U.Sales.trend)* U.Imp.Unit]

SE   0.44   0.11 E -07

                        -.00084 (U.Prod)
                        .00018

SEE = 0.019 $\overline{R}^2$ = .64   D.W. = 1.5

Estimation period: Q2 1975 to Q4 1978. Estimation method: 2SLS.

215

Table 5 (continued)

(5)   U.Imp.Uvi = -2.02 + 0.016 T + 0.6 Ln (J.Exp.pi* J.ER)

    SE   0.9   0.002   0.2

                          -.027 Ln [(U.Sales/U.Sales(-1))**2]
                          .024

SEE = 0.04 $\bar{R}^2$ = .90   D.W. = 1.9

Estimation period: Q1 1975 to Q3 1979. Estimation method: 2SLS.

(6)   J.Exp.pr = -9.03 + 0.06 CU + 0.14 J.WP + 0.89 J.Exp.pi(-1)

    SE   6.6   0.04   0.08   0.05

SEE = .16 $\bar{R}^2$ = .98   D.W. = 1.85

Estimation period: April 1975 to September 1979. Estimation method: 2SLS.

(7)   J.WP1 = 2.13 -6.3 J.Prod + 0.8 J.WP1(-1)

    SE   9.8   2.9   0.08

SEE = 1.55 $\bar{R}^2$ = .94   D.W. = 2.03

Estimation period: February 1975 to September 1979. Estimation method: OLS.

<u>Notes:</u> $\bar{R}^2$ = Error based R^2, adjusted for degrees of freedom.

---

(3)

— *Exports from Japan to the United States* of colour receivers (J.Exp*) are determined by expectations of consumer durable expenditure (U.Dur.Pr), current US sales of receivers (U.Sales*) and the ratio of Japanese export prices for receivers to US producer prices for receiver (J.Rel.pr*).

(4)

— *US producer prices* for colour receivers (U.PP1 *) are determined by apparent labour productivity in the US colour receiver industry (U.Prod) and by import unit values (U.Imp.Unit*). However, price levels are allowed to vary with the deviation of current period sales from the trend level of sales (U.Sales — U.Sales.Trend). This "strength of demand" factor is assumed to affect the mark-up in producer prices over import unit values.

(5)

— *US import unit values* (U.Imp.Unit*) are a function of the one period change in sales, export prices for colour receivers from Japan (J.Exp.pi*), and the yen-dollar exchange rate (J.ER).

      — *Export prices* for colour receivers from Japan (J.Exp.pi*) are determined by an export margin over wholesale prices for colour receivers in Japan (J.WP1*). This margin is assumed to adjust, with a lag, to changes in capacity utilisation (CU)[2], which is proxied by the ratio of shipments to the domestic market to the trend value (6) shipments.

      — Finally, *wholesale prices* for colour receivers in Japan (J.WP1*) are determined by the level of productivity in the electrical engineering industries in Japan (J.Prod). Attempts to incorporate wages and input prices into the equation failed because of (7) extensive multicollinearity.

2.   The system as a whole is simultaneous: sales affect prices, which in turn affect sales; sales and prices jointly determine import volumes, which affect prices and, through prices, sales. This simultaneity imposes care both in model specification and estimation. Table 6 summarises the identification conditions on an equation-by-equation basis. As can be seen from this table, the

Table 6

IDENTIFICATION CONDITIONS

Equation number	Dependent variable	Number of included endogenous variables	Number of excluded predetermined variables	Identification conditions met ? (1)
(1)	Sales	2	11	√
(2)	U.Imp	5	13	√
(3)	J.Exp	5	12	√
(4)	U.PP1	3	12	√
(5)	U.Imp.Uvi	3	11	√
(6)	J.Exp.pi	3	11	√
(7)	J.WP1	1	11	√

1.   The identification conditions are as follows. Let G be the total number of endogenous variables, g the number of endogenous variables included in equation x, K the total number of predetermined (lagged and exogenous) variables, k the numbher of predetermined variables included in equation x. Then equation x is fully identified if:

   i) $K - k \geqslant g - 1$
   ii)   rank $(A \phi) = G - 1$ where A is the matrix of co-efficients and ϕ is a matrix with one column for each restriction on the structural parameters.

model is adequately identified. To eliminate simultaneous equation bias from the coefficients, the equations were estimated by two stage least squares (2SLS). In general, 2SLS will be superior to OLS when:

- the model is strongly interdependent;
- there is little multicollinearity among the exogenous variables

Both these conditions appear to be met in the present case.

3.   As a test on the robustness of the results, the model was re-estimated with three major modifications:

- Univariate Box-Jenkins models were constructed to provide continuous time proxies for expectations on the following variables: income in the sales equations and expected sales in the wholesale price model. These replace proxies based on linear auto-regressive models.
- All equations were estimated using quarterly data: while this leads to a loss of degrees of freedom it also reduces the noise arising from reporting errors in monthly data.
- The model was estimated using 3 stage Least Squares so as to fully correct for simultaneity.

4.   The results of this estimation are reproduced in Table 7. These results were used as a check on the simulations reported in Part III below; the estimates obtained did not differ significantly from those reported.

Table 7

ESTIMATION BY 3SLS

I.   Sales = $13.6 + 1.14$ Income$_A$ $+ 0.9$ Income$_W$ $- 2.05$ W.P.I$_A$

t - Value	-4.1	7.2	8.3	-4.2
t - Probability	1.0	1.0	1.0	1.0

Income A : ARIMA model : $\Theta_o = (1 - \Theta_1 B - \Theta_2 B^4 - \Theta_3 B^{12})$ wt

$$w_t = (1 - B)(1 - B^{12}) \, Ln \, (Z_t)$$

Income W = Income - Income A = residual of Univariate Box -- Jenkins model.

II.   Imports

Imports = $-131.2 - 4.21$ (Import U.V.I./W.P.I.) $+ 4.9$ Income$_A$ $+ 1.6$ Sales

t - Value	-8.5	-9.5	8.0	8.1
t - Probability	1.0	1.0	1.0	1.0

Estimation: 3SLS   [2SLS $R^{-2} = .99$ SEE = .005]

218

III. Wholesale Prices (WPI)

$$W.P.I. = 0.5 + .028 \text{ (Sales} \div \text{Sales}_A \text{) Import U.V.I}$$

t - Value   2.47   1.71
t - Probability .99   .90

$$- .15 \text{ Prod} \qquad\qquad + .28 \text{ W.P.I. } (-1)$$
- 2.9   1.5
  .99   .87

Estimation   3SLS   [2SLS $\bar{R}^2$ = .85   SEE = 0.02]

Sales A : ARIMA model: $W_t = (1. - \Theta_1 B^1 - \Theta_2 B^{12}) (Z_t - \delta_t)$

IV. Import Unit Values (UVI)

$$\text{Import U.V.I.} = -3.9 + .08 \text{Time} + 0.92 \text{ J.Exp.pr} - .68 \text{ (Sales} \div \text{Sales}_A\text{)}$$

t - Value   -8.0   7.5   9.0   -3.6
t - Probability 1.0   1.0   1.0   1.0

Estimation: 3SLS   [2SLS : R^{-2} = .97   SEE = .01]

V. Japanese Export Prices (J.Exp.Pr)

$$\text{J.Exp.pr} = -1.6 - .052 \text{ (J.Exp} \div \text{J.Prod)} + .599 \text{ J.WP1} + .726 \text{ J.Exp.pr}(=1)$$

t - Value   -5.6   3.9   5.5   9.5
t - Probability 1.0   1.0   1.0   1.0

Estimation: 3SLS   [2SLS : R^2 = .996   SEE = .003]

VI. Japan Exports (J.Exp.)

$$\text{J.Exp.} = -39.9 + .06 \text{ Sales} + 2.96 \text{ Income}_A -6.2 \text{ (J.Exp.pr} \div \text{WP1)}$$

t - Value   -2.8   2.6   4.6   -10.2
t - Probability .99   .99   1.0   1.0

Estimation: 3SLS [2SLS : R^2 = .98   SEE = .01]

II. Predictive Performance

5.   What is important from a forecasting point of view is the ability of the equations to predict the direction and extent of changes in the dependent variables. To assess this ability, the root mean square error (RMSE) between predicted and realised period-on-period percentage changes *within* the sample period was calculated for each of the dependent variables, together with the correlation between the predicted and realised changes (Table 8). Examination of this table suggests that the predictive performance of the model in terms of percentage changes is best for US imports, US producer prices and US import unit values. Performance is poor for US sales and Japanese wholesale prices, and mediocre for Japanese export prices and export volumes. However, performance on these last two variables may be adversely affected by the use of monthly data in estimations, since this data is subject to stochastic noise from reporting error, random fluctuations, and from seasonality.

Table 8

PREDICTIVE PERFORMANCE

Equation number	Dependent variable	RMSE	RMSE/SD	Correlation between predicted and realised % changes
(1)	U.Sales	89	1.1	- .380
(2)	U.Imp	134	0.5	.870
(3)	J.Exp	109×10^3	0.3	.440
(4)	U.PPI	9	0.9	.350
(5)	U.Imp.Unit	20	0.9	.265
(6)	J.Exp.pi	29	1.2	.220
(7)	J.WPI	26	1.5	- .450

Notes: RMSE = Square root of the mean of the squared difference between realised and predicted period-on-period percentage changes.

RMSE/SD = RMSE divided by the standard deviation of the realised changes.

6.   A more detailed assessment of the causes of disparities in predictive performance is provided in Table 9. This table decomposes the mean square error of prediction for each equation into three components[3]: a bias proportion, U^m, which measures the difference between the mean

Table 9

DECOMPOSITION OF THE MEAN SQUARE ERROR

Equation number	Dependent variable	U^m	U^s	U^c
(1)	U.Sales	.08	.52	.40
(2)	U.Imp	.06	.02	.92
(3)	J.Exp	.03	.94	.03
(4)	U.PP1	.01	.17	.82
(5)	U.Imp.Unit	.01	.36	.63
(6)	J.Exp.pi	0	0	1.00
(7)	J.WP1	.01	0	.99

Notes: A = realised % period-on-period change;
        P = predicted % period-on-period change.

$$(i)\ U^m = \frac{(\bar{P} - \bar{A})^2}{\frac{1}{n}\sum (Pi - Ai)^2} \qquad (ii)\ U^s = \frac{(S_P - S_A)^2}{\frac{1}{n}\sum (Pi - Ai)^2}$$

$$iii)\ U^c = \frac{2(1 - r)\, S_p S_A}{\frac{1}{n}\sum (Pi - Ai)^2}$$

where S_p, S_A are the standard deviations of predicted and realised changes respectively and r is the correlation between predicted and realised changes.

predicted and realised percentage changes; a variance proportion, U^s, which measures the difference between the variance of the predicted and realised percentage changes; and a co-variance proportion, U^c, which measures the difference in the co-variance of the series.

7.   Examination of Table 9 confirms that all of the equations — with the possible exception of equation (1) — perform well in predicting the average of the period-on-period changes over the estimation samples. In addition, equations (2), (4), (6) and (7) perform well in terms of the variance of the changes. The poor performance of equations (1) and (3) seems largely due to a disparity between the extent of the seasonal fluctuation in the dependent variable and the coefficient-weighted fluctuation in the independent variables. These equations could probably be improved by

appropriate transformation of the dependent variable. In contrast, the poor performance of equation (7) seems almost entirely due to the fact that the predicted changes do not lie on a straight line[4]; this source of error is difficult to correct.

III.   Assessing the Impact of Trade Restrictions

8.   In this Section, the model outlined in Section I will be used to assess the impact of trade restrictions, subject to the provisos about forecasting performance advanced above.

9.   In general, a volume restriction on imports will raise import prices and domestic prices and reduce domestic sales and imports. The hypothesis that import prices will increase follows from the assumption of profit-maximising behaviour: faced with an effective upper volume on imports, importers will bid up import prices to the point at which further increases reduce their economic rents. Exporters in the restricted country will find that the profit margin on exports has increased, so that in the exporting country the relation between export prices and domestic prices will change. At the same time, domestic prices in the importing country will rise: first because an increase in domestic prices will be necessary under conditions of increasing cost to stimulate the import-replacing increase in domestic production; second, because domestic producers face less competition from imports. The increase in domestic prices will, in turn, reduce sales and imports. The extent of the import displacement will therefore be the difference between:

- the level of imports which would have been observed had import prices, domestic prices and sales assumed their "no restriction" values; and
- the level of imports actually observed.

10.   In the case of colour television receivers, two sets of restrictions are involved. The first restrictions, which entered into effect in June 1977, limited US imports from Japan. The second restrictions, which entered into effect in February 1979, extended these limits to Korea and Taiwan. Both of these restrictions were partial, in that no limits were set on US imports from other sources. One would therefore expect the impact of the restrictions to depend on the elasticity of supply from other sources: if alternative sources of supply are readily available, one would not expect restricting one of these sources to have much impact either on export prices in the restricted country — since the price elasticity of export demand will be high — or on the total volume of imports in the restricting country.

11.   In fact, the econometric evidence suggests that because of the availability of alternative sources of supply, the June 1977 restrictions had little independent impact. If these restrictions had had an independent impact, instability over time would have been observed in the estimated coefficients for equations (3) and/or (6): equation (6) if exporters captured the entire rents arising from the restrictions; equation (3) if the increase in the export margin was insufficient to reduce exports to the restricted level. The impact of the restrictions can therefore be assessed by examining the stability of these equations. This was done in three ways:

- by introducing dummy variables into equations (3) and (6);
- by estimating the equations over the period from January 1975 to September 1979 with the regression coefficients as polynomials in time;
- by testing the cumulative sum and the cumulative sum of squares of the regression residuals from recursive regressions over this period, and then using the Quandt Log-Likelihood ratio to identify the discontinuity in the relationship.

Table 10(a)

STABILITY TESTS FOR EQUATIONS (3) AND (6): F TESTS

Equation number	Dependent variable	1st Degree Polynomial in time	2nd Degree Polynomial in time
(3)	J.Exp	8.7**	13.7**
(6)	J.Exp.pi	1.9	1.9

** = Significant at 1% level.

1. The F ratio is calculated on the sum of squares removed by each of the following nested hypotheses:

$$(0) \quad Y = X_t^1 \, \underline{B} + E_t$$

$$(1) \quad Y = X_t^1 \, (\underline{B}_{(o)} + \underline{B}_{(1)} t) + E_t$$

$$(2) \quad Y = X_t^1 \, \underline{B}_{(o)} + \underline{B}_{(1)} \, t + \underline{B}_{(2)} \, t^{-2}) + E_t$$

The results of the second and third of these methods are presented in Table 10[5]. These results suggest that the export quantities equation may have been unstable over the period, but that the export prices equation probably was not. Further, the Quandt Log-Likelihood ratio implies that to the extent to which the coefficients of the equations did shift, this shift occurred towards the end of 1978 — when the second set of restrictions came into effect — rather than in 1977. These results can be interpreted as implying that the rise in the external value of the Yen — which put upward pressure on export prices — was more significant than the 1977 restrictions in reducing export volumes[6].

12. In contrast, the February 1979 restrictions appear to have had a major impact on the volume of trade. The extent of this impact was calculated in the following manner:

— Equations (1), (3), (5), (6) and (7) were re-estimated over the sample Q1 1975 to Q4 1978.
— The equations were checked for coefficient stability over the sample period; all of the equations were stable.
— The estimated equations were then solved for the "no-restriction" import prices, domestic prices and import volumes for Q1 1979 to Q3 1979. This was done using simulation by Newton's method, that is, by solving the Taylor series expansion of the equation system. The iterations were continued up to a tolerance of 0.00001.

Table 10(b)

STABILITY TESTS FOR EQUATIONS (3) AND (6): CUSUM TESTS (1)

Equation number	Dependent variable	Cumulative sum of residuals	Cumulative sum of squared residuals	Minimun points for Quandt L-L ratio
(3)	J.Exp.	.35	.36**	Nov. -- Dec. 1978
(6)	J.Exp.pi	.58	.11	Dec. -- Jan. 1978/79

** = Significant at 1 per cent level.

1. The method underlying these tests is, briefly stated, as follows: define W_r as the difference between the observed value of y at time r and the value "predicted" from the regression on the time segment from 1 to and including r-1, standardized by a positive quantity independent of the residuals. Further, define Ho as the hypothesis that the regression relationship is stable. Under Ho, the W_i's will be independent with mean zero; that is, the sequence W_{kH} ......W_r is a sequence of approximately normal variables such that:

$$E (W_r) = 0$$

$$Var (W_r) = r - K \qquad \text{(K is the number of regressors)}$$

$$Cov (W_r, W_s) = Min (r, s) - K$$

It can be shown that the significance of the deviation of the cumulative sum of the W_i's from zero can be evaluated in terms of a continuous Gaussian process. Similarly, the cumulative sum of the squared residuals will have a Beta distribution -- under Ho -- with mean $(r - K)/(T - k)$. The test statistic for this distribution is a modified Kolmogorov-Smirnov statistic. It should be noted that the cumulative sum of the (unsquared) residuals test tends to give a significant result more often than an exact test would.

Finally, the Quandt Log-Likelihood ratio is derived as follows: for each observation, r, from r=K+1 à r=T-K-1, we calculate:

$$Q_r = \log_{10} \frac{\text{max. likelihood of the observations given Ho}}{\text{max. likelihood of the observations given H1}}$$

where H_1 is the hypothesis that the observations in time segments (1, ..., r) and (r + 1, ..., T) come from two different regressions. No exact test has yet been devised for Qr; but since the ratio is likely to be at a minimum at a true change point, the position of the least value of Qr is revealing.

Table 11

IMPACT OF FEBRUARY 1979 TRADE RESTRICTIONS

Variable name		Q1 1979	Q2 1979	Q3 1979
			(% change over Q4 1978)	
U.Imp.Unit	(i) Forecast	0.8	0.0	1.4
	(ii) Observed	5.0	13.5	9.3
U.PP1	(i) Forecast	-3.3	-5.0	-3.9
	(ii) Observed	-1.0	-0.2	1.1
U.Imp	(i) Forecast	-22.0	12.9	-6.9
	(ii) Observed	-45.0	-58.0	-57.5

13.   The principal results are presented in Table 11. These results can be adjusted, using the linear correction coefficients presented in Table 9 to obtain a range estimate of the impact of the restrictions. The adjusted estimates suggest that over the first three quarters of 1979, the restrictions:

- increased import unit values by 4 to 8 per cent;
- increased producer prices by 4 to 6 per cent;
- reduced import volumes by 0.6 to 1.1 million units.

NOTES

1. Experiments were made with alternative weightings of the expected values. The best results were obtained with a simple arithmetic mean.

2. For estimation purposes, capacity utilisation is treated as endogenous. It is a function of the lagged change in constant price consumer durable expenditure in Japan and of the yen-dollar exchange rate.

3. See Theil, H.: 1966, *Applied Economic Forecasting;* North-Holland Publishing Company, Amsterdam.

4. That is, in a graph with predicted change on the Y axis and realised change on the X axis.

5. The results for dummy variable estimation are not presented because a very large number of combinations was tested. In no case were the dummy variables significant.

6. It might be argued that one of the reasons for which the Japanese exporters were willing to accept voluntary export restraint was that they were expecting a decline in exports to occur.

BIBLIOGRAPHY

Adams, W.J., 'Producer-Concentration as a Proxy for Seller-Concentration: Some Evidence from the World Automotive Industry", *Journal of Industrial Economics,* Vol. XXIX, No. 2, pp. 185-202, December 1980.

Adams, W. and Mueller, H., "The steel industry" in Walter Adams (Ed.) *The Structure of American Industry,* 6th ed., Macmillan, New York, 1982.

Adams, W., Dirlam, J.N., "The Trade Laws and their Enforcement by the International Trade Commission", National Bureau of Economic Research, Conference on Recent Issues and Initiatives in US Trade Policy, Cambridge, Massachusetts, August 1983.

Aggarwal, V.K., "The unraveling of the Multi-Fiber Arrangement, 1981: an examination of international regime change, *International Organization,* Autumn 1983.

Aggarwal, V.K. with Haggard, S., in Zysman, J. and Tyson, L. (Eds.), *American Industry in International Competition,* Cornell University Press, 1983.

Aggarwal, V.K., *Liberal Protectionism: The International Politics of Organised Textile Trade,* University of Ca., Berkeley, 1985.

Aharoni, Y., *The No-Risk Society,* Chatham House, New Jersey, 1981.

Ahearn, R.J. and Reifman, A., "Trade Policy Making in the Congress", Conference on Recent Issues and Initiatives in US Trade Policy, Cambridge, Massachusetts, August 1983.

Aho, C.M. and Carney, R.D., "Is the United States Losing its Comparative Advantage in Manufacturing?: An Empirical Analysis of the Structure of Manufactures Trade 1964-1976", Economic Discussion Paper 3, US Department of Labor, Washington D.C., June 1979.

Aho,C.M. and Orr, J., "Demographic and Occupational Characteristics of Workers in Trade-Sensitive Industries", Economic Discussion Paper 2, Office of Foreign Economic Research, Bureau of International Labor Affairs, US Department of Labor, Washington D.C., December 1979.

Aho, C.M. and Bayard, T.O., "Costs and Benefits of Trade Adjustment Assistance", Conference on the Structure and Evolution of Recent US Trade Policy, Cambridge, Mass., December 1982.

Aislabie, C.J., "The Australian Tariff as a Selective Employment Policy Instrument: An Empirical Study", *Australian Economic Papers,* June 1984.

Akerlof, G.A., "The Economics of 'Tagging' as applied to the Optimal Income Tax, Welfare Programs, and Manpower Planning", *The American Economic Review,* March 1978.

Akerlof, G.A. and Main, B.G.M., "Unemployment Spells and Unemployment Experience", *The American Economic Review,* December 1980.

Andersen, J.E., "Effective Protection in the US: A Historical Comparison", *Journal of International Economics,* 2, 1972.

Anderson, K. and Baldwin, R.E., "The Political Market for Protection in Industrial Countries: Empirical Evidence", World Bank Staff Working Paper No. 492, October 1981.

Anderson, R.G., and Kreinin, Mordechai E., "Labour Costs in the American Steel and Auto Industries", *The World Economy,* Vol. 4, No. 2, June 1981, pp. 199-208.

Anjaria, S.J. *et al.,* "Trade Policy Developments in Industrial Countries", International Monetary Fund, Occasional Paper No. 5, Washington D.C., July 1981.

Arpan, J.S., de la Torre, J., Toyne, B. *et al., The US Apparel Industry: International Challenge/Domestic Response,* Business Publishing Division of the College of Business Administration, Georgia State University, Research Monograph No. 88, Atlanta, Georgia, 1982.

Ashworth, M.M., Kay, J.A. and Sharpe, T.A.E., "Differentials between car prices in the UK and Belgium", Institute for Fiscal Studies, Report Series No.2, London.

Asselain, J-C, "Croissance, Dépression et Récurrence du Protectionisme Française", Colloque GRECO-EFIQ, 1983.

Aylen, J., "The Imperatives of Kanban Steel Production", *Steel Times,* Vol. 211, No. 11, November 1983, pp. 558-561.

Aylen, J., "Plant size and efficiency in the steel industry: an international comparison", *National Institute Economic Review,* No. 100, May 1982, pp. 65-76.

Aylen, J., "Innovation in the British steel industry" in K. Pavitt (ed.) *Technical Innovation and British Economic Performance,* Macmillan, London, 1980.

Aylen, J., "Prospects for Steel", *Lloyds Bank Review,* April 1984, pp. 13-30.

Bailey, E.E. and Friedlaender, A.F., "Market structure and multiproduct industries", *Journal of Economic Literature,* Vol. XX, September 1982, pp. 1024-1048.

Balassa, B., *Changing Patterns in Foreign Trade and Payments,* New York, 1964.

Balassa, B., "Tariff Protection in Industrial Countries: An Evaluation", *Journal of Political Economy,* December 1965.

Balassa, B., "La Montée des Protectionnismes et La Recherche des Voies Alternatives", GRECO-EFIQ, Colloque, Aix-Marseille, June 1983.

Balassa, B. and Balassa, C., "Industrial Protection in the Developed Countries", mimeo, 1984.

Baldwin, J. and Gorecki, P., with McKey, J. and Crysdale, J., *Entry and Exit to the Canadian Manufacturing Sector: 1970-1979,* Discussion Paper No. 225 prepared for the Economic Council of Canada, 1983.

Baldwin, R.E., *Nontariff Distortions of International Trade,* The Brookings Institution, Washington D.C., 1970.

Baldwin R.E., *The Inefficacy of Trade Policy,* Essays in International Finance, Princeton University, 1982.

Baldwin, R.E., "The Changing Nature of US Trade Policy since World War II", Conference on the Structure and Evolution of Recent US Trade Policy, Cambridge, Massachusetts, December 1982.

Baldwin, R.E., "Trade Policies under the Reagan Administration", Conference on Recent Issues and Initiatives in US Trade Policy, Boston, August 1983.

Baldwin, R.E., "Trade Policy and Employment" in OECD: *Employment Growth and Structural Change,* 1985.

Barbe, D., "Pour une réforme des aides aux entreprises en difficulté", *Problèmes Economiques,* No. 1787, 1st September 1982.

Barker, T.S. and Han, S.S., "Effective rates of Protection for United Kingdom Production", *The Economic Journal,* June 1971.

Barna, T., *Investment and Growth Policies in British Industrial Firms,* The National Institute of Economic and Social Research, Cambridge University Press, 1962.

Barnett, D.F. and Schorsch, Louis, *Steel: Upheaval in a Basic Industry,* Ballinger, Cambridge, Mass., 1983.

Baroin, D. and Fracheboud, P., *Les PME en Europe et leur contribution à l'emploi,* La Documentation Française, Notes et Etudes Documentaires No. 4715-4716, 29th April 1983.

Barry, B., *Sociologists, Economists and Democracy,* Collier-Macmillan, London/Toronto, 1970.

Bartel, R.D., "Changing nominal and effective tariff structures: German protection 1960 to 1972", Research Paper No. 7404, Federal Reserve Bank of New York, March 1974.

Barth, J.R., Cordes, J.J. and Tassey, G., *Evaluating the impact of securities regulation on venture capital markets,* US Department of Commerce, NBS Monograph 166, June 1980.

Basevi, G., "The United States Tariff Structure: Estimates of Effective Rates of Protection of United States Industries and Industrial Labour", *The Review of Economics and Statistics,* May 1966.

Batchelor, R.A., Major, R.L., Morgan, A.D., *Industrialisation and the Basis for Trade,* National Institute of Economic and Social Research Economic and Social Studies XXXII, Cambridge University Press, 1980.

Baumol, W.J., "Contestable Markets: an uprising in the theory of industry structure", *The American Economic Review,* March 1982, pp. 1-15.

Bayard, T. and Orr, J., "Trade and Employment Effects of Tariff Reductions agreed to in the MTN", Economic Discussion Paper 1, Office of Foreign Economic Research, Bureau of International Labor Affairs, US Department of Labor, June 1979.

Berger, S. (Ed.), *Organizing interests in Western Europe: Pluralism, corporatism, and the transformation of politics,* Cambridge University Press, 1981.

Berry, M., *Une Technologie Invisible? L'impact des instruments de gestion sur l'évolution des systèmes humains,* Centre de Recherche en Gestion, Ecole Polytechnique, Paris, June 1983.

Berthelemy, J.C., "La montée des protectionnismes et la recherche des voies alternatives", Colloque GRECO-EFIQ, Aix-Marseille, 30th June-1st July 1983.

Berthelot, Y. and De Bandt, J., *Impact des relations avec le Tiers Monde sur l'économie française,* La Documentation française, 1982.

Bhagwati, J.N., "Directly Unproductive, Profit-seeking (DUP) Activities, *Journal of Political Economy,* Vol. 90, No. 5, 1982, pp. 988-1002.

Bhisault, L., Blandinières, J.P. and Mormiche, P., "Le système productif régional", *Économie et Statistiques,* 1983.

Birnberg, T.B., "Trade Reform Options: Economic Effects on Developed Countries", in: Cline, W.R., *Policy Alternatives for a New Economic Order: An Economic Analysis,* 1979.

Black, J. and Hindley, B. (Eds.), *Current Issues in Commercial Policy and Diplomacy*, Macmillan Press for the Trade Policy Research Centre, London, 1980.

Black, A.P., *Long-run theories of growth and development with reference to the American and British automobile industries*, unpublished PhD thesis, University of London.

Black, A.P., "Product Pricing Cycles in the Automobile Industry", EARIE Conference, Bergen, August 1983.

Black, A.P., "International Trade in the Automobile Industry", International Institute of Management, Berlin, August 1983.

Black, A.P., "Intra-Industry Trade and Industrial Adjustment: The Case of the Automobile Industry", International Institute of Management, Berlin, 1984.

Black, A.P., "A Survey of Recent Developments in the World Automotive Industry: some causes and consequences", International Conference on Sectoral Crisis Management in Europe and the USA, June 1984.

Blackburn, J.A., "The vanishing UK Cotton Industry", *National Westminster Bank Quarterly Review*, November 1982, pp. 43-53.

Bloch, H., "Prices, costs, and profits in Canadian manufacturing: the influence of tariffs and concentration", *Canadian Journal of Economics*, Vol. VII, No. 4, November 1974.

Boussemart, B. and Rabier, J.C., *Le Dossier Agache Willot*, Presses de la Fondation Nationale des Sciences Politiques, 1983.

Bowen, H.P. and Pelzman, J., "US Export Competitiveness: 1962-77", *Applied Economics*, 1984.

Boyle, S.E. and Hogarty, T.F., "Pricing behaviour in the American automobile industry 1957-1971", *Journal of Industrial Economics*, December 1975.

Brander, J.S., and Barbara J. Spencer. "Tariffs and the Extraction of Foreign Monopoly Rents under Potential Entry," *Canadian Journal of Economics*, 16, August 1981, pp. 371-89.

Breitenacher, M., "The Textile Industry in the Process of Structural Adjustment", *Ifo-Digest*, 2, 1980, pp. 28-37.

Bright, Samuel L., and McKinney, Joseph A., "The Economics of the Steel Trigger Price Mechanism", *Business Economics*, Vol. 19, No. 4, July 1984, pp. 40-46.

Brincard, M., "The Textile Industry in Europe", *Europe's Textile Industry*, 1977.

British Business, "Analyses of British Businesses by Turnover Size", 23rd January 1981, pp. 183-185.

Brock, G., "Optimal Pricing with Endogenous Barriers to Entry", manuscript, University of Arizona, 1978.

Brock, W.A. and Magee, S.P., "The Economics of Special Interest Politics: The Case of the Tariff", *Review — American Economic* Vol. 68, No. 2, pp. 246-250.

Bröckel, I.G., "The Point of View of the Textile Machinery Industry", University of Stuttgart, West Germany, September 1978.

Brown, D., "Success brings problems for Swedish steel: Booming exports have raised the spectre of foreign restrictions", *Financial Times*, Tuesday, 21st August 1984.

Brown, F. and Whalley, J., "General equilibrium evaluations of tariff-cutting proposals in the Tokyo Round and comparisons with more extensive liberalisation of world trade", *The Economic Journal*, 90, 1980.

Bulow, J.I. and Shoven, J.B., "The Bankruptcy Decision", *The Bell Journal of Economics,* 1979.

Bureau of Economics, Federal Trade Commission, *Economic Papers 1966-69,* Washington D.C., 1969.

Bureau of Labor Statistics, *International Comparisons of Productivity and Labor Costs in the Steel Industry; United States, Japan, France, Germany, United Kingdom; 1964 and 1972-82,* BLS, Office of Productivity and Technology, US Department of Labor, unpublished mimeo, Washington D.C., January 1984.

Bureau of Labor Statistics, *Estimated Hourly Compensation of Production Workers in the Iron and Steel Industries, 16 Countries, 1975-1981,* BLS, unpublished mimeo,, Washington DC, January 1982.

Business Week, "A Chrysler-VW Hookup is still far down the road", July 1983.

Business Week, "A New Weapon against Japan: R&D Partnerships", 8th August 1983.

Business Week, "Can Don Lennox save Harvester?", 15th August 1983.

Business Week, "High-Tech Companies team up in the R&D Race", 15th August 1983.

Business Week, "How the GM-Toyota deal buys time", February 1983.

Business Week, "Ideas & Trends", September 1983.

Business Week, "Imports are still ripping into the Textile Industry", 5th September 1983.

Business Week, "J.P. Stevens takes the Designer Route", 19th September 1983.

Business Week, "Suddenly US Companies are teaming up", 11th July 1983.

Business Week, "The Dispute over Lead-Free Gasoline Catches up with Europe", August 1983.

Business Week, "The tiny cars that women are wild about", February 1983.

Business Week, "US Car Quotas: How less is more for Japan?", November 1983.

Business Week, "US Textile Quotas: Mending Loopholes has frayed Nerves", 21, 10th September 1984.

Buxton, J., "Italian fibres group with a new name for arms", Financial Times, 8th March 1983.

Buzzell, R., and Wiersema, F.: "Successful Share - Building Strategies", *Harvard Business Review,* Jan-Feb 1981.

Buzzell, R.D., Gale, B.T. and Sultan, R.G.M., "Market share — a key to profitability", *Harvard Business Review,* January-February 1975.

Cable, V., "World Textile Trade and Production", Economist Intelligence Unit Special Report No. 63, London, 1979.

Cable, V., "An Evaluation of the MultiFibre Arrangement and Negotiating Options", Commonwealth Economic Papers, No. 15, 1981.

Cable V. *Protectionism and Industrial Decline,* Hodder and Stoughton, London 1983.

Cameron, D.R., "The expansion of the public economy: a comparative analysis", *The American Political Science Review,* Vol. 72, No. 4, December 1978.

Candot, Z. and Dubarry, J.P., "Les importateurs sont-ils aussi exportateurs?", INSEE, *Économie et Statistique,* 1982.

Canto, V.A., "The Effect of Voluntary Restraint Agreements: a Case Study of the Steel Industry", *Applied Economics,* Vol. 16, No. 2, April 1984, pp. 175-186.

Capie, F., *Depression and Protectionism: Britain between the Wars*, George Allen & Unwin, London, 1983.

Carlsson, B. "The Measurement of Efficiency in Production: An Application to Swedish Manufacturing Industries, 1968," *Swedish Journal of Economics*, 74, December 1972, pp. 468-85.

Carlsson, B., "Steel", paper for the European Association for Research in Industrial Economics, Milan Conference, 1981.

Carlsson, B., "Industrial Subsidies in Sweden: Macroeconomic Effects and an International Comparison", *The Journal of Industrial Economics*, Vol. 32, No. 1, September 1983.

Carmoy, G. de, "Subsidy policies in Britain, France and West Germany: An Overview," in Warnecke, S.J., *International Trade and Industrial Policies*, Macmillan, London, 1978.

Cavanagh, J. and Machel, J., "Contracting Poverty", *Economic Weekly*, Bombay, 1983, pp. 1347-48.

Caves, R.E., Khailzadeh-Shirazi, J. and Porter, M.E., "Scale Economies in Statistical Analyses of Market Power", *Review of Economics and Statistics*, May 1975.

Caves, R.E. and Uekusa, M., *Industrial Organization in Japan*, Brookings Institution, Washington D.C., 1976.

Caves, R.E., Michael E. Porter and A. Michael Spence, *Competition in the Open Economy: A Model Applied to Canada*, Harvard University Press, Cambridge, 1980.

Caves, R.E., *Multinational Enterprise and Economic Analysis*, Cambridge University Press, 1982.

Caves, R.E., *International Trade and Industrial Organisation: Problems, Solved and Unsolved*, mimeo, Harvard University, prepared for European Association for Research on Industrial Economics, Bergen, August, 1983.

Caves, R.E., *Scale, openness, and productivity in Australian industries*, The Brookings Survey of the Australian Economy Conference, Canberra, 9th-11th January 1984.

Caves, R.E., Fortunato, M. and Ghemawat, P., "The Decline of Dominant Firms, 1905-1929", *The Quarterly Journal of Economics*, August 1984.

Centre d'Etudes Prospectives et d'Informations Internationales, *Économie mondiale : la montée des tensions*, Économica, Paris, 1983.

Centre d'Études et de Recherches sur les Qualifications, *Création de Produits Nouveaux et Industries de Mode : Le Cas de l'Habillement et de la Chaussure*, Dossier No. 31, January 1982.

Chenery, H. and Keesing, D., "The Changing Composition of Developing Country Exports", World Bank Staff Working Paper, No. 314, 1979.

Chichilnisky, G. and Heal, G., "Trade and Development in the Eighties", Graduate School of Business, Columbia University, Research Working Paper No. 540A, November 1983.

Chiplin D., and Wright, M.: "Divestment and Structural Change in U.K. Industry", *National Westminster Bank Quarterly Review*, Feb 1980.

Clark, K.B., "Competition, Technical Diversity and Radical Innovation in the US Auto Industry", Working Paper HBS.82-25, Graduate School of Business Administration, Harvard University, August 1981.

Clarke, R., "Profit Margins and Market Concentration in UK Manufacturing Industry: 1970-1976", *Applied Economics*, 16, 1984., pp. 57-71.

231

Clifford, D.K., "Thriving in a Recession", *Harvard Business Review,* Jul-Aug. 1977.

Cline, W.R. *et al., Trade Negotiations in the Tokyo Round, A Quantitiative Assessment,* The Brookings Institution, Washington D.C., 1978.

Cline, W.R., "Exports of Manufactures from Developing Countries: Performance and Prospects for Market Access", February 1982.

"Clothing and Footwear in France", *Marketing in Europe,* 225, August 1981.

CNUCED, *Commerce international des textiles de coton et pays en voie de developpement : Problèmes et perspectives,* United Nations, New York, 1968.

Cockerill, A., "Steel and the State in Great Britain", *Annals of Public and Co-operative Economy,* Vol. 51, No. 4, October-December 1980, pp. 439-457.

Cohen, C.M., "Textile : stopper l'hécatombe", le Nouvel Economiste, No. 317, Paris, 1981, pp. 38-43.

Cohen, S.D., *The Making of United States International Economic Policy: Principles, Problems, and Proposals for Reform,* Praeger Publishers, New York, 1981.

Cohen, S.D. and Metzler, R.I, *United States International Economic Policy in Action,* Praeger, New York, 1982.

COMITEXTILE, *The European Textile and Clothing Industries and the International Division of Labour,* Brussels, 1976.

Commission of the European Communities, *Thirteenth Report on Competition Policy,* Brussels/Luxembourg, 1984.

Condliffe, J.B., *The Commerce of Nations,* Allen and Unwin, London, 1951.

Connidis, L.A., "The effective rate of protection for motor vehicle manufacturing in Canada", *Canadian Journal of Economics,* 16, No. 1, 1983.

Consumers' Association, *A Study of the Effect of Import Controls on the Cost of Imported Clothing: A Which? Campaign Report,* London, August, 1979.

Corden, W.M., "The calculation of the cost of protection", *Economic Record* Vol. 33, April 1957, pp. 29-51.

Corden, W.M., *Trade Policy and Economic Welfare,* Clarendon Press, Oxford, 1974.

Corden, W.M. and Fels, G., *Public Assistance to Industry, Protection and Subsidies in Britain and Germany,* Macmillan Press, 1976.

Corden, W.M., "The Revival of Protectionism", Occasional Papers No. 14, The Group of Thirty, New York, 1984.

Corden, W.M., "Market Disturbances and Protection: Efficiency versus the Conservative Social Welfare Function", Discussion Paper No. 92, The Australian National University, Centre for Economic Policy Research, March 1984.

Cornes, R. and Dixit, A., "Comparative Effects of Devaluation and Import Controls on Domestic Prices", *Economica,* 49, February 1982, p. 1-10.

Correale, G., Gaeta, R., "Mutamenti structurali nell'industria tessile — abbigliamento", *Economia e Politica industriale,* No. 38, 1983, pp. 146-191.

Council on Wage and Price Stability, *Report to the President on Prices and Costs in the United States Steel Industry,* US Government Printing Office, Washington DC, October 1977.

Coutts, K., Godley, W.A.H., and Nordhaus, W.D. *Industrial Pricing in the United Kingdom,* Cambridge: OUP, 1978.

Cowhey, P.F. and Long, E., "Testing Theories of Regime Change: Hegemonic Decline or Surplus Capacity?", *International Organization*, Vol. 37, 2, Spring 1983.

Cox C.C. "The Enforcement of Public Price Controls," *Journal of Political Economy*, Vol. 99, No. 51, University of Chicago, 1980.

Cox, D. and Harris, R., "Trade Liberalisation and Industrial Organisation: some estimates for Canada", Discussion Paper 523, Queen's University (Canada), April 1983.

Crandall, R.W., *The US Steel Industry in Recurrent Crisis: Policy Options in a Competitive World*, The Brookings Institution, Washington DC, 1981.

Crandall, R.W., "Rationalising the US Carbon Steel Industry: A Critical Perspective", Paper for Institute for International Economics Project on Structural Adjustment, Washington D.C., Institute for International Economics, November 1984.

Crandall, R.W., "Competition and Trade Protection in the US Steel Market", Brookings Institution, draft mimeo, Washington D.C., November 1984b.

Cripps, N.B. and Godley, W.A.H., "Control of Imports as a Means to Full Employment and the Expansion of World Trade: the U.K. Case", *Cambridge Journal of Economics*, 1978.

Cronin, M.R., "Protection and employment in the Motor Car Sector", *Australian Economic Papers*, Vol. 23, No. 42, June 1984, p. 38-51.

Crouch, C., "New thinking on pluralism", in *The Political Quarterly*, October-December 1983, pp. 363-374.

Dahl, R.A., *Dilemmas of Pluralist Democracy*, Yale University Press, 1982.

Daily News Record, "Textile Technology", Section 2, 6th December 1982.

Dalton, J.A. and Rhoades, S., "Growth and product differentiability as factors influencing changes in concentration", *Journal of Industrial Economics*, 1974.

Dancet, G., "Nominal and effective tariffs and the protection of labour in Belgium", *Cahiers Économiques de Bruxelles*, No. 85, 1980.

Davidson, F.G., and Stewardson, B.R., *Economics and Australian Industry*, Victoria, Australia, 1974.

Deardorf, A.V. and Stern, R.M., "The effects of the Tokyo Round on the structure of protection", National Bureau of Economic Research, Conference on the structure and evolution of recent US Trade Policy, Cambridge, Mass., December 1982.

Deardorf, A.V., and Stern, R.M., "Input-Output Technologies and the Effects of Tariffs and Exchange Rates", Bureau of International Labor Affairs, US Department of Labour, April 1984.

Deardorf, A.V. and Stern, R.M., "Economic Effects of the Tokyo Round", *Southern Economic Journal*, Vol. 49, No. 3, 1983.

De Cecco, M., *Economia e finanza internazionale dal 1890 al 1914*, Editori Laterza, Siena, November 1970.

De Grauwe, P., Kennes, W., Peeters, T., and Van Straelen, R., "Trade Expansion with the Less Developed Countries and Employment: A Case Study of Belgium", *Weltwirtschaftliches Archiv.*, Vol. 3 1979.

De la Torre, J., *Corporate Responses to Import Competition in US Apparel Industry*, Research Monograph-College of Business Administration, Georgia State University, No. 74, Atlanta, 1978.

De la Torre, J. and Bacchetta, M., *Decline and Adjustment: European Policies Toward Their Clothing Industries,* European Institute of Business Administration, Fontainebleau, France, June, 1979.

De la Torre, J., "Public Intervention Strategies in the European Clothing Industries", *Journal of Trade Law,* January-June 1981.

De Menton, J., *Compétitivité et stratégie des firmes dans les secteurs textile habillement,* Centres d'Études et de Prévision, Ministère de l'Industrie, March 1981.

Demsetz, H., *Economic, Legal and Political Dimensions of Competition,* North-Holland, Amsterdam, 1982.

Denton, G., O'Cleireacain, S. and Ash, S., *Trade Effects of Public Subsidies to Private Enterprise,* Macmillan, 1975.

Department of Commerce, *The US Automobile Industry,* 1982, Report to the Congress from the Secretary of Commerce, Washington D.C. 1983.

De Rosa, D.A., and Goldstein, M., "Import Discipline in the US Manufacturing Sector," *IMF Staff Papers,* 28, September, 1981,pp. 600-34.

Dethomas, B., "Faut-il sauver les entreprises en difficulté?", *Le Monde,* 3rd March 1984.

Deutscher Bundestag, *9. Subventionsbericht,* Bonn, 1983.

De Vany, A. and Frey, G., "Backlogs and the Value of Excess Capacity in the Steel Industry", *The American Economic Review,* Vol. 72, No. 3, 1982 pp. 441-451.

De Witt, F., "La Troisième Mort de Boussac", *L'Expansion,* 2nd/15th April 1982.

Dicke, H. *et al., Beschäftigungswirkungen einer verstärkten Arbeitsteilung zwischen der Bundesrepublik und den Entwicklungslandern,* Kieler Studien Nr. 137, Institut für Weltwirtschaft an der Universitat Kiel, Hrg. Herbert Giersch, Tübingen, 1976.

Diebold, W.J., "The End of the ITO", Essays in International Finance, No. 16, Princeton University, October 1952.

Diebold, W.J., "The United States in the world economy: a fifty year perspective", *Foreign Affairs,* 1984, pp. 81-104.

Dion, R., *An Econometric Model of the Steel Trade,* Bank of Canada Technical Report 33, mimeo, Ottawa, October 1982.

Dirlam, J.B. and Mueller, H., "Import restraints and reindustrialization: the case of the US steel industry", *Middle Tennessee State University Conference Paper Series,* No. 67, published in *Journal of International Law,* Vol. 14, Summer 1982, No. 3, pp. 419-445.

Dixit, A., "A model of duopoly suggesting a theory of entry barriers", *The Bell Journal of Economics,* Vol. 10, No. 1, Spring 1979.

Dixit, A., "The role of investment in entry-deterrence", *The Economic Journal,* 90, March 1980, pp. 95-106.

Doeringer, P.B. and Piore, M.J., *Internal Labour Markets and Manpower Analysis,* D.C. Heath & Co., Boston, 1976.

Donnadieu, G., "Les nouvelles stratégies de la concurrence internationale dans l'industrie textile", Problèmes économiques, Documentation française, 1758, Paris, 1982, pp. 19-27.

Dreze, J., "Quelques réflexions sereines sur l'adaptation de l'industrie belge au Marché Commun", No. 275, Comptes Rendus des travaux de la Société Royale d'Économie Politique de Belgique, 20th December 1960.

Duchesneau, T. D., Cohn, S.F. and Dutton, J.E., *A Study of Innovation in Manufacturing: Determinants, Processes and Methodological Issues,* Executive Summary, The Social Science Research Institute, University of Maine at Drono, 1980.

Dunne, Nancy, "Washington faces hard slog in steel talks", *Financial Times,* Wednesday, 30th January 1985.

Dunnett, P.J.S., *The Decline of the British Motor Industry: The Effects of Government Policy, 1945-1979,* Croom Helm Ltd., London, 1980.

Dunning, John H., *International Production and the Multinational Enterprise,* George Allen and Unwin, London 1981.

Eastman, H.C. and Stykoit, S., *The Tariff and Competition in Canada,* St. Martin's Press, New York, 1967.

Easton, S.T. and Messerlin, P., "The French Tariff During the Twentieth Century: An Aggregate Analysis", June 1982.

Eaton, C. and Lipsey, R.G., "Exit barriers are entry barriers: the durability of capital as a barrier to entry", *The Bell Journal of Economics,* 1980,pp. 721-729.

Economic Commission for Europe, *Structural Changes in the Iron and Steel Industry,* United Nations, New York, 1979.

Ehrenberg, R.G., *The Regulatory Process and Labor Earnings,* Academic Press, New York, 1979.

Elliott, J., "Government Policy Faces Significant Tests", *Financial Times,* Tuesday, 22nd June 1982.

Encaoua, D., *Price dynamics and industrial structure: a theoretical and econometric analysis,* Working Paper No. 10, OECD, July 1983.

Ergas, H., "Corporate Strategies in Transition", in Jacquemin, A. (Ed.), *European Industry: Public Policy and Corporate Strategy,* Oxford University Press, 1984.

Ethier, W.J. "National and International Returns to Scale in the Modern Theory of International Trade," *American Economic Review* 72, June 1982, pp. 389-405.

Evans, P., *Dependent Development,* Princeton University Press, 1979.

Ewing, A.F., "Non-tariff barriers and non-adjustment on international trade", *Journal of World Trade Law,* Vol. 18, No. 1, January-February 1984, pp. 63-80.

Fedele, M., *La Deriva del Potere* De Donato, Bari, 1981.

Federal Trade Commission, Bureau of Economics, *Staff Report on the United States Steel Industry and its International Rivals: Trends and Factors Determining International Competitiveness,* Government Printing Office for FTC, Washington DC, 1977.

Federtessile, *Il settore tessile e abbigliamento in Italia,* Angeli, Milan, 1980.

Feenstra, R.C., "Voluntary Eport Restraint in US Autos, 1980-81: Quality, Employment and Welfare Effects", mimeo January 1983.

Feinberg, R.E. and Kallab, V. (Eds.), "Adjustment Crisis in the Third World", *US Third World Policy Perspectives,* No. 1, Overseas Development Council, New Brunswick, London, 1984.

Feldstein, M., Horioka, C., "Domestic Saving and International Capital Flows", *The Economic Journal,* 90, June 1980, pp. 314-329.

Ferreira, M.P., and Reyment, P., "Exports of Manufactures from South European Countries," *Journal of World Trade Law,* May-June 1984.

Field, A., *An Analysis of the Changing Patterns of International Trade in Textiles and Clothing*, International Division of Labour Programme, International Labour Organisation, September 1979.

Financial Times, "US Steel Pushes for Greater Protection", Tuesday, 1st May 1984.

Finger, J.M., "Tariff Provisions for off-shore Assembly and the Exports for Developing Countries", *Economic Journal*, June 1975.

Finger, J.M., De Rosa, D.A., Nye, W.W., Golub, S.S., Shelton, J.R. and Suddeth, L., "Countervailing duties against foreign indirect tax remissions on exports, and retaliation: estimates of the impacts", Office of Policy Research Discussion Paper Series, Treasury Department, 7th September 1977.

Finger, J.M., "Industrial Country Policy and Adjustment to Imports from Developing Countries", World Bank Staff Working Paper No. 470, July 1981.

Finger, J.M., Hall, H.K. and Nelson, D.R., "The Political Economy of Administered Protection", *The American Economic Review*, Vol. 72, No. 3, June 1982, pp. 452-466.

Fisher, F.M., Griliches, Z. and Kaysen, C., "The Costs of Automobile Model Changes Since 1949", *Journal of Political Economy*, 70, October 1962, pp. 433-51.

Fitzgerald, F., "Energy in Iron and Steelmaking", Keynote speech to South East Asia Iron and Steel Institute Conference, Singapore, September 1984.

Flax, S., "How Detroit is Reforming the Steelmakers", Fortune, May 1983.

Fleisig, H. and Hill, C., "The benefits and costs of official export credit programs", National Bureau of Economic Research, Conference, Cambridgem Mass., 3rd-4th December 1982.

Forcellini, P. *Rapporto sull'industria italiana*, Editori Riunti, Roma, November 1978.

Fornengo, G., *L'industria italiana dell'abbigliamento*, Il Mulino, Bologna, 1978.

Fornengo, G., "The Impact of Protectionism on the Textiles and Clothing Industries of Western Europe", Laboratorio di Economica Politica, Università degli Studi di Torino, Turin, 31st August 1983.

Fortune, "How Japan manages declining industries", 10th January 1983.

Fortune, "Anatomy of an Auto-Plant Rescue", 4th April 1983.

Fortune, "Benetton Takes on the World", 13th June 1983, pp. 114-117.

Fouquin, M., Messler, V., Richemond, A. and Desaigues, M.J., *Redéploiements géographiques et rapports de force industriels*, Économie Prospective Internationale, No. 5, January 1981.

Frank, C.R., *Foreign Trade and Domestic Aid*, The Brookings Institution, Washington D.C., 1977.

Franko, L.G., *Joint Venture Survival in Multinational Corporations*, Praeger, New York, 1971

Franko, L.G., *European Industrial Policy*, Conference Board in Europe, Brussels, 1980.

Franko, L.G., "Adjusting to export thrusts of newly industrialising countries", *Economic Journal*, Vol. 91, June 1981, pp. 486-505.

Franko, L.G. and Stephenson, S., "The Micro Picture: Corporate and Sectoral Developments", in: Turner and McMullen, *The Newly Industrialising Countries: Trade and Adjustment*, Allen & Unwin, 1982.

Freeman, R.B., "Manpower requirements and substitution analysis of labor skills: a synthesis", in Ehrenberg, R.G. (Ed.), *Research in Labor Economics: An Annual Compilation of Research*, JAI Press, Greenwich, 1977.

Frey, B., *International Organization,* 1984.

Frey, L., *Lavoro a domicilio e decentramento dell'attività produttiva nei settori tessile e abbigliamento in Italia,* Angeli, Milan, 1975.

Friden, L., *Instability in the International Steel Market: A Study of Import and Export Fluctuations,* Beckmans, Stockholm, 1972.

Friendlaender, A.F., Winston C. and Wang U. "Costs, Technology and Productivity in the US Automobile Industry" *Bell Journal of Economics,* Vol. 14 n° 1 Spring 1983.

Fröbel, F., Henrichs, J., Kreye, O., *The New International Division of Labour,* Cambridge University Press, Cambridge, 1980.

Gale, B.T. and Branch, B.S., "Concentration vs. market share", *The Anti-Trust Bulletin,* Spring 1982.

Gardiner, R.N., *Sterling-Dollar Diplomacy in Current Perspective: The Origins and the Prospects of our International Economic Order,* Columbia University Press, New York, 1965.

Gaskins, D.W. Jr, "Dynamic Limit Pricing: Optimal Pricing under Threat of Entry", *Journal of Economic Theory 3,* September 1971, pp. 306-22.

GATT, "Arrangement regarding international trade in textiles", Geneva, 1974.

GATT, Studies in International Trade, *Trade Liberalisation Protectionism and Interdependence,* Geneva: GATT, No. 5, 1977.

GATT, *Adjustment, Trade and Growth in Developed and Developing Countries,* Geneva: GATT No. 6, 1978.

GATT, "The Tokyo Round of Multilateral Negotiations", Report by the Director-General of GATT, Geneva, April, 1979.

GATT, "Committee on Safeguards", Document Spec(82)18/Rev.2, September 1982.

GATT, "Textiles and Clothing in the World Economy", GATT document Spec(84)24, May 1984.

Gavioli, N, "Cosi piccoli, cosi bravi", *Mondo economico,* 3rd November 1983.

General Accounting Office, *New Strategy required for aiding distressed Steel Industry: Report to the Congress of the United States by the Comptroler General,* Government Printing Office for FTC, Washington DC, 1981.

Genevaz, P., *Industrial and Financial Indicators of the Steel Industry,* La Chambre des Contes, 1982.

Gennard, J., *Job security and industrial relations,* OECD, Paris, 1979.

George, K.D. and Ward, T.S., *The Structure of Industry in the EEC: An International Comparison,* University of Cambridge, Department of Applied Economics, Occasional Paper 43, Cambridge University Press, 1975.

Geroski, P.A., Hankub, A.P., Knight, K.G., "Wages, Bargaining Power and Market Structure", mimeo, May 1979.

Geroski, P.A., and Alexis Jacquemin. "Imports as a Competitive Discipline," *Recherches Économiques de Louvain 47,* September 1981, pp. 197-208.

Geroski, P.A., Jacquemin, A., "Dominant Firms and their Alleged Decline", *International Journal of Industrial Organisation,* 2, 1984, pp. 1-27.

Giersch, H. (Ed.), *Emerging Technologies: Consequences for Economic Growth, Structural Change, and Employment Symposium 1981,* J.C.B. Mohr (Paul Siebeck), Tübingen.

Gilpin, R., *War and Change in World Politics*, Cambridge University Press, Cambridge, 1981.

Glezer, L., *Tariff Politics: Australian Policy-making 1960-1980*, Melbourne University Press, 1982.

Glismann, H.H. and Weiss, F.D., "On the political economy of protection in Germany", World Bank Staff Working Paper No. 427, October 1980.

Gold, Bela, "Evaluating scale economies: the case of Japanese blast furnaces", *Journal of Industrial Economics,* 1974.

Gold, Bela, "Changing Perspectives on Size, Scale and Returns: An interpretive Survey", *Journal of Economic Literature,* Vol. XIX, March 1981.

Gold, Bela, "Pressures for Restructuring the World Steel Industry in the 1980's: A Case Study in Challenges to Industrial Adaptation", *Quarterly Review of Economics and Business,* 22 No. 1, Spring 1982, pp. 45-66.

Goldthorpe, J.H., "Problems of Political Economy after the End of the postwar Period", Nuffield College, Oxford, August 1982.

Gorecki, P.K., "An inter-industry analysis of diversification in the UK manufacturing sector", *Journal of Industrial Economics,* 1975, pp. 131-46.

Grant, R.M., "Corporate Adjustment to Import Competition and Trade Protection with a Case Study of the UK Cutlery Industry 1973-83", London Business School, Decemmber 1983.

Grant, R.M., "Strategy Options for Firms in Mature Industries Facing Low Cost International Competition", London, 1984.

Griliches, Z, "Automobile Prices and Quality: Did the Gasoline Price Increase Change Consumer Tastes in the US?", mimeo, 1984.

Grilli, E. and La Noce, M., "The Political Economy of Protection in Italy: Some Empirical Evidence", *Banca Nazionale del Lavoro,* Quarterly Review, 1982, pp. 144-161.

Grjebine, V., "L'ajustement structurel dans l'industrie du textile et de l'habillement", mimeo, 1985.

Gronhang, K. and Lorentzen, T., "Exploring the impact of Government export subsidies", *European Journal of Marketing,* Vol. 17, No. 2, 1983.

Grossman, G.M., "Imports as a cause of injury: the case of the US steel industry", Princeton University, July 1984.

Grubel, H.G. and Johnson, H. (Eds.), *Effective Tariff Protection,* Geneva, 1971.

Guillochon, B., "La France des années 1970, est-elle protectionniste?", *Revue Économique,* Vol. 33, No. 6, November 1982.

Guttman, J.M., "Understanding Collective Action: Matching Behaviour", *American Economic Association,* Vol. 68, No. 2, May 1978, pp. 251-255.

Hacche, G., "The Determinants of Exchange Rate Movements", OECD Economics and Statistics Department, Working Paper No. 7, 1983.

Hambrick, D.C. and Schecter, S.M. "Turnaround strategies for mature industrial-product business units", *Academy of Management Journal,* 26, 1983, pp. 231-48.

Hamermesh, R., Anderson M. and Harris, J.: "Strategies for Low Market Share Businesses", *Harvard Business Review,* May-Jun 1978.

Hamermesh R., and Silk S.: "How to Compete in Stagnant Businesses", *Harvard Business Review,* Sep-Oct 1979.

Hamilton, C., "A new approach to estimation of the effects of non-tariff trade barriers: an application to the Swedish textile and clothing industry", *Weltwirtschaftliches Archiv,* 1981.

Hanusek, E.A., "Statement before the Subcommittee on Trade on Ways and Means, US House of Representatives", 20th June 1984.

Harrigan, K.R., *Strategies for Declining Businesses,* Lexington, 1980.

Harrigan, K.R., "Strategic planning for endgame", *Long Range Planning,* 15, 1982, pp. 45-8.

Harrigan, K.R., "Exit Decisions in Mature Industries", *Academy of Management Journal,* 1982.

Harrigan, K.R. and Porter, M.E., "Endgame strategies for declining industries", *Harvard Business Review,* July-August 1983, pp. 111-20.

Harris, R.G., "Applied general equilibrium analysis of small open economies with scale economies and imperfect competition", Queen's University Discussion Paper, No. 524, 1983.

Harris, R.G. (with the assistance of David Cox), "Trade, industrial policy, and Canadian manufacturing", Economic Council, 1984.

Hart, J., "An Industrial Policy for the United States", mimeo, 1982.

Hartle, D.G., "The Theory of 'Rent-Seeking': some reflections", Canadian *Journal of Economics,* XVI, No. 4, November 1983, pp. 539-554.

Havrylyshyn, O. and Civan, E., "Intra-Industry Trade and Stage of Development", Discussion paper No. 8309, Centre d'Economie Mathématique et d'Econométrie, Brussels.

Havrylyshyn, O. and Civan, E., "Intra-Industry Trade Among Developing Countries", Division Working Paper No. 1982-86, November 1982.

Havrylyshyn, O., "The Increasing Integration of Newly Industrialized Countries in World Trade: A Quantitative Analysis of Intra-Industry Trade", Symposium on Intra-Industry Trade, Brussels, May 1983.

Hawke, G.R., "The United States Tariff and Industrial Protection in the Late Nineteenth Century", *Review of Economic History,* 1975.

Hazledine, Tim, "Testing Two Models of Pricing and Protection with Canada / United States Data," *Journal of Industrial Economics* 29, December 1980, pp. 145-54.

Hekman, J.S., "An Analysis of the Changing Location of Iron and Steel Production in the Twentieth Century", *The American Economic Review,* Vol. 68, No. 1, March 1978, pp. 123-133.

Helleiner, G.K., *The Impact of the Exchange Rate System on the Developing Countries: Report to the Group of Twenty-Four,* UNCTAD/MFD/TA/13, April 1981.

Henner, H.F. *et al., La protection effective dans les pays industrialisés,* Éditions Économica, Paris, 1972.

Hesselman, L., "The Macroeconomic Role of Relative Price Variability in the USA and the UK", *Applied Economics,* 15, Chapman and Hall Ltd., 1983, pp. 225-233.

Hindley, B., "Britain's Economy as seen by the Cambridge group" in Corbet *et al., On How to Cope with Britains Trade Position,* Trade Policy Research Centre, London, 1977.

Hindley, B., "Trade Policy, Economic Performance, and Britain's Economic Problems" in Alan Winters (ed.), *Trade Policy and Economic Performance* (Macmillan, forthcoming), 1983.

Hitiris, T., "Effective protection and economic performance in UK manufacturing industry, 1963 and 1968", *The Economic Journal,* 88, March 1978.

Hocking, R.D., "Trade in Motor Cars between the Major European Producers", *Economic Journal*, No. 90, pp. 504-519.

Hogan, W.T., *The 1970s: Critical Years for Steel*, D.C. Heath, Lexington, 1972.

Holden, K. and Peel, D.A., "The Benefit/Income Ratio for unemployed Workers in the United Kingdom", *International Labour Review*, Vol. 118, No. 5, September-October 1979.

Holmes, P. and Shepherd, G., "Protectionism in the European Community: internal and external aspects", International Economics Study Group, 8th Annual Conference, Isle of Thorns, Sussex, 16th-18th September 1983.

Holsti, O.R., Siverson, R.M. George, A.L. (Eds.), *Change in the International System*, Westview Press, Boulder, Colorado, 1980.

Hood, N. and Young, S., *Multinationals in Retreat: The Scottish Experience*, Edinburgh University Press, 1982.

House of Commons, *The British Steel Corporation's Prospects*, HMSO, London, 1983.

Houtte, H.V., "The EEC Draft Regulation on Selective Distribution of Automobiles", *Journal of World Trade Law*, 1983, pp. 349-357.

Howe, W.S., "The Dundee Jute Industry 1967-1977: A Study of Individual Industry Response to Decline", paper presented at the 7th Conference of the European Association for Research in Industrial Economics, Milan, September 1980.

Hufbauer, Gary and Rosen, Howard, "Managing comparative disadvantage", paper for Institute of International Economics Project on Structural Adjustment, Institute for International Economics, Washington D.C., November 1984.

Hughes, G.A., Newbery, D.M.G., "The effect of protection on manufactured exports from developing countries", Discussion Paper Series No. 14, Centre for Economic Policy Research, London, 1984.

Hughes, H. and Krueger, A., "Effects of Protection in Developed Countries on Developing Countries' Exports of Manufactures", paper contributed to Conference on the Structure and Evolution of Recent US Trade Policy Cambridge, Mass, December 1982.

Hunker, J.A., *Structural Change in the US Automobile Industry*, Lexington Books, Massachusetts, 1984.

Hürni, B.S., "Restrictions on international competition through government measures", *Intereconomics*, March/April, 1983.

HWWA — Institut für Wirtschaftsforschung, "Analyse der strukturellen Entwicklung der deutschen Wirtschaft", Strukturbericht, 1983, Hamburg, 1983.

Imai, K. and Sakuma, A., "An Industrial Organisation Analysis of the Semiconductor Industry: A US-Japan Comparison", Discussion Paper No. 113, Institute of Business Research, Hitotsubashi University, Kunitachi-shi, Tokyo.

Imlah, A.H., *Economic Elements in the Pax Britannica*, Oxford University Press, 1958.

Industries Assistance Commission, *Annual Report*, 1973-74, Canberra, 1974.

Industries Assistance Commission, *Annual Report*, 1979-80, Canberra, 1980.

Industries Assistance Commission, *Annual Report*, 1980-81, Canberra, 1980.

Industries Assistance Commission, *Annual Report*, 1981-82, Canberra, 1980.

Industries Assistance Commission, *Approaches to General Reductions in Protection*, Information Paper No. 1, Trends in the Structure of Assistance to Manufacturing, Canberra, 1980.

Industries Assistance Commission, *Approaches to General Reductions in Protection,* Canberra, 1982.

Industries Assistance Commission, *Passenger and Light Commercial Vehicles — Substitution,* 14th December 1983, No. 35, Australian Government Publishing Service, Canberra, 1983.

Industries Assistance Commission Report, *Certain Iron and Steel Products and Certain Alloy Steel Products,* Australian Government Publishing Service, Canberra, 1983.

Industries Assistance Commission Report No. 330, *Polyvinyl Chloride Homopolymer (anti-dumping),* Australian Government Publishing Service, Canberra, 4th October 1983.

INSEE, "La Situation Financière des entreprises", Mimeo, February 1985.

Isard, P., "Employment Impacts of Textile Imports and Investment: a vintage Capital Model", *American Economic Review,* June 1973, pp. 402-16.

Itoh, Motoshige, and Yoshiyasu Ono. "Tariffs, Quotas and Market Structure," *Quarterly Journal of Economics* 97, May 1982, pp. 195-305.

Jacobson, L.S., *Earnings Losses and Worker Displacement When Employment Declines in the Steel Industry,* PhD dissertation, Northwestern University, August 1977.

Jacobson, L.S. and Thomason, J., *Earnings Loss due to Displacement,* The Public Research Institute of the Center for Naval Analyses, Virginia, 25th July 1979.

Jacquemin, A. and Thisse, J., "Strategy of the Firm and Market Structure: An Application of Optimal Control Theory", in Cowling, K. (Ed.), *Market Structure and Corporate Behaviour,* Gray-Mills, London, 1972.

Jacquemin, A., De Ghellinck, E. and Huveneers, C., "Concentration and profitability in a small open economy", *Journal of Industrial Economics,* XXIX, December 1980, pp. 131-44.

Jacquemin, A. "Imperfect Market Structures and International Trade", *Kyklos* Vol. 35 n° 1 1982.

Jager, H. and Lanjouw, G.J., "An alternative method for quantifying international trade barriers", *Weltwirtschaftliches Archiv,* Vol. 113, No. 4, 1977.

Jenkins, G.P., *Costs and Consequences of the New Protectionism: The Case of Canada's Clothing Sector,* North-South Institute/World Bank Monograph, 1980.

Johansen, L., "The bargaining society and the inefficiency of bargaining", *Kyklos,* Vol. 32,3, 1979, pp. 497-522.

Johansen, L., "Cores, aggressiveness and the breakdown of cooperation in economic games", *Journal of Economic Behavior and Organisation,* North Holland, Vol. 3, 1982, pp. 1-37.

Johnson, P.S. and Cathcart, D.G., "New Manufacturing Firms and Regional Development: Some Evidence from the Northern Region", *Regional Studies,* Vol. 13, Pergamon Press Ltd., Great Britain, 1979.

Jondrow, M., "Effects of trade restrictions on imports of steel" in *The Impact of International Trade and Investment on Employment,* US Government Printing Office, Washington DC, 1978, pp. 11-25.

Jones, C.D., *Visible Imports Subject to Restraint,* Department of Trade & Industry, Government Economic Service Working Paper No. 62, London, 1983.

Jones D.T., "Motor Cars: a maturing industry" in G. Shepherd, Duchêne F., and Saunders C. (Eds.), *Europe's Industries,* Frances Pinter, London.

Jones, K., "Forgetfulness of things past: Europe and the steel cartel", *The World Economy,* Vol. 2, No. 2, May 1979, pp. 139-154.

Katrak, H., "Foreign competition, tariffs and industrial concentration in Britain, 1963 and 1968", in: Black, J. and Hindley, B. (Eds.), *Current Issues in Commercial Policy and Diplomacy*, The Macmillan Press for the Trade Policy Research Centre, London, 1980.

Katzenstein, P.J. (Ed.), *Between Power and Plenty, Foreign Economic Policies of Advanced Industrial States*, Madison, University of Wisconsin, 1978.

Keeling, B., *The World Steel Industry: Structure and Prospects in the 1980s*, Economist Intelligence Unit Special Report 128, London, 1982, summarised in "The West European steel crisis", *EFTA Bulletin*, 3/82, pp. 5-8.

Keesing, D.B. and Wolf, M., *Textile Quotas Against Developing Countries*, Thames Essays No. 23, Trade Policy Research Centre, London, 1980.

Keesing, D.B., "Linking up to Distant Markets: South to North Exports of Manufactured Consumer Goods", *AEA Papers and Proceedings*, Vol. 73, No. 2, May 1983, pp. 338-342.

Kenen, P.B., "United States Commercial Policy: A Programme for the 1960s", in: Balassa, B., *Changing Patterns in Foreign Trade and Payments*, New York, 1964.

Keohane, R.O. and Nye, J.S., *Power and Interdependence: World Politics in Transition*, Little, Brown & Co., Boston, 1977.

Keohane, R.O., "The Demand for International Regimes", *International Organization*, Vol. 36,2, Spring 1982.

Khan, M.S. and Zhaler, R., *The Macroeconomic effects of changes in barriers to trade and capital flows: a Simulation Analysis*, IMF, Washington, 1982.

Kindleberger, C.P., "Group Behaviour and International Trade", *Journal of Political Economy*, 1951, pp. 30-46.

Kindleberger, C.P., *Economic Response*, Harvard University Press, Cambridge, Massachusetts, 1978.

Kitching, J., "Winning and losing with European acquisitions", *Harvard Business Review*, March-April, 1974.

Knickerbocker, F.T., *Oligopolistic Reaction and Multinational Enterprise*, Harvard University Press, Boston, 1973.

Knight, A., "Government Intervention: its Impact on the Textile Industry", *Journal of General Management*, No. 3-1, August 1975.

Kochan, Thomas A and Piore, Michael J. "Will the New Industrial Relations Last? Implications for the American Labor Movement", Working Paper, Alfred P. Sloan School of Management, Massachusetts, December 1983.

Koekkek, K.A., "The effective protection of Dutch industry, 1970", Centre for Development Planning, Erasmus University, Rotterdam, Discussion Paper No. 44, Rotterdam, 1979.

Koenig, H. and Nerlov, M., "Response of prices and production to unanticipated demand shocks: some microeconomic evidence", University of Manheim and University of Pennsylvania, Draft, May 1983.

Korpi, W., *The Democratic Class Struggle*, RKP, London, 1984.

Koskinen, M., "Excess documentation costs as a non-tariff trade measure: an empirical analysis of the import effects of documentation costs", Working Paper, Swedish School of Economics and Business Administration, August 1983.

Krasner, S.D., "Structural Causes and Regime Consequences: Regimes as intervening Variables", *International Organization*, Vol. 36, 2, Spring 1982.

Krasner, S.D., *International Regimes*, Cornell University Press, Ithaca, New York, 1983.

Krause, L.B., "Australian International Trade", *Brookings Survey of the Australian Economy Conference*, Canberra, 9th-11th January 1984.

Krauss, M.B., *The New Protectionism*, New York University Press for the International Center for Economic Policy Studies, 1978.

Kreinin, M.E. and Officer, L.H., "Tariff Reductions under the Tokyo Round", *Journal of the Kiel Institute of World Economics*, Vol. 115, 1979.

Krueger, A.O., "Alternative Trade Strategies and Employment in LDCs", International Trade and Developing Countries, Vol. 68, No. 2, May 1978.

Krueger, A.O., "Protectionist Pressures,, Imports and Employment in the United States", *Scandinavian Journal of Economics*, 1980.

Krugman, Paul, "The Macroeconomics of Protection with a Floating Exchange Rate", *Carnegie-Rochester Conference Series on Public Policy* 16, 1982.

Kurt Salmon Associates, "The 1980s: The Decade for Technology?, A Study of the State of the Art of Assembly of Apparel Products", prepared for the EEC Commission, December 1979.

Kwoka, J.E. Jr., "Market Power and Market Change in the US Automobile Industry", *Journal of Industrial Economics*, Vol. XXXII, No. 4, June 1984.

Lafay, G., *Dynamique de la specialisation internationale*, Economica, Paris, 1979.

Laird, S., "Intra-Industry Trade and the Expansion, Diversification and Integration of the Trade of the Developing Countries", pp. 79-101.

Lambert, J.T., *Clothing Industry Scheme*, Government Economic Service Working Paper No. 61, Department of Trade and Industry, London, 1983.

Lamfalussy, A., *Investment and Growth in Mature Economies: The Case of Belgium*, MacMillan, London, 1961.

Lapan, H.E., "International Trade, Factor Market Distortions, and the Optimal Dynamic Subsidy", *The American Economic Review*, June 1976.

Lassudrie-Duchene, B., "Les Incidences régionales des Echanges internationaux", *Revue d'Économie Politique*, No. 1, 1984.

Laursen S., and Metzler, Lloyd "Flexible Exchange Rates and the Theory of Employment", *Review of Economics and Statistics*, 1950.

Lawrence, R.Z., "Growth, Trade and the Global Trading System", The Brookings Institution, April 1982.

Lawrence, R.Z., *Can America Compete?*, The Brookings Institution, Washington D.C., 1984.

Lawson, F., "Hegemony and the structure of international trade reassesed: a view from Arabia", *International Organization*, Vol. 37, No. 2, Spring 1983.

League of Nations, Economic, Financial and Transit Department, *Commercial Policy in the Interwar Period*, Geneva, 1942.

Le Monde, "La France suspend ses aides à l'industrie textile", 7th October 1983.

Lerdan, E., "On the measurement of tariffs: the US over forty years", in: *Economia Internazionale*, May, 1957.

Lesourne, J., *Les Systèmes du Destin*, Dalloz, Paris, 1976.

Lillen, D.M., "Sectoral Shifts and Cyclical Unemployment", *Journal of Political Economy*, Vol. 90, No. 4, 1982.

Lindert, P.H. and Kindleberger, C.P., *International Economics,* 7th Edition, 1982.

Lipsey, R.E., "Recent Trends in US Trade & Investment", NBER Working Paper No. 1009, October 1982.

Lipson, C., "The Transformation of Trade: The Sources and Effects of Regime Change", *International Organization,* Vol. 36,2, Spring 1980.

Litan, R.E. and Nordhaus, W.D., *Reforming Federal Regulation,* Yale University Press, 1983.

L'Usine Nouvelle, "Textile : la technique va tout changer", No. 39, Paris, 27th September 1979.

L'Usine Nouvelle, "Fibres chimiques : les Européens se spécialisent", No. 44, Paris, 28th October 1982.

Lustgarten, S.H. and Thomadaki, S.B.,"Valuation Response to New Information: A Test of Resource Mobility and Market Structure", *Journal of Political Economy,* No. 5, 1980.

Lydall, H., "Protection Policy: The Choices facing Australia", The Australian National University, Centre for Economic Policy Research, Discussion Paper No. 81, November 1983.

Lyons, B., "International Trade, Industrial Pricing and Profitability: a Survey", University of Sheffield, September 1979.

MacPhee, C., *Restrictions on International Trade in Steel,* D.C. Heath, Lexington, 1974

Magaziner, I.C. and Reich, R.B., *Minding America's Business: The Decline and Rise of the American Economy,* Harcourt Brace Jovanovich Publishers Law & Business Inc., New York, 1982.

Magee, S.P., "The welfare effects of restrictions on US trade", *Brookings Papers on Economic Activity,* 1972, Vol. 3, pp. 645-707.

Main, J., "Ford's Drive for Quality", Fortune, April 1983.

Maizels, A., *Industrial Growth and World Trade,* NIESR, Cambridge University Press, 1963.

Major, R.L., *Trade and Exchange Rate Policy,* Heinemann, 1979.

March, J.G., "Bounded Rationality, ambiguity, and the engineering of choice", *The Bell Journal of Economics,* March 1979.

Marchesini, E. and Masiero, A., *Il Caso Tessile: Ciclo produttivo e forza-lavoro Lanerossi 1963-1974,* Milan, 1975.

Marcus, Peter and Kirsis, Karlsis M., *World Steel Dynamics Core Reports,* Paine Webber Mitchell Hutchins Inc., New York, 1984.

Mariotti, S., *Efficienza e Struttura Economica: Il Caso Tessile-Abbigliamento,* Angeli, Milan, 1982.

Marketing in Europe, "Clothing and Footwear in Italy", 246, May 1983.

Marsden, J.S. and Anderssen, H.E., "Employment Change in Manufacturing: The Role of Imports, Productivity and Output Growth", Industries Assistance Commission, Canberra, June 1979.

Martin, D.D., "The Davignon Plan: whither competition policy in the ECSC?", *The Antitrust Bulletin,* Vol. 24, No. 4, 1979, pp. 837-887.

Martin, J.P. and Page, J.M., Jr., "The impact of subsidisation on X-efficiency in LDC industry: theory and an empirical test", *The Review of Economics and Statistics,* Vol. LXV, No. 4, November 1983.

Mattera, A., "Protectionism inside the European Community", *Journal of World Trade Law,* 1984, pp. 283-307.

Maxcy, G., *Multinationales de l'automobile,* Institut de recherche et d'information sur les multinationales, IRM, Paris, 1982.

Mayer, W., "The Infant Export Industry Argument", *Canadian Journal of Economics,* May 1984.

Mayes, D.G., "The determinants of marked, sharp and sustained improvement in company performance", Paper presented at the Fourth International Meeting of the Association Française de Finance at Carry-le-Rouet, 9th-10th June 1983.

McCormack, G.P., "The reinstated steel Trigger Price Mechanism: reinforced barrier to import competition", *Fordham International Law Journal,* Vol. 4, No. 2, 1980, pp. 289-339.

McFetridge, "Determinants of pricing behaviour: a study of the Canadian cotton textile industry", *Journal of Industrial Economics,* 1973.

McGee, J.S., "Economies of Size in Auto Body Manufacture", *Journal of Law and Economics,* 16, October 1973, pp. 248-53.

McKeown, T., "Hegemonic Stability Theory and 19th Century Tariff Levels in Europe", *International Organization,* Vol. 37,1, Winter 1983.

Melvin, J.R. and Wilkinson, B.W., "Effective Protection in the Canadian Economy", Special Study No. 9 prepared for the Economic Council of Canada, Ottawa, 1968.

Menge, J.A., "Style Change Costs as a Market Weapon", *Quarterly Journal of Economics,* 76, November 1962, pp. 632-47.

Messerlin, P., *La Révolution Commerciale,* Bonnel Éditions, Paris, 1982.

Messerlin, P., "Bureaucracies and the Political Economy of Protection: Reflections of a Continental European", World Bank Staff Working Papers, No. 568, 1983

Messerlin, P., "Les impacts sectoriels et macroéconomiques des politiques de promotion des exportations", FNSP-SEAE, Paris, October 1983.

Messerlin, P., "Note sur les Barrières non tarifaires aux Importations françaises", GRECO-EFIQ, Colloque, Aix-Marseille, June 1983.

Messerlin, P., "Commerce extérieur et crédits à l'exportation", Fondation Nationale des Sciences Politiques, Service d'Étude de l'activité économique, Paris, March 1984.

Metals Intelligence International, *South Korea's Pohang Iron and Steel: Strong Company Excellent Prospects,* Paine Webber Mitchell Hutchins Inc., New York, 22nd February 1984.

Metals Intelligence International, *Carbon Steel Price Track No. 12,* Paine Webber Mitchell Hutchins Inc., New York, 25th May 1984.

Michalski, W, "Long-term Prospects for World Development", *Intereconomics,* November/December 1979.

Michalski, W., "Les politiques d'ajustement positives. Un concept stratégique pour les années 80", *Revue d'économie industrielle,* No. 23, 1er trimestre 1983. (For an English version of this paper, see INTERECONOMICS, January/February 1983.

Michalski, W., "Les nouvelles dimensions du Protectionnisme", GRECO-EFIQ, Colloque, Aix-Marseille, June 1983.

Midler, C., "L'Organisation du Travail et ses Déterminants : Enjeux Economiques et Organisationnels des Réformes de Restructuration des Tâches dans le Montage Automobile", Paris, Ph.D Thesis, October 1980.

Miles, C., *Lancashire Textiles. A Case Study of Industrial Change*

Mintzberg, Henry, *Power in and around Organizations,* (Theory of Management Policy Series), Prentice-Hall, 1983.

Mitnick, B.M., *The Political Economy of Regulation: Creating, Designing, and Removing Regulatory Forms,* Columbia University Press, New York, 1980.

Morandi, L and Pantini, G., *Dialogo sull'industria chimica,* Gruppo Editoriale Fabbri, Bompiani, Sonzogno, Etas Libri, 1982.

Moreton, A., "Textile Nations fear North American Curbs", Financial Times, Tuesday, 13th September 1983.

Moreton, A., "Why Europe is Putting out More Flags", Financial Times, Friday, 21st October 1983.

Moreton, A., "US Curbs Imports of Textiles", Financial Times, 24th October 1983.

Morgan, A.D. and Martin, D., "Tariff Reductions and UK Imports of Manufactures: 1955-1971", *National Institute Economic Review,* No. 72, May 1975.

Morici, P. and Megna, L.L., *US Economic Policies Affecting Industrial Trade: a Quantitative Assessment,* NPA Committee on Changing International Realities, National Planning Association, Washington D.C., 1983.

Morkre, M.E. and Tarr, D.G., *Effects of Restrictions on US Imports: Five Case Studies and Theory,* Federal Trade Commission Staff Report, US Government Printing Office, 1980.

Mosconi, A. and Velo, D., *Crisi e Ristrutturazione del Settore Automobilistico,* il Mulino, Bologna, 1982.

Mueller, H. and Kawahito, K., *Steel Industry Economics: A Comparative Analysis of Structure, Conduct and Performance,* International Public Relations, New York, 1978.

Müller, J., "Competitive performance and trade with the EEC: generalizations from several case studies with specific reference to the West German economy", mimeo, 1983.

Müller, J.and Owen, N., *Economic Effects of Free Trade in Manufactured Products within the EC: A pilot study of some European Industries,* mimeo, Berlin, 1984.

Mundell, R.A., "Flexible Exchange Rates and Employment Policy", *Canadian Journal of Economics.,* 1961.

Murray, T. *et al.,* "Alternative forms of protection against market disruption", *Kyklos,* Vol. 31, 1978.

Mutti, J., *Taxes, subsidies and competitiveness internationally,* NPA Committee on Changing International Realities, Washington D.C., January 1982.

Mutti, J. and Grubert, H., "D.i.s.c. and its effects", National Bureau of Economic Research, Conference, Cambridge, Mass., 3rd-4th December 1982.

Mutti, J. and Morici, P., *Changing Patterns of US Industrial Activity and Comparative Advantage,* NPA Report No. 201, Washington D.C., 1983.

National Academy of Engineering, Committee on Technology and International Economic and Trade Issues, Automobile Panel, National Research Council (US) and Committee on Engineering and Technical Systems, *The Competitive Status of the US Auto Industry: A Study of the Influences of Technology in Determining International Industrial Competitive Advantage,* National Academy Press, Washington D.C., 1982.

Nelson, P.B., *Corporations in Crisis: Behavioral Observations for Bankruptcy Policy,* Praeger Publishing, New York, 1981.

Nowzad, B., *The Rise in Protectionism,* IMF Pamphlet Series No. 24, Washington D.C., 1978.

Nunn, S., "The Opening and Closure of Manufacturing Units in the United Kingdom, 1966-75", Government Economic Service Working Paper No. 36, Department of Industry, November 1980.

Ochel, W., "Die asiatischen Schwellenländer – eine Gefahr für die deutsche Investitionsgüterindustrie?", ifo, Schnelldienst, 28, 1984.

OECD, *Rapports traitant de l'adaptation des secteurs industriels,* Paris, 1965.

OECD, *La Prévision de la Consommation d'Acier : Approches synchronique et chronologique,* Paris, 1974.

OECD, *The Impact of Newly Industrialising Countries on Production and Trade in Manufactures,* Paris, 1979.

OECD, *Facing the Future,* Paris, 1979.

OECD, *Steel in the 80s,* Symposium February 1980, Paris 1980.

OECD, *The Impact of the Newly Industrialising Countries on Production and Trade in Manufactures: Updating of Selected Tables from the 1979 Report,* Paris, 1981.

OECD, *Forecasting Car Ownership and Use,* Paris, 1982.

OECD, *Long Term Outlook for the World Automobile Industry,* Paris, 1983.

OECD, *Positive Adjustment Policies: Managing Structural Change,* Paris, 1983.

OECD Observer, "Towards a World Auto Industry", No. 123, Paris, July 1983.

OECD, *Textiles and Clothing Industries,* Paris, 1983.

OECD, *The Generalised System of Preferences. Review of the First Decade,* Paris, 1983.

OECD, *Employment Growth and Structural Change,* 1985.

Olechowski, A. and Sampson, G., "Current Trade Restrictions in the EEC, the United States and Japan", *Journal of World Trade Law,* Vol. 14, No. 3, 1980.

Olson, M., "Symposium on the Rise and Decline of Nations", *International Studies Quarterly,* Vol. 27, No. 1, March 1983.

Ono, Y., "Price Leadership: a Theoretical Analysis", *Économica,* 43, February 1982, pp. 11-20.

Orr, D., "An index of entry barriers and its application to market structure-performance relationships", *Journal of Industrial Economics,* 1974.

Oster, S., "The Diffusion of Innovation among Steel Firms: The Basic Oxygen Furnace", *The Bell Journal of Economics,* Vol. 13, No. 1, Spring 1982.

Oster, S., "Intra-industry structure and the ease of strategic change", *Review of Economics and Statistics,* August 1983.

Owen, N., "Competition and structural change in unconcentrated industries", *Journal of Industrial Economics,* 1971.

Owen, N., *Economies of Scale, Competitiveness and Trade Patterns in the European Community,* Ph.D Dissertation, University of London, 1981.

Padioleau, J.G., *Quand la France s'enferre : la politique sidérurgique de la France depuis 1945,* Presses Universitaires de France, Paris, 1981.

Page, S.A.B., "The Increased Use of Trade Controls by the Industrial Countries", *Intereconomics,* May-June 1980

Parry, T.G., "The Employment Consequences of Adopting the Industries Assistance Commission Post-1984 Assistance Recommendations for the Australian Motor Vehicle Industry", Federal Chamber of Automotive Industries, N.S.W., June 1981.

Parsons, D.O. and Ray, E.J., "The United States Steel Consolidation: the creation of market control", *Journal of Law and Economics,* Vol. 18, April 1975, pp. 181-220.

Parsons, D.O., "Unemployment, the Allocation of Labor and Optimal Government Intervention", *The American Economic Review,* September 1980.

Pashigian, B.P., *The Distribution of Automobiles: An Economic Analysis of the Franchise System,* Englewod Cliffs, N.J., Prentice-Hall, 1961,

Passeron, H., "Developper la productique : l'exemple de l'habillement", *Économie et Statistiques,* Economie et Statistiques n° 159, Oct. 1983. INSEE, Paris.

Pastor, R., "The Political Implications of US Trade Policy in the 1980s", Appendix A, Brookings Institution, Phase I Report — International Trade to the National Science Foundation, Essay No. 10, April 1982.

Pavitt, K., "Some Characteristics of Innovative Activities in British Industry", Science Policy Research Unit, University of Sussex, 1982.

Pavitt, K., "International patterns of technological accumulation", Science Policy Research Unit, University of Sussex, Draft, 24th July 1984.

Pelzman, J. and Andrews, J., *The Competitiveness of the US Textile Industry,* Research Division, College of Business Administration, The University of South Carolina, Colombia.

Pelzman, J. and Bradberry, C.E., "The Welfare Effects of Reduced US Tariff Restrictions on Imported Textile Products", *Applied Economics,* Vol. 12, Chapman & Hall Ltd., 1980, pp. 455-465.

Pelzman, J. and Martin, R.C., "Direct Employment Effects of Increased Imports: A Case Study of the Textile Industry", *Southern Economic Journal,* Vol. 48, No. 2, October 1981.

Pelzman, J. and Martin, R.C., "The Regional Welfare Effects of Tariff Reductions on Textile Products", *The Journal of Regional Science,* September 1982.

Pelzman, J., "The Impact of the Multifiber Arrangement on the US Textile Industry", NBER Conference, Boston, January 1983.

Pelzman, J. "Economic Costs of Tariffs and Quotas on Textile and Apparel Products Imported into the United States: A Survey of the Literature and Implications for Policies", *Weltwirtschaftliches Archive,* No.3, 1983.

Pelzman, J., "The US Generalized System of Preferences: An Evaluation and an Examination of Alternative Graduation Programs", Report prepared for the Office of International Economic Affairs, Division of Foreign Economic Research, Bureau of International Labor Affairs, US Department of Labor, September 1983.

Pelzman, J., "The Impact of the Caribbean Basin Economic Recovery Act on Caribbean Exports", mimeo 1984.

Pelzman, J., "The Multifiber Arrangement and its Effect on the Profit Performance of the US Textile Industry", mimeo, 1984.

Penrose, E.T., *The Theory of the Growth of the Firm,* Basil Blackwell, Oxford, 1980.

Perry, R., *The Future of Canada's Auto Industry: The Big Three and the Japanese Challenge,* Canadian Institute for Economic Policy, James Lorimer & Co., Toronto, 1981.

Pike, T., "Relative earnings in counties with SDAs", *Employment Gazette,* September 1983.

Pointon, T., "Measuring the gains from government export promotion", *European Journal of Marketing*, Vol. 12, No. 6, 1978.

Poncelet, C., "Rapport sur les difficultés actuelles de l'industrie de textile et de l'habillement", Senat No. 282, Paris, June 1981.

Porter, M.E., "Consumer Behavior, Retailer Power and Market Performance in Consumer Goods Industries", *The Review of Economics and Statistics*, November 1974.

Porter, M.E., "Interbrand Choice, Media Mix and Market Performance", *American Economic Review*, Papers and Proceedings, May 1976.

Porter, M.E., "The Structure within Industries and Companies' Performance", *Review of Economics and Statistics*, May 1979.

Porter, M.E., *Competitive Strategy: Techniques for Analyzing Industries and Competitors*, The Free Press, New York, 1980.

Porto, M.C.L., "The Political Economy of Protection: A case study of Portugal", 8th Annual Conference of the International Economics Study Group, University of Sussex, 16th-18th September 1983.

Potter, D., Davies, G. and Gibbs, R., *Wool Textile Industry*, Government Economic Service Working Paper No. 60, Department of Trade and Industry, London, 1983.

Problèmes Économiques, Bulletin hebdomadaire de la Kredietbank, "L'industrie de la chaussure dans les pays de la Communauté Européenne", No. 1574, 24th May 1978.

Problèmes Économiques No. 1787, "Les Entreprises et les Echanges extérieurs", 1st September 1982.

Prodi, R. and Bianchi, P., *The Case of Motor Car Industry*, European University Institute, Colloquium: the management of euro-american trade conflicts in the 80s, Florence, 2nd-4th April, 1984.

Pugel, T.A., "Foreign Trade and US Market Performance," *Journal of Industrial Economics* 29, December 1980, pp. 119-30.

Pugel, T.A. and Walter, I., "US Corporate Interests and The Political Economy of Trade Policy", University of Reading Discussion Papers in International Investment and Business Studies, No. 78, January 1984.

Putnam, Hayes & Bartlett, *Economics of International Steel Trade; Policy Implications for the United States; An Analysis and Forecast for American Iron and Steel Institute*, Putnam, Hayes & Bartlett, Newton, Mass., May 1977.

Quinn, J.B., "Managing Structural Change", *Sloan Management Review*, MIT, Vol. 21., No. 4, Summer 1980.

Ranci, P., *I Trasferimenti dello Stato alle Imprese Industriali negli Anni Settanta*, Il Mulino, Bologna, 1983.

Redwood, John, *Going for Broke*, Blackwell, London, 1983.

Reich, R.B., "Beyond Free Trade", *Foreign Affairs*, Spring 1983.

Reynolds, R.J. and Masson, R.T., "Predation: the 'Noisy Pricing Strategy'", Paper for the US Department of Justice, Cornell University.

Richardson, J.J. and Jordan, A.G., *Governing Under Pressure: The Process in a Post-Parliamentary Democracy*, Martin Robertson, Oxford, 1979.

Richter, R. and Stolper, W.F. (Eds.), "Economic Reconstruction in Europe: The Reintegration of Western Germany: A Symposium, Zeitschrift für die gesamte Staatswissenschaft, 3rd September 1981.

Riedel, J., "Tariff concessions in the Kennedy Round and the structure of protection in West Germany", *Journal of International Economics*, Vol. 7, 1977.

Riedel, J., "Trade as the Engine of Growth in Developing Countries", Washington D.C., 1983

Rodger, Ian, "Back in the European first division", *Financial Times*, Thursday, 7th June 1984.

Roningen, V. and Yeats, A., "Nontariff Distortions of International Trade: Some Preliminary Empirical Evidence", *Weltwirtschaftliches Archiv*, Vol. 112, No. 4, 1976.

Rosen, S., "Hedonic Prices and Implicit Markets", *Journal of Political Economy*, Vol. 82, pp. 34-55, 1974.

Rotemberg, J.J. and Saloner, G., "A Supergame-Theoretic Model of Business Cycles and Price Wars during Booms", MIT Working Paper No. 349, Massachusetts Institute of Technology, July 1984.

Rothwell, R., "Innovation in the UK Textile Machinery", *R&D Management*, Vol. 6,3, 1976.

Ruggie, J.G., "International regimes, transactions, and change: embedded liberalism in the postwar economic order", *International Organization*, Vol. 36,2, Spring 1982.

Rumelt, R.P., "Towards a Strategic Theory of the Firm", paper prepared for Conference on "Non-Traditional Approaches to Policy Research", Graduate School of Business, University of Southern California, November 1981.

Rush, H. and Hoffmann, K., "Information Technology and Economic Perspectives: Microelectronics and the Clothing Industry", OECD July 1984.

Salmans, S., "The Woes of Woollens", Management Today, October 1980, pp. 91-96.

Salter, M.S. and Weinhold, W.A., *Diversification through Acquisition: Strategies for Creating Economic Value*, The Free Press, New York, 1979.

Sapir, A. and Schumacher, D., "The Employment Impact of Shifts in the Composition of Commodity and Services Trade", in OECD: *Employment Growth and Structural Change*, 1985.

Saxonhouse, G.R., "What is all this about 'industrial targeting' in Japan?", *The World Economy*, 1984, pp. 253-273.

Schatz, K.W. and Wolter, F., International Division of Labour Programme, International Trade, Employment and Structural Adjustment: The Case Study of the Federal Republic of Germany, ILO, World Employment Programme Research Working Paper, Geneva, 1982.

Schelling, T.C., *The Strategy of Conflict*, Harvard University Press, Boston, 1980.

Scherer, F.M., *Industrial Market Structure and Economic Performance*, 2nd Ed., Rand McNaly College Publishing Co., Chicago, 1981

Schumacher, D., "Trade with Developing Countries and Employment in the European Community", Study No. 82/22, European Economic Commission.

Schumacher, D., "The Employment Impact of Shifts in the Composition of Goods and Services Trade", Berlin, September 1983.

Scitovsky, T., *Economic Theory and Western European Integration*, Unwin University Books, London, 1962.

Scott, A., "Property Rights and Property Wrongs", *Canadian Journal of Economics*, XVI, No. 4, November 1983, pp. 555-573.

Scott, M. F., Corden, W.M., and Little, I.M.D., *The Case Against General Import Restrictions*, London: Trade Policy Research Centre, 1980.

Scwarting, U., 'Strategies for survival: the example of the clothing industry", *Intereconomics*, January/February 1979.

Séguin, P., "Rapport sur le textile habillement en France", Assemblée Nationale, Paris, No. 2254, 1981.

Shepherd, G., *Public and Private Strategies for Survival in the Textile and Clothing Industries of Western Europe and The United States*, Sussex European Research Centre, Sussex, September 1981.

Shepherd, G., *Textile-Industry Adjustment in Developed Countries*, Thames Essay, No. 30, Trade Policy Research Centre, London, 1981.

Shepherd, G. and Duchêne, F., "Industrial Change and Intervention in Western Europe", in Shepherd, G. Duchêne F., and Saunders, C. (eds.), *Europe's Industries*, Frances Pinter, London 1983.

Shoeffler, S., Buzzell, R.D. and Heany, D.F., "Impact of strategic planning on profit performance", *Harvard Business Review*, March-April 1974.

Shonfield, A., *The Use of Public Power*, Oxford University Press, 1982.

Silberston, Z.A., *The Multi-Fibre Arrangement and the UK Economy*, HMSO, London, 1984.

Silva, F., Grillo, M. and Prati, M., *Il Mercato italiano dell Auto nel Contesto Europeo*, Franco Angeli Editore, Milan, 1982.

Simison, R.L. and Koten, J., "High-Gear Profits: Auto Makers' Earnings in US are Increasing Despite Mediocre Sales", Wall Street Journal, December 1983.

Skidelsky, R., "Britain under Mrs Thatcher", Hudson Research Europe SA, France, June 1984.

Smith, R.J., "Shuttleless Looms" in L. Narbeth and G.F. Ray (Eds.), *The Diffusion of New Industrial Processes: An International Study*, Cambridge University Press, 1974, pp. 251-293.

Soete, L., Clark, J. and Turner, R., *Technology and Employment — Textiles and Clothing*, Science Policy Research Unit, University of Sussex, 1982.

Solomon Report, *Report to the President: A Comprehensive Program for the Steel Industry (December 1977) reprinted in Hearings on the Administration's Comprehensive Program for the Steel Industry before the Subcommittee on Trade of the House Committee on Ways and Means*, US Government Printing Office, for 95th Congress, 2nd Session, Washington DC, 1978.

Somers, G.G. (Ed.), *Collective Bargaining: Contemporary American Experience*, Industrial Relations Research Association Series, Pantagraph Printing, Wisconsin, 1980.

Soras, C.G. and Stodden, J.R., *The US Automobile Market: Structure & Outlook*, Chemical Bank, Economic Research Department, New York, May 1983.

Spence, A. Michael, "Investment Strategy and Growth in a New Market," *The Bell Journal of Economics*, Spring 1979.

SSRC Government and Industry Relations Subcommittee, "Government and Industry Relationships: A Framework for Analysis", December 1983.

Stanback, T.M. Jr., Bearse, P.J., Noyelle, T.J. and Karasek, R.A., *Services: The New Economy*, Conservation of Human Resources series: 20, Allanheld, Osmun & Co., New Jersey, 1981.

Stein, A.A., "Coordination and Collaboration: Regimes in an anarchic World", *International Organization,* Vol. 36,2, Spring 1982.

Stein, A.A., "The Hegemon's Dilemma: Great Britain, the United States, and the International Economic Order", *International Organization,* Vol. 38.2, Spring 1984.

Stock, Schuman S. and Owen, Verrill C. Jr., "Recent Developments in Countervailing Duty Law and Policy", National Bureau of Economic Research, Conference on recent issues and initiatives in US trade policy, 8th August 1983.

Stoffaes, C., *Politique Industrielle,* Institut d'Études Politiques de Paris, 1984.

Strange, S., "The management of surplus capacity, or how does theory stand up to protectionism 1970s style?", *International Organization,* Vol. 33,3, Summer 1979.

Strange, S. and Tooze, R., *The International Politics of Surplus Capacity: Competition for Market Shares in the World Recession,* George Allen & Unwin, London, 1981.

Streeck, W. and Hoft, A., "Manpower management and industrial relations in the restructuring of the world automobile industry", IIM/LP Discussion Paper 83-5, 1983.

Strolz, H., "Some Reflections on Textile Industrial Development", Silver Jubilee Celebrations of the Cotton Textiles Export Promotion Council, Bombay, 1st-3rd December 1979.

"Subsidies in the Federal Republic of Germany", in: *European Economy,* No. 16, July 1983.

Sugden, R. and Cowling, K., "Exchange rate adjustment and oligopoly pricing dynamics", paper for the Workshop on Price Dynamics and Economic Policy, OECD, 1984.

Sultan, R.G.M., *Pricing in the Electrical Oligopoly,* Vol. 1: Competition or Collusion, Harvard University Press, 1974.

Sutton, J., Pearce, J. and Batchelor, R., *Europe and Protection,* Routledge and Kegan Paul, London, 1985.

Swedish Ministry of Industry, *The Net Costs of Government Support to Swedish Industry,* Stockholm, 1982.

Szenberg, M., Lombardi, J.W. and Lee, E.Y., *Welfare Effects of Trade Restrictions: a Case Study of the US Footwear Industry,* Academic Press, New York, 1977.

Tackacs, W., *Quantitative Restrictions in International Trade,* PhD dissertation, John Hopkins University, 1975.

Tamister, M-H., "Les restructurations marquent la vie des entreprises et des groupes", *Économie et Statistique,* INSEE, 1983.

Teece, D.J., "Towards an Economic Theory of the Multiproduct firm", *Journal of Economic Behavior and Organization,* No. 3, 1982.

"The common scandal of the uncommon market", *The Economist,* September 1981, pp. 68-72.

Thompson, .A., "Strategies for staying cost competitive", *Harvard Business Review,* January-February 1984, pp. 110-17.

Till, L., "La Montée des Protectionnismes et La Recherche des Voies Alternatives", GRECQ-EFIQ, Colloque, Aix-Marseille, June 1983.

Toyne, B. *et al., The US Textile Mill Products Industry: International Challenges and Strategies for the Future,* University of South Carolina Press, Columbia, SC, 1983.

Toyne, B., Arpan, J.S., Ricks, D.A., Shirup, T.A. and Barnett, A., *The Global Textile Industry,* World Industry Studies No. 2, George Allen & Unwin, London, 1984.

Trade Policy Research Centre, "Public Scrutiny of Protection", Draft Report on Policy Transparency and Public Assistance to Industries, London, November 1983.

Transport Canada Research & Development Centre, "The Future of the Automobile in Canada", TP.1148, April 1979.

Tsoukalis, L. and Da Silva Ferreira, A., "Management of Industrial Surplus Capacity in the European Community", *International Organization,* Vol. 34,3, Summer 1980.

Tsurumi, Yoshi, *The Japanese Are Coming,* Ballinger, Cambridge, Mass., 1976.

Turner, L., "The newly industrialising countries: growth and prospects", paper given at *A new Investment Era: an International Investment Symposium,* Cambridge, June 1983.

Turner, Philip P. "Import Competition and the Profitability of United Kingdom Manufacturing Industry," *Journal of Industrial Economics,* No.29, December, 1980, pp. 1013-20.

UNCTAD, *The Kennedy Round estimated effects on tariff barriers,* United Nations, New York, 1968.

United Nations, "Fibres and Textiles: Dimensions of Corporate Marketing Structure", Study by the UNCTAD Secretariat, United Nations, Geneva, February 1981.

United Nations, New York, *Economic Bulletin for Europe,* Vol. 34, Trade (XXXI)/1, New York, 1982.

United Nations, New York, *Transnational Corporations in the International Auto Industry,* ST/CTC/38, UN Publications, New York, 1983.

United Nations Centre on Transnational Corporations, *Transnational corporations in world development: third survey,* United Nations, 1983.

United States Congress, Committee on Finance, *Hearings before the Committee on Finance ... Proposals to Impose Import Quotas on ... Steel,* US Government Printing Office for 90th Congress, 1st Session, 2 vols, October 1967.

United States Congress, Committee on Finance, *Steel Imports,* Staff Report, Government Printing Office, for 90th Congress, 2nd Session, Washington DC, 1968.

United States International Trade Commission, "The Effectiveness of Escape Clause Relief in Promoting Adjustment to Import Competition", US ITC Publication 1229, March 1982.

United States International Trade Commission, *A Review of Recent Developments in the US Automobile Industry Including an Assessment of the Japanese Voluntary Restraint Agreements,* USITC Publication 1648, Washington D.C., 1985.

Utton, M.A., *The Political Economy of Big Business,* Martin Robertson & Co., Oxford, 1982.

Valdes, A. and Zeitz, J., "Agricultural Protection in OECD: Its Costs to Less Developed Countries", International Food Policy Research Institute, December 1980.

Vellas, F., *Échange International et Qualification du Travail,* Économica, Paris, 1981.

Vernon, R., *Storm over the multinationals. The real issues,* Harvard University Press, Cambridge, Mass., 1977.

Vernon, R., *Two Hungry Giants: The United States and Japan in the Quest for Oil and Ores,* Harvard University Press, Boston, 1983.

Waelbroeck, J. and Messerlin, P., "Le Déclenchement du Protectionnisme : Résultats pour l'Europe", GRECO-EFFIQ : Colloque, June 1983.

Warnecke, S.J., (Ed.), *International Trade and Industrial Policies,* Macmillan, London, 1978.

Weinstein, M.M., *Recovery and Redistribution under the NIRA,* Studies in Monetary Economics, Vol. 6, North-Holland Publishing Co., New York, 1980.

Weizsäcker, C.C.von, *Barriers to Entry: A Theoretical Treatment,* Lecture Notes in Economics and Mathematical Systems, Vol. 185, Springer-Verlag Berlin Heidelberg, 1980.

Werner International Management Consultants, "Spinning and Weaving: Labour Cost Comparisons", Brussels/New York, Spring 1980.

Westphal, L.E., Kim, L., Amsden, A., "Capacity augmentation trade and Korean industrialisation", The World Bank, May 1983.

White, L.J., *The Automobile Industry Since 1945,* Harvard University Press, Cambridge, Mass., 1971.

White, L.J., "Industrial Organization and International Trade: Some Some Theoretical Considerations," *American Economic Review* 64, December 1974, pp. 1013-20.

Whiting, A., (Ed.), Department of Industry, *The Economics of Industrial Subsidies,* UK, February 1976.

Wieman, J., "Selective Protectionism and Structural Adjustment", German Development Institute, Berlin, 1983.

Willard, J.C., "Conditions d'emploi et salaires de la main d'œuvre étrangère", *Économie et Statistiques,* No. 162, January 1984.

Williamson, O.E., *Markets and Hierarchies: Analysis and Antitrust Implications, A Study in the Economics of Internal Organization,* The Free Press, New York, 1975.

Willoughby, J., "The changing role of protection in the world economy", *Cambridge Journal of Economics,* June 1982, pp. 195-211.

Worcester, D.A., "Why Dominant Firms Decline", *Journal of Political Economy,* August 1957, pp. 338-47.

Yamawaki, Hideki. "Market Structure, Capacity Expansion, and Pricing; The Cases of the United States Iron and Steel Industry, 1970-1930, and the Japanese Iron and Steel Industry, 1957-1975." Ph.D. dissertation, Harvard University, 1982.

Yates, P.L., *Forty Years of Foreign Trade,* Allen & Unwin, London, 1959.

Yeats, A.J., "Effective tariff protection in the United States, the European Economic Community and Japan", *Quarterly Review of Economics and Business,* 1974.

Yoffie, D.B., "Adjustment in the Footwear Industry: The Consequences of Orderly Marketing Agreements", in Zysman and Tyson (Eds.), *American Industry in International Competition,* 1983.

Yoffie, D.B., *Power and Protectionism: Strategies of the Newly Industrializing Countries,* Columbia University Press, New York, 1983.

Yoshino, M.Y., *Japan's Multinational Enterprises,* Harvard University Press, Cambridge, 1976.

Yoshoka, M., "Overseas Investment by the Japanese Textile Industry", *The Developing Economies,* 18(1), 1979.

OECD SALES AGENTS
DÉPOSITAIRES DES PUBLICATIONS DE L'OCDE

ARGENTINA – ARGENTINE
Carlos Hirsch S.R.L., Florida 165, 4° Piso (Galería Guemes)
1333 BUENOS AIRES. Tel. 33.1787.2391 y 30.7122

AUSTRIA – AUTRICHE
OECD Publications and Information Center
4 Simrockstrasse 5300 Bonn (Germany). Tel. (0228) 21.60.45
Local Agent/Agent local :
Gerold and Co., Graben 31, WIEN I. Tel. 52.22.35

BELGIUM – BELGIQUE
Jean De Lannoy, Service Publications OCDE
avenue du Roi 202, B-1060 BRUXELLES. Tel. 02/538.51.69

CANADA
Renouf Publishing Company Limited/
Editions Renouf LimitéeHead Office/Siège social – Store/Magasin :
61, rue Sparks Street,
OTTAWA, Ontario KIP 5A6
Tel. (613)238-8985. 1-800-267-4164
Store/Magasin: 211, rue Yonge Street,
TORONTO, Ontario M5B 1M4
Tel. (416)363-3171
Regional Sales Office/
Bureau des Ventes régional :
7575 Trans-Canada Hwy., Suite 305,
SAINT-LAURENT, Québec H4T 1V6
Tél. (514)335-9274

DENMARK – DANEMARK
Munksgaard Export and Subscription Service
35, Nørre Søgade
DK 1370 KØBENHAVN K. Tel. +45.1.12.85.70

FINLAND – FINLANDE
Akateeminen Kirjakauppa
Keskuskatu 1, 00100 HELSINKI 10. Tel. 65.11.22

FRANCE
Bureau des Publications de l'OCDE,
2 rue André-Pascal, 75775 PARIS CEDEX 16. Tel. (1) 524.81.67
Principal correspondant :
13602 AIX-EN-PROVENCE : Librairie de l'Université.
Tel. 26.18.08

GERMANY – ALLEMAGNE
OECD Publications and Information Center
4 Simrockstrasse 5300 BONN Tel. (0228) 21.60.45

GREECE – GRÈCE
Librairie Kauffmann, 28 rue du Stade,
ATHÈNES 132. Tel. 322.21.60

HONG-KONG
Government Information Services,
Publications (Sales) Office,
Beaconsfield House, 4/F.,
Queen's Road Central

ICELAND – ISLANDE
Snaebjörn Jónsson and Co., h.f.,
Hafnarstraeti 4 and 9, P.O.B. 1131, REYKJAVIK.
Tel. 13133/14281/11936

INDIA – INDE
Oxford Book and Stationery Co. :
NEW DELHI-1, Scindia House. Tel. 45896
CALCUTTA 700016, 17 Park Street. Tel. 240832

INDONESIA – INDONÉSIE
PDIN-LIPI, P.O. Box 3065/JKT., JAKARTA, Tel. 583467

IRELAND – IRLANDE
TDC Publishers – Library Suppliers
12 North Frederick Street, DUBLIN 1 Tel. 744835-749677

ITALY – ITALIE
Libreria Commissionaria Sansoni :
Via Lamarmora 45, 50121 FIRENZE. Tel. 579751/584468
Via Bartolini 29, 20155 MILANO. Tel. 365083
Sub-depositari:
Ugo Tassi
Via A. Farnese 28, 00192 ROMA. Tel. 310590
Editrice e Libreria Herder,
Piazza Montecitorio 120, 00186 ROMA. Tel. 6794628
Costantino Ercolano, Via Generale Orsini 46, 80132 NAPOLI. Tel. 405210
Libreria Hoepli, Via Hoepli 5, 20121 MILANO. Tel. 865446
Libreria Scientifica, Dott. Lucio de Biasio "Aeiou"
Via Meravigli 16, 20123 MILANO Tel. 807679
Libreria Zanichelli
Piazza Galvani 1/A, 40124 Bologna Tel. 237389
Libreria Lattes, Via Garibaldi 3, 10122 TORINO. Tel. 519274
La diffusione delle edizioni OCSE è inoltre assicurata dalle migliori librerie nelle
città più importanti.

JAPAN – JAPON
OECD Publications and Information Center,
Landic Akasaka Bldg., 2-3-4 Akasaka,
Minato-ku, TOKYO 107 Tel. 586.2016

KOREA – CORÉE
Pan Korea Book Corporation,
P.O. Box n° 101 Kwangwhamun, SÉOUL. Tel. 72.7369

LEBANON – LIBAN
Documenta Scientifica/Redico,
Edison Building, Bliss Street, P.O. Box 5641, BEIRUT.
Tel. 354429 – 344425

MALAYSIA – MALAISIE
University of Malaya Co-operative Bookshop Ltd.
P.O. Box 1127, Jalan Pantai Baru
KUALA LUMPUR. Tel. 577701/577072

THE NETHERLANDS – PAYS-BAS
Staatsuitgeverij, Verzendboekhandel,
Chr. Plantijnstraat 1 Postbus 20014
2500 EA S-GRAVENHAGE. Tel. nr. 070.789911
Voor bestellingen: Tel. 070.789208

NEW ZEALAND – NOUVELLE-ZÉLANDE
Publications Section,
Government Printing Office Bookshops:
AUCKLAND: Retail Bookshop: 25 Rutland Street,
Mail Orders: 85 Beach Road, Private Bag C.P.O.
HAMILTON: Retail: Ward Street.
Mail Orders, P.O. Box 857
WELLINGTON: Retail: Mulgrave Street (Head Office),
Cubacade World Trade Centre
Mail Orders: Private Bag
CHRISTCHURCH: Retail: 159 Hereford Street,
Mail Orders: Private Bag
DUNEDIN: Retail: Princes Street
Mail Order: P.O. Box 1104

NORWAY – NORVÈGE
J.G. TANUM A/S
P.O. Box 1177 Sentrum OSLO 1. Tel. (02) 80.12.60

PAKISTAN
Mirza Book Agency, 65 Shahrah Quaid-E-Azam, LAHORE 3.
Tel. 66839

PORTUGAL
Livraria Portugal, Rua do Carmo 70-74,
1117 LISBOA CODEX. Tel. 360582/3

SINGAPORE – SINGAPOUR
Information Publications Pte Ltd.
Pei-Fu Industrial Building,
24 New Industrial Road N° 02-06
SINGAPORE 1953, Tel. 2831786, 2831798

SPAIN – ESPAGNE
Mundi-Prensa Libros, S.A.
Castelló 37, Apartado 1223, MADRID-28001. Tel. 275.46.55
Libreria Bosch, Ronda Universidad 11, BARCELONA 7.
Tel. 317.53.08, 317.53.58

SWEDEN – SUÈDE
AB CE Fritzes Kungl Hovbokhandel,
Box 16 356, S 103 27 STH. Regeringsgatan 12,
DS STOCKHOLM. Tel. 08/23.89.00
Subscription Agency/Abonnements:
Wennergren-Williams AB,
Box 30004, S104 25 STOCKHOLM.
Tel. 08/54.12.00

SWITZERLAND – SUISSE
OECD Publications and Information Center
4 Simrockstrasse 5300 BONN (Germany). Tel. (0228) 21.60.45
Local Agents/Agents locaux
Librairie Payot, 6 rue Grenus, 1211 GENÈVE 11. Tel. 022.31.89.50

TAIWAN – FORMOSE
Good Faith Worldwide Int'l Co., Ltd.
9th floor, No. 118, Sec. 2,
Chung Hsiao E. Road
TAIPEI. Tel. 391.7396/391.7397

THAILAND – THAILANDE
Suksit Siam Co., Ltd., 1715 Rama IV Rd,
Samyan, BANGKOK 5. Tel. 2511630

TURKEY – TURQUIE
Kültur Yayinlari Is-Türk Ltd. Sti.
Atatürk Bulvari No : 191/Kat. 21
Kavaklidere/ANKARA. Tel. 17 02 66
Dolmabahce Cad. No : 29
BESIKTAS/ISTANBUL. Tel. 60 71 88

UNITED KINGDOM – ROYAUME-UNI
H.M. Stationery Office.
P.O.B. 276, LONDON SW8 5DT.
(postal orders only)
Telephone orders: (01) 622.3316, or
49 High Holborn, LONDON WC1V 6 HB (personal callers)
Branches at: EDINBURGH, BIRMINGHAM, BRISTOL,
MANCHESTER, BELFAST.

UNITED STATES OF AMERICA – ÉTATS-UNIS
OECD Publications and Information Center, Suite 1207,
1750 Pennsylvania Ave., N.W. WASHINGTON, D.C.20006 – 4582
Tel. (202) 724.1857

VENEZUELA
Libreria del Este, Avda. F. Miranda 52, Edificio Galipan,
CARACAS 106. Tel. 32.23.01/33.26.04/31.58.38

YUGOSLAVIA – YOUGOSLAVIE
Jugoslovenska Knjiga, Knez Mihajlova 2, P.O.B. 36, BEOGRAD.
Tel. 621.992

Les commandes provenant de pays où l'OCDE n'a pas encore désigné de dépositaire peuvent être adressées à :
OCDE, Bureau des Publications, 2, rue André-Pascal, 75775 PARIS CEDEX 16.
Orders and inquiries from countries where sales agents have not yet been appointed may be sent to:
OECD, Publications Office, 2, rue André-Pascal, 75775 PARIS CEDEX 16.

68837-08-1985

OECD PUBLICATIONS, 2, rue André-Pascal, 75775 PARIS CEDEX 16 - No. 43333 1985
PRINTED IN FRANCE
(03 85 02 1) ISBN 92-64-12758-5